I0810149

"From a renowned expert on children's spirituality in the tradition of Robert Coles comes a book whose insights into children's religious imagination will turn common assumptions upside down. Loaded with thought-provoking interview stories, this book is a reminder that attentive listening to children is itself an invaluable 'faith practice' that has the power to transform *us* as adults."

—**Bonnie J. Miller-McLemore,** author of *Let the Children Come: Reimagining Childhood from a Christian Perspective*

"There has been a flurry of research in recent years about the way children understand God: about whether they are confident that God is real, about what God knows, about what children learn from adults about God, and so forth. This engaging book deepens that work with rich accounts of the way that children not only reason about God but relate to him."

—**Tanya Marie Luhrmann,** author of *How God Becomes Real: Kindling the Presence of Invisible Others*

"In the tradition of Robert Coles's landmark work, Brad Wigger's *When Children Imagine God* centers the voices of children and takes seriously the wisdom and insight only the youngest among us can offer. Wigger creates space for children to lead us into fresh imaginings about age-old questions of who God is and who we are in relation to the Divine. For those who believe 'a little child shall lead them,' this book is a brilliant example of why we must listen to the voices of children and how they lead us in imagining a God beyond the confines of our adult perspectives. Professors, parents, grandparents, congregational leaders, and teachers will find in these pages an invaluable and inspiring conversation partner for nurturing the life of faith with children and families."

—**Rebecca L. Davis,** director of the Font and Faith Initiative in Nurturing Faith in Children and Families

"*When Children Imagine God* ushers readers into a beautiful and creative space—a realm awash in spiritual wisdom. Refusing to treat children's spirituality as simply a source for cute stories and giggles, Brad Wigger invites us to listen to children with patience and care. When we make time to attend to these observant souls, Wigger observes, we inevitably discover that they have a lot more going on spiritually than we may imagine. In fact, through these conversations, we discover reliable and winsome guides for our own spiritual journeys."

—**Scott Black Johnston,** senior pastor of
Fifth Avenue Presbyterian Church, New York

"As a scholar, pastor, and grandmother, I'm fascinated by Wigger's reflections on children and their imaginative encounters with God. Each chapter provides new insights into childhood faith and suggests how religious leaders, parents, grandparents, and others can support children's spiritual flourishing."

—**Karen-Marie Yust,** author of *Real Kids, Real Faith:
Practices for Nurturing Children's Spiritual Lives*

WHEN CHILDREN IMAGINE GOD

Conversations with Church Kids

J. BRADLEY WIGGER

William B. Eerdmans Publishing Company
Grand Rapids, Michigan

Wm. B. Eerdmans Publishing Co.
2006 44th Street SE, Grand Rapids, MI 49508
www.eerdmans.com

Published 2026
Printed in the United States of America

32 31 30 29 28 27 26 1 2 3 4 5 6 7

ISBN 978-0-8028-8631-6

Library of Congress Cataloging-in-Publication Data

Names: Wigger, J. Bradley author
Title: When children imagine God : conversations with church kids / J. Bradley Wigger.
Description: Grand Rapids, Michigan : William B. Eerdmans Publishing Company, 2026. | Includes bibliographical references. | Summary: "Based on interviews with children conducted by an expert in religious education and childhood studies, this book book provides insights into how children imagine God"—Provided by publisher.
Identifiers: LCCN 2025054158 | ISBN 9780802886316 paperback | ISBN 9781467471015 epub
Subjects: LCSH: Christian children—Religious life—United States | Christian children—Religious life—Mexico—Yucat·n Peninsula | Parenting—Religious aspects—Christianity | Parents—Religious life—United States | Parents—Religious life—Mexico—Yucatán Peninsula | BISAC: RELIGION / Christian Ministry / Children | RELIGION / Spirituality | LCGFT: Anecdotes | Interviews
Classification: LCC BV4571.3 .W54 2026
LC record available at https://lccn.loc.gov/2025054158

To Elly and Jacob

Contents

Introduction

Our son, David, was three years old and praying at bedtime.[1] He asked God to bless his friends and family, as well as his stuffed animals. He ended the prayer saying, "And, God, I miss you."

I was stunned. Did David just say he misses God? Yes, he did. What is that about? What should I do? Part of me wanted to offer him a comforting story or thoughtful words that would assure him of God's presence. But another part of me was paralyzed by the stark words of a three-year-old, "God, I miss you." So instead of saying anything, I kissed him goodnight and went to tell Jane, his mother, so she could worry too. Jane, a pastor, was equally puzzled and concerned. The truth is, a parent cannot easily make a three-year-old or any-aged child feel something they do not, let alone the presence of God. Whatever we could say or do would fall short of the depth generating the prayer, the sense of absence. This was from the heart.

The next morning over our peanut butter and toast, with a touch of fear and trembling, I said to our son, "David, last night, when you were praying, you said you missed God."

"Oh yeah," he answered, "but that's okay now."

"What do you mean?"

"Well," he said. "God came to me last night–"

I interrupted. "David, you mean like in a dream?" (My modern brain was a little too quick to explain.)

"I dunno," he said. "I guess. Anyway, I was playing in the sandbox behind our old house," David explained. We had recently moved across town into an apartment. "And God came and said, 'Come, David,' so I followed, and we came here, and now God is here with us in our new home!" He smiled.

David has young children of his own now, but that event still holds power over my imagination. Through the years I've thought about multiple layers going on in it, for example, the intimacy of a young child in conversation with an invisible figure, God, and how easily that came. I've thought of the paradox of praying to a God you miss, somehow there and not there at the same time. I've reflected upon that dream sandbox where God met David in play. Play, that relaxed realm rounding off the limits of the world of our senses, where sand can become castles and holes can tunnel to the other side of the globe. And there's dreaming, that liminal land that sits between the hard edges of the daylight world and the softer reflective glow of moonlight. I've considered the setting of this compact drama playing out in a three-year-old's soul. That is, at the time, like many pastor families, we lived in a church-owned house. The sandbox sat in a backyard plot shared by the church where Jane was a pastor, our backyard, as well as the preschool run by the church. Church, home, school—all blended together to create a meaningful place. And then there's God, a figure who is in a three-year-old's deepest attachments alongside family, friends, and stuffed animals, the One who shows up in the religious imagination to be with a child in a new home. Finally, there's the smile. A simple expression of delight born from resting in the assuring presence that nothing separates us from Holy Love.

The event with David occurred over three decades ago, when I was a PhD student hoping to one day teach religious education in a theological school. That eventually happened. And while teaching adults who would become ministers and chaplains and therapists and more, I found much of my teaching focused upon the hearts and minds of children—encouraging our students to do the same. Typically, students' main concerns in relation to young people were how to give a good children's sermon or what to say to a child who is having a hard time. Those are good things to learn and will play into their professional roles. Yet the approach can be a bit bossy, that is, the minister or therapist or teacher is the expert and passes along their expertise to the less knowledgeable. The great philosopher of education Paolo Freire calls it the banking method.[2] The experts make deposits into the empty minds of others. These deposits are most often in the form of talking—especially in the theological world! And again, talk, words, advising, instructing, directing, and passing along expertise can be very good things to do in the right situation. As a minister, a PhD student, a father—this was my internal first response to David's "God, I miss you." I wanted to tell him something, deposit some expertise. But what I stumbled onto through my own shock and inability to know what to say is that even a three-year-old is the expert of their own experience. And I learned that something deep may be moving in the soul of a young child, a spirit of grace that makes a home. I learned the power of listening.

Only in retrospect can I see how much this lesson has affected my vocations as teacher, researcher, and parent. Oh, I can be as bossy and play the expert and try to bank deposits as the next professor or dad. I stomp over my own values as much as anyone. Even so, I have tried to create opportunities for listening to the experiences of my students, my children, my grandchildren. I continue to hope to honor their agency by letting their voices, creativity, and insights enrich our shared learning and life together.

Somewhat paradoxically, therefore, the "expertise" I have been trying to pass along to students is less a batch of professional information and more a posture—a receptive, attentive, listening way of being with others, especially children. For nearly thirty years now, I have been asking students to listen to children—to conduct interviews in which they ask kids about God and church and prayer and beliefs, that is, the subjects of students' developing expertise. More often than not, students were moved, if not stunned, by what they found. Over and over, I heard, "I had no idea so much was going on," or "I was surprised by how thoughtful she was," or, my favorite, "Kids are awesome!" As important as what we say to children can be, our words are no match for the power at work when we listen—when we pay attention, be with, take seriously, honor, delight in, and learn from children themselves.

This is the spirit in which the book you hold has been written. It took some time, but eventually I was able to focus upon children not only in my teaching but also in my research and writing. Thanks to funding from various foundations, I've been interviewing children all over the world, trying to better understand how they think and learn and how they themselves understand others and the world around them.[3] I've tried to hear and then describe the contours of children's imaginations, from the wild world of their fantasy play to their thoughtful reflections upon God and church. In short, I've been trying to better appreciate the religious imaginations of children. And through this experience, I've come to believe that listening to children is itself a faith practice, one that glows with life and a sense that something irreducible, something powerful yet subtle, is at work in them.

Parents too. I've been listening to parents and grandparents describe their religious lives in relation to children, including their motivations for wanting the ones they love to be part of a community of faith. In addition to the sheer support they feel by being part of a community that values love, in addition to being in the company of other parents and caretakers struggling to raise children, in addition to wanting their children to have other caring adults in their lives—from pastors and Sunday school teachers to surrogate grandparents and youth leaders—in addition to these and other reasons, the same adults described how much parenting has affected their own spiritual lives.

* * *

The conversations that form the heart of this book flow from a project called The Religious Imagination of Children, in which our research team interviewed 151 children mostly between the ages of three and twelve. We also interviewed 93 parents, including several grandparents. We set out to find as much geographic, denominational, and ethnic diversity as we could.

Religiously, with a couple of exceptions, all the children and parents were Christian. After some attempts at interviewing beyond Christianity, we made the decision to stick within the church world (of which I am part) where we had more connections and were less likely to ask questions that, even unconsciously, reflect a Christian set of interests and biases. Christianity, with all its various denominations, is complicated enough. Indeed, we were able to interview children and parents from multiple denominational backgrounds: Presbyterian (Presbyterian Church [USA], Presbyterian Church of America), Roman Catholic, Episcopalian, Independent Baptist, American Baptist, nondenominational evangelical, Russian Orthodox, Church of Jesus Christ of Latter-day Saints (LDS), Apostolic/ Pentecostal, Reformed Church of America, nondenominational expat, United Methodist, Society of Friends, interdenominational, as well as one Jewish parent and one atheist parent. Many of these parents were raised in still other traditions, for example, Christian Scientist, Armenian Orthodox, or Greek Orthodox, before settling in their current churches.

Geographically the interviews took place all across the United States—in nearly every major region—as well as in the Yucatan of Mexico. In all, including the Yucatan, we interviewed in eleven different states and nineteen cities, towns, or villages. Most of the time, in the following chapters, the location of the interview is described in only the most general terms, for example, "a city in the Southwest." This is to protect the anonymity of the speakers (whose names have been changed).

Ethnically, children and parents were European American, African American, Hispanic American, indigenous Mexican (Yucatec Mayan), Ethiopian (recently adopted), Ghanaian (recent immigrants), Kenyan, South Asian, and Korean American.

In the research world, the method for finding interviews would be called "convenience sampling," which makes it sound too much like dropping by a local market for some bread. What it really means is that I reached out to connections I had with people all over the country (pastors, professors, former students, friends, and so forth), who in turn put me in touch with connections they had with church or community leaders. We interviewed in homes, libraries, churches, parks, and religious schools. We intentionally sought out households that were actively engaged in church, a fact crucial to our findings. This was not a study to find out why people don't go to church or don't believe in God or practice their faith. Such a choice limits the relevance of our research for other communities, specifically, children who are not part of any religion. How do children of atheist homes, or with "spiritual but not religious" parents, or simply practitioners of "nothing," think about God or religion? That is a good thing to study, but our interests were more about the ways faith is reflected in the hearts and minds of children and parents actively engaged with their churches.

The questions we asked are described in the pages that follow. The protocol and study generally were approved by the Institutional Review Board of my school concerned with ethical practices for human research. Parents who participated gave written consent to talk to them and their children, but importantly, the children themselves gave either written or oral assent. They were assured that the interview was not a test, that there were no wrong answers ("We want to understand how kids think"). The interviews were recorded and transcribed so that they could be accurately reflected here. I personally either conducted the interviews or listened to them, reading the transcript as I listened.

Generally, with school-aged children, we began with descriptive-type questions: *Tell me about your church. What do you like about it? Not like about it? Tell me what you do there.* Then we would move into more theological territory: *Does your church talk about God? Tell me about God. What makes God happy? Sad? Tell me about Jesus. The Holy Spirit. What is baptism? Communion? How do you pray?* We posed questions that explored other ways they might think about church: *If you have kids when you're older, do you think you would want your children to go to church? Why?* Most of these interviews lasted anywhere from twenty minutes to an hour, depending upon age and talkativeness. With younger children, the interviews were much simpler and might last only a few minutes, often in the company of a parent. *Do you like your church? Tell me about it.* Or the parent might report how they pray at bedtime. *Can you tell me the prayer?* We also experimented with interviewing groups of children, in a Sunday school class, or in pairs, or siblings together. That created a slightly different dynamic as children played off the thoughts of one another. The goal was not to create exactly the same conditions or questions for each interview as a way of generating quantitative comparisons statistically analyzed (something I have done for other projects). Our procedure was looser, more journalistic perhaps, in the sense that we were looking for the story or stories at work in those we talked with. Or to use another metaphor, the goal was a kind of linguistic portraiture—depicting the faces of faith through conversation.

One of the greatest surprises through all the interviews was how willingly and easily parents and children whom we had just met spoke with us. Even when speaking with children whose parents warned might be shy, when we took it slowly, the interviews grew into wonderful conversations. Of course, we never pressured anyone to speak, and we were ready to abandon an interview if a child changed their mind or found the conversation uncomfortable. This happened only once. Anna, a nine-year-old Orthodox girl, had warmed to us immediately, and we chatted about school and life and friends for fifteen minutes. Then, when it came time to actually conduct the interview, she changed her mind. It was a little surprising given how talkative she already had been, and I worried we'd said something that bothered her. Regardless, we assured her that this was not a problem, and that if she changed her mind again, she should let us know. The next day we went to her (Orthodox) school to interview a family. We sat in on a religion class, and several of the other children we had interviewed were there and told Anna they had spoken with us.

"Can I ask you something?" Anna said after class.

"Sure, what do you want to know?"

Anna asked, "Is an interview just talking?"

"Yes," I answered. "We talk. I'll ask you some questions—about your church, about God, but it's just talking."

"Oh," she said. "If you had just called it talking, we could have done it last night. I thought an interview was something different." She smiled at the misunderstanding. I assured her I was going to call it "talking" in the future.

After a phone call with her mother, Anna and I had a delightful "talk," if a little rushed to finish before her recess was over. The incident shows how easily misunderstanding can happen and deepens my appreciation for the children and adults to hand over such a precious gift as their time, if not their spiritual hearts.

Parent interviews often lasted an hour or more. Typically, the parents had to stop because it was time for swim lessons, a doctor's appointment, or a trip to the grocery store. The bulk of the child interviews were conducted by me, while most of the parent interviews were conducted by Jane Larsen-Wigger (a longtime pastor to whom I'm married). She is a great listener and why many of the interviews with parents lasted so long. While there was a set of questions we started from with parents, usually it only took a few to get to the ways that their faith lives and parenting lives intersect. Questions like: *Why do you take your kids to church?* Or *What values or practices do you hope to pass on?* But the one that often generated the most conversation, as alluded to above, was: *How has being a parent affected your faith?*

As psychologist Janis Clark Johnston puts it in her book *It Takes a Child to Raise a Parent*, "In most families, children join raising their parents just as much as parents raise children."[4] What's true in the psychological realm is often true in the spiritual realm. More on this point will follow, but it reveals how faith formation is not simply a top-down or banking operation from parent to child. Children, too, are forming parents. Or perhaps it is more accurate to say that faith itself is larger than parent or child and generates relationships and love in multiple directions. I know my own spiritual adventures have been bound up with joining my children in theirs. More recently, this has included grandchildren whose sheer presence in the world is a source of grace. And, of course, I include in this venture the hundreds of children I've had the privilege of interviewing.[5]

To this point, looking back, I can now see how many of the themes of my research and reflection show up, along with God, in a backyard dream sandbox. I am struck by the communion of it all, how my eyes were opened at the breakfast table, over the breaking of bread and simple conversation, to the Sacred Presence.

1

Imagination

DAVID SENT A VIDEO of our granddaughter, Elly, sixteen months old at the time.[1] "I think you'll get a kick out of this!" he wrote. In the clip, just eight seconds long, Elly is standing in front of her plush monkey friend, Curious George. She holds a plastic cup and a small toddler's fork—a utensil that she was just learning to use. She looks down into the cup, dips the fork in, and with one quick stroke, she brings the fork to the mouth of George, then to her own mouth for a bite. The video ends with Elly smiling as she hugs her stuffed friend while still hanging onto the cup. When I asked our son about it, he didn't believe she had done that before, not that he'd noticed. And David made it clear that he had not invited or suggested or encouraged Elly to feed George. The action was spontaneous.

David was right; I did get a kick out of the video. Not only is the scene extraordinarily cute, it is profoundly revealing of a budding imagination. From a child-development perspective, the fascinating fact is that the cup in the video is completely empty. Our mostly preverbal grandchild is pretending. She is "feeding" her inanimate companion an invisible forkful of pretend food and delighting in the shared occasion.

* * *

What is going on in a young mind that plays out such an imaginative act with a toy? The answer depends a lot on how one views childhood imagination.[2] Once upon a time in the psychological literature, pretend play was considered evidence of confusion in a child sixteen months old, one too young to differentiate fantasy from reality. Sigmund Freud believed that children come into this world as a bundle of needs—true enough. They need to be held, fed, burped, changed, washed, kept safe, and generally loved. But not all needs are met all the time, and the result, according to Freud, is that the infant id generates fantasies to satisfy unmet needs. Think of the stereotypical movie scene in which a thirst-ridden soul lost in the desert hallucinates an oasis. The difference, in the case of a baby, is that the illusion satisfies the need. For Freud, young children are awash in these fantasies compensating for frustrated desires.[3] So, when Elly pretends to eat—in a Freudian interpretation—she was simply hungry, and her imagination compensates with the fantasy of food. Why would she feed George first? I do not know. Perhaps she is projecting her hunger onto the doll?

Development then, for Freud, is the process of working through the Greek drama of childhood in order to shed our wish-fulfilling fantasies and face reality as it is. Otherwise, in adulthood, neurotic, irrational symptoms continue to plague us—trying to satisfy unmet childhood needs. Of significance to a religious imagination is that "God," for Freud, is one such fantasy.[4] God is an illusion generated by the need to feel secured and loved in a world that is often cold and hostile.

Jean Piaget, playing off Freud, characterized the young mind as "ludistic,"[5] that is, full of magical thinking that compensates for frustrated desires. For example, when Piaget's daughter, Jacqueline, was two years old, she was told not to play with the water used for washing. In response, Jacqueline "took an empty cup, went and stood by the forbidden tub and went through the actions, saying: 'I'm pouring out water.'" In another instance when she was nearly four, Jacqueline was told not to go into the kitchen where pails of hot water were prepared for a bath. (This was the late 1920s.) She responded, "Then I'll go into a pretend kitchen."[6] Like Freud, Piaget saw these events of pretend play as forms of compensation, egocentrically bending reality through fantasy to fit her thwarted desires. Jacqueline can't play with the real water, so she pretends with imagined water. She can't go into the kitchen, so she'll go to the pretend kitchen. Children are so full of this magical thinking, according to Piaget, they have a hard time differentiating fantasy from reality until seven or eight years of age.

Child development, in the tradition of these two giants of psychology, is the process of moving from the foggy magical thinking that compensates for frustrated desires to the pure light of scientific, logical, real-world-oriented thought—moving from the ludicrous to the truth.

I am not convinced. Perhaps my grandparent love enchants me into reading too much into the video, but I don't think so. It is not just Elly. I have spent a lot of time in near and faraway places exploring children's thinking, play, and imaginations. The results lead me in a different direction.

I see in the feeding event something deeply relational and flowing with joy—a form of communion.

* * *

This chapter, then, explores an alternative picture of the imagination—as well as the religious imagination—as a corrective to assumptions about childhood that have been baked into our imaginations about imagination. Prior to the Religious Imagination of Children project, I traveled across the globe interviewing children about the wild and wonderful world of imaginary or invisible friends—IFs. (For the record, my use of the acronym predates the movie *IF*, about imaginary friends, by over a decade.) This IF research was built upon a new generation of work in cognitive psychology.[7] The imagination, untethered from Freudian fantasy about fantasy, is much more complex and social, and it can be seen as deepening children's ability to engage the world.

* * *

My curiosity about the subject of childhood imagination was first piqued when my three-year-old daughter, Cora, developed an IF named

Crystal. The standard explanation, based on the Freudian-Piagetian framework, was that Cora was either (1) compensating for loneliness or (2) splitting off a part of herself to blame for misbehavior (another type of compensation). Neither explanation fit well. First, Cora had plenty of friends, the kind anyone could see. Second, Cora did not blame Crystal for anything. In fact, one day when I playfully blamed Crystal for some trash on the floor, Cora got mad at me and declared, "Crystal didn't do that, I did!"

Twenty years later, I found myself asking children about IFs not only in Louisville, Kentucky, where I live but in places like Malawi and Nepal, as well as Kenya and the Dominican Republic, over five hundred children total. I was introduced to a marvelous menagerie of invisible figures. There was Dino, the dinosaur friend of eight-year-old Kent. Dino was often a prehistoric reptile, but sometimes, according to Kent, Dino was a space alien. Four-year-old Nathan, instead of one IF taking multiple forms, had multiple IFs: Stella (a one-hundred-year-old robin); eight-year-old brothers, Jump Jump and Jump Jax; as well as his favorite, Quack Quack, a four-year-old pretend duck.

Kids were not only from various geographic areas but from different religious backgrounds: Christian, Muslim, Hindu, Jewish, and Buddhist. One question we sought to answer was whether children from very different parts of the world from the United States even have IFs. They do! The prevalence of them varied to some degree between locations. It seems that different cultures—be those of a household, religion, or society—can discourage, encourage, or ignore children having IFs.[8] But the potential for them appears to be as close to universal as the potential for language or play among kids.

One of the key findings from these interviews—as Cora and Crystal would foreshadow—is how deeply relational children's pretend play often is. These were invisible *friends*, after all. And the children described doing the kinds of things kids do with friends—playing together, talking, going places, reading, coloring, doing homework together, playing house or family or school, eating snacks or meals, taking turns pushing on swings, dancing, practicing sports, and more. Of course, this does not eliminate the possibility that children are compensating for loneliness. But when I asked the same children whether they had friends of the more ordinary sort, visible, they all named several. In fact, some of the children with IFs shared them with their visible friends. A little boy in Pokhara, Nepal, had a whole "pretend family" that he and his brother played with. A girl in Santo Domingo, Dominican Republic, told me how she shares her IF with her friends at school. Siblings in Louisville discovered Baby Bear together while camping in a forest. The brothers played with Baby Bear individually at times, and at other times they played with him together.

Relationships with IFs, as described by these children, are a deeply social phenomenon. Not only social in the sense of having company, but also in the sense of social practice. When a child pretends with IFs, they are generating relationships, playing out scenarios and roles, and using play as a way to practice social life—just as children might do with dolls or action figures, but without the props. After all, in pretend play, children are moving back and forth between their own point of view and that of another. Plus, they're having a good time.

And, by the way, I never heard a child blame an IF for anything.

* * *

Of religious significance, we also discovered children who, when asked about an invisible friend, named the Holy Spirit, or Jesus Christ, or God, as an invisible—but not imaginary—friend. And others named a Pawpaw (deceased grandfather), angels, and a friend who died. These types of figures have led me to use most often the term "invisible" rather than "imaginary" when speaking generally about these friends (or the ambiguous "IF"). A point from this finding is that the cognitive scaffolding that allows children to play with imaginary companions may also allow them to have meaningful relationships with gods, angels, ancestors, or the dead. An important, perhaps central, component of that scaffolding is the imagination. The imagination makes possible reflection upon, or relationship to, invisibles. Children, it seems, are not always as "concrete" as they are accused of, especially when the imagination is at work. Not only gods and angels but children can imagine all kinds of other invisibles, such as germs and oxygen, or they can imagine otherwise invisible times like their parents' childhood or even the beginning of the universe.[9]

Another finding from listening to children discuss their IFs is that the children knew they were pretend. In the very first interview we conducted, Nicole (two years, eleven months) told me all about Leah and Coda, her IFs. When I offered to give Leah and Coda stickers (as I had given Nicole), she looked at me completely puzzled and said, "They're pretend!" Nicole, not even three, was taken aback when I seemed not to understand. In other words, children are not confused. Using language like "pretend friends" or "imagination friends," children consistently differentiated IFs from the kinds of figures anyone could see. When pressed on what it means for a friend to be imaginary or pretend, children said things like "I made her up," or "He's only in my head," or "Nobody else can see them because they're pretend."

Even so, these friendships forged in the imagination can be very important to children. The relationships are real and often heartfelt. (I never used the terms "real" or "not real" with kids when referring directly to their IFs.) Children can become attached to IFs the same way they get attached to stuffed animals or the way an adult can get attached to characters in novels or films—all more evidence of how deeply social this form of play can be.

In addition to asking children about their IFs, we also conducted simple cognitive tests called *theory of mind* tasks with them. For example, we'd show a child a crayon box and ask what was inside. "Crayons," children would say. (We used a matchbox outside the United States.) When we opened the box, the children were surprised to see that there were actually rocks inside. We'd close the box and ask what their best friend would think is inside. School-aged kids (five and up) typically said their best friend would be fooled and think crayons were inside. We asked what God would think. The vast majority said something like, "Oh, God would know rocks are in the box."[10] In other words, even five-year-olds could differentiate a human mind from a divine one. We asked what their IF would think, and the answers were more complex. Some children thought their IF would know the truth; others did not. On average, IFs were significantly less likely to know rocks were in the box than God, but significantly more likely to know than humans. They were in-between. And depending upon the culture, we asked about angels, spirits, fairies, ancestors, and even Santa Claus. They all came out in-between as well. We also asked about an animal (dog or chicken, depending upon the country), and children treated an animal's knowledge like a human's—they wouldn't know. In other words, children were differentiating various mental capacities for various kinds of minds, including extraordinary ones like God's or an angel's.[11]

Younger children (three and four) were a different story. They were most likely to say that any or all of the figures we asked about would know rocks were in the box. That is, once young children knew, they tended to say everyone would know. Conventional explanations would be that young children are particularly egocentric in their perspectivetaking. That is, they don't realize others have a different point of view or knowledge than they have—young children project the state of their own knowledge onto everyone else. This could lend credence to Piaget's idea that children base their understanding of God upon their understanding of humans.[12] Young children think humans, or, for that matter, animals, will know rocks are in the box; therefore God will too.

However, we found a different result when we conducted another type of theory-of-mind test, one that I think is even more revealing. Instead of showing surprising contents (rocks) in a crayon box or matchbox, we showed children a very generic, nondescript cloth bag and asked them what was inside. Some guessed, but eventually all children admitted to not knowing the contents. Then we asked whether their best friend, God, and the other figures would know the contents. The results: these youngest children believed God would know the contents of the bag even when they themselves did not know. Best friends—no. Animals—no. IFs and other in-betweens? They were again less likely to know than God and more likely to know than a human or animal. That is, even three-year-olds could differentiate various kinds of minds.[13]

This is only a brief summary of the studies that went into the book *Invisible Companions: Encounters with Imaginary Friends, Gods, Ancestors, and Angels*, but a large theme emerging from this research is that children's thinking and imaginations are much more sophisticated than much of the Freudian-Piagetian framework has allowed. Children are not confused about their IFs. They don't seem to be compensating or scapegoating for misbehavior. They engage in social practice with IFs and even share them with visible friends or classmates. Children understand the pretend status of IFs. And, offering clues to the religious imagination, children are able to differentiate different kinds of minds and easily attribute extraordinary knowing to divine minds.

This is the background that eventually led to our exploring the *religious* imagination of children more deeply. That is, if children's imaginations as such are more sophisticated than thought, perhaps children's religious imaginations are more sophisticated than our theories have allowed. In my imagination, Elly's communion with Curious George bridges the two projects.

* * *

Given this background, it may not be surprising that, even as I asked children about church and God and prayer or communion itself, I also included questions specifically about *imaginary* friends in the latest round of research. That is, because of the cognitive overlap between imaginary friends and invisible figures like God or angels, I asked children who had imaginary friends what the difference was, if any, between them and God. Even though children are able to differentiate between IFs and ordinary, visible friends, would they distinguish between an invisible friend and an invisible God? Typically, this line of questioning took place near the end of an interview, after asking more explicitly religious questions. "Now I've got an easy question for you. Do you like to play?" All the children did. "What do you like to play?" Children named all kinds of games and activities. When I asked whether they ever played with pretend friends, about half said they did and could name them.

Eve was one of them. Seven years old, Eve was the daughter of a pastor, and her favorite part of church was the singing, she told me, and her favorite song was "Jesus Loves Me." After talking about church and God and playing, I asked, "Do you ever pretend play?" She looked at me, curious, waiting for more. I added, "Like playing with an imaginary or pretend friend?"

Eve smiled and said she did. "Her name is Moe and she's a taco." She said this like she knew it was funny. I smiled as well. I had encountered all kinds of imaginary characters and figures—lots of animals, shape-shifting aliens, and more human-like friends, but this was the first taco.

"And what do you do with Moe that's a taco?"

"We play hide and seek."

I chuckled at the idea, then asked, "How do you play hide and seek with an invisible friend?"

"I just find the spot and pretend to not know where she is."

My thoughts spun as I tried to dissect the layers of pretense going on in this seven-year-old's mind. Pretending to have a friend that is a taco. Pretending the invisible taco can hide. Pretending not to know where the hiding spot is that you have found for your invisible taco friend to hide. Anyway, after hearing a bit more about Moe, I asked, "So Moe the taco is invisible?" She agreed. "And God is invisible?" Again, she agreed. "So, what's the difference between an invisible God and an invisible friend?"

Eve immediately offered, "One's imaginary and one is real," she answered.

"And what does imaginary mean?"

"Fake," she said.

Eve's answer was representative. Again, children appreciate the pretend nature of their imaginary friends—the qualitative difference between them and the visible kind. In addition, these same children consistently differentiated their invisible, imaginary friends from an invisible God. "I know that God is real, and I know that because he created us," ten-year-old Bob said. He and a friend had invented "Billy the ghost" one day when the wind kept blowing open the door. He went on to explain that pretend games are "not real." His five-year-old sister said God was her invisible friend. I asked whether she had any other invisible friends that were not God. She said she liked to pretend with a character from television. But she clarified, "God is real," she said, "but shows are not."

Nine-year-old Eli told me about his IF, a dragon named Sparky! I laughed at the clever name for the fire-breather. Eli was clear about the difference between his imaginary friends and God, but along the way he made a fascinating point. "God can see my pretend friends, because he brought us to Earth. So, he can see things after we've been sent to Earth."

"God is in heaven," six-year-old Sarah told me, "and my [imaginary] friends are in my mind."

An eight-year-old boy, Jordan, whose IF was a dinosaur, said, "Well, imaginary friends aren't real, but God is real."

Other responses include: "I think God stays with you for all of your life. Whereas invisible friends don't because as you grow up, you maybe forget about them"; God is "in my heart"; "God is powerful"; "God is a lot more important"; "God made people"; "imaginary friends are completely invisible, but God has a way of talking to us. My imaginary friends don't talk"; "Delilah [IF] didn't create the world and make people"; "God is always with me all the time, but Angela [IF] is like off running around with her invisible family."

Some children, in making the distinction between an invisible God and invisible friend, pointed to Jesus, creating some ambiguity and complexity. "God is human"; "God is a person"; or "you can see Jesus, he's invisible but you can see him." Another child offered: "Because God actually did something, while Jesus actually did something. And guardian angels do something. They protect you. So does Jesus, but imaginary friends, you play with."

* * *

The chapters to follow provide fuller conversations with children and parents about their religious beliefs and practices. Here, in the most theoretical chapter of the book, I simply want to make the case that some of the basic popular assumptions about childhood have distorted our imaginations about imagination, if not a religious imagination. I want to offer a different starting point.

In fairness to Freud and Piaget, their work flowed from centuries of distorted assumptions about the minds and bodies of babies coming into the world. The primary assumption was that sense-based perceptions are nothing but points of sensation, flat and impoverished. The mind has to fill in the depth and richness of reality, and that takes time. The baby's world is a "blooming, buzzing confusion," as William James put it. The implications of this historical theory of perception for early childhood are tremendous.[14]

These assumptions about babies and impoverished perception have not held up. (For example, you may have heard that babies don't perceive color or depth, which is not true.) More recent work has shown that the information that the senses provide is robust from the beginning. The minds of babies don't have to learn how to fill in the sensed world any more than children have to be taught how to blink or breathe. Increasingly, over the last thirty years, researchers have discovered not only how robust the senses are from the beginning but how sophisticated even the youngest minds are. Shaped by millions of years of evolution, babies come into the world with (or rapidly develop) all kinds of realistic expectations about the world around them. For example, Piaget believed that children don't grasp "object permanence" until eight or nine months of age. Place a ball out of view, and the six-month-old thinks it no longer exists—out of sight, out of mind, out of existence. So thought Piaget. But more recently, it's become clear that even three-month-old babies expect that a ball rolled behind a screen will come out the other side. Their eyes look for the ball, and if it doesn't appear they keep staring, presumably surprised. Babies can orient themselves by surfaces and angles in a room, and they even have a sense of more or less. In short, very young children operate with a kind of intuitive physics. And what's true in the realm of objects is true in the realm of people. Babies appear to come into the world with an intuitive psychology. They pick up on the emotions of caregivers. Infants seek and prefer human faces to other objects, even stuffed animals and dolls. Babies are drawn to mutual eye-gazing, and they expect animate creatures (humans, animals) to move about under their own power but are surprised if objects seem to do the same (like a Roomba vacuum).[15]

In other words, these findings suggest a very real-world orientation on the part of babies. Add to this the fact that children show no sign of pretend play until the second year of life (like Elly above), and we have to reimagine the imagination and child development.[16] If anything, the capacity for pretense is the developmental achievement. Rather than a world of buzzing confusion and ludic hallucinations, babies come into a world primed for relationships—relationship to the physical world via the senses and an intuitive physics; relationship to an animate, human world via an intuitive psychology. And what a turnaround. Rather than lost in an egocentric fog, the youngest among us are the clear-eyed realists primed for relationships.

If the developmental psychologist Alison Gopnik is right, "babies are, at least by some measures, *more* conscious than we are."[17] Gopnik has done as much research as anyone to demonstrate, contra the Freudian-Piagetian framework, how logical, caring, thoughtful, and creative children, even very young children, can be. In her book *The Philosophical Baby*, she explores the question, "What's it like to be a baby?"[18] The baby experience—from the first-person baby point of view—is so opaque to us as adults that some philosophers and psychologists have assumed babies are simply not conscious. But Gopnik suggests that the evidence from both neuro- and cognitive science implies just the opposite. Babies may be even more in tune with the world around them than adults, at least in certain ways.

Gopnik is talking about a specific quality of attention to the world. She describes two basic forms of awareness in humans: one works like a spotlight, the other more like a lantern. When we attend to something in the world around us, say the road while we're riding a bicycle in traffic, it's as if our minds shine a spotlight on certain features of the world (cars, the road ahead, potential hazards, pedestrians) but largely shut out other features of the environment (the shape of the clouds overhead, the type of trees or birds or buildings around us). The spotlight illumines more brightly some things and leaves others in the relative dark.

As Gopnik points out, there are bodily chemicals–neurotransmitters–that enhance our spotlighting ability. They facilitate information processing in relation to whatever we're attending to, that is, they brighten the light. But that is only part of the story. In spotlight awareness the brain also releases transmitters that activate neurons that inhibit other parts of the brain, the parts that are irrelevant to the matter at hand. Those parts of our awareness grow dimmer. "So," as Gopnik puts it, "paying attention literally boosts some parts of your brain and shuts down others."

Adults are generally better at spotlight attention than children because the parts of the brain that allow us to inhibit some features of perception take time to develop. As Gopnik puts it, babies' brains are soaking in the neurotransmitters that open up the sights and sounds of the world around them. They have few of the inhibitory transmitters that would allay their effects. The result is a more vivid, intense awareness of the sensed world in general because babies don't have the option to tamp down some experiences for some purpose (like riding a bike).

Gopnik calls this baby awareness lantern consciousness, "that vivid panoramic illumination of the everyday." The attention of a baby becomes absorbed by the stuff of the world. In fact, Gopnik thinks the best analogy for adults comes in travel. The more different from your familiar world, the more you are like a baby struck by the strange sounds and smells, the way the light shines on the buildings in a city or on the glacier in the mountains. Our perceptual systems are in an "I don't know" state, which opens us to the environment. We "lose our selves by becoming part of the world."[19] Our senses, and our minds, are open, especially if we're not hurrying to a meeting or preoccupied with a purpose or panicked by not knowing exactly what we're seeing. In such a state, the lantern illuminates our experiences. We remember the meals, the hike, the people in the streets. There's a loss of self-consciousness in favor of other-consciousness because everything is fresh and new. And it is the very novelty of the experience that overwhelms the inhibitory processes that allow for spotlight attention in the first place. Paradoxically, such unself-conscious experiences enliven and invigorate our lives.

Gopnik likens the experience to those invoked by Romantic poets, such as William Wordsworth or William Blake, or to a Zen "beginner's mind," a deep state of wonder. Of course, babies can be fussy and colicky as well, and these experiences of distress may be illuminated and intensified also, in effect narrowing awareness. So, children are not always in a broad state of lantern consciousness. But as Gopnik says, "I think they spend much more of their time in that state. That's more like their natural state than adults are in."[20]

I have a hunch that this lantern consciousness can rub off babies and onto adults. One of the most profound experiences of wonder in my own life occurred soon after the birth of our daughter, Cora.[21] There was, of course, the incredibly hard work of pregnancy, labor, and delivery on Jane's part. However, there were no complications, no extra worries, no medical challenges. Mother and daughter were exhausted but in good health. After lots of holding and smiles and tears of joy and relief, maybe an hour or so later while Jane rested, a nurse and I were cleaning Cora up. Something hit me. I was entranced by my daughter's sheer presence. The sense of wonder overcame me, beyond words, beyond tears even. She and the room even seemed to glow. The nurse, wiping my daughter's precious body, gently commented, "You have to believe in God, don't you?" I think the nurse saw that lantern glow too.

* * *

What a different starting point for considering children, their imaginations, and their religious imaginations. Rather than beginning life in a fantasy-soaked world of compensating illusions that have to be overcome to face reality, babies are immersed in a sense-based illumination, a state of wonder directed at the world around them.

So, what if we think of pretense and fantasy play as built upon this foundation of wonder—even an expression of it—deepening the potential for connections to the world around us? That is, the imagination allows for all kinds of relationships to invisibles whether in play (invisible friends), science (invisible germs), or church (invisible God). The *religious* imagination can allow for taking another's point of view, critical to the moral life and justice. The religious imagination understands that God knows in extraordinary ways. God's love can be imagined, or the creation of the universe, or a peaceable kingdom, or what it means to love self and others.

* * *

In Mark's Gospel, Jesus gets upset with the disciples because they are trying to keep children away from him. "Let the little children come to me; do not stop them; for it is to such as these that the kingdom of God belongs" (10:14). I don't know if this means, as is sometimes claimed, that children are closer to God somehow. Maybe. But at the least, it could be that children are more "porous," as philosopher Charles Taylor puts it, more open to a world teeming with God and angels and the irreducible mystery at the heart of reality.[22]

In *A Secular Age*, Taylor traces the emergence of secular cultures in North Atlantic societies and the effects upon our religious imaginations. He calls it a story of subtraction. We've gone from a porous self that is open to a reality shot through with God's glory to a buffered self in an impersonal universe devoid of soul. It is a tale of disenchantment. Transcendence, the sense of more, if not wonder, is subtracted out and a religious imagination becomes more and more difficult to attain or sustain. It seems no accident, then, that in such a context, theories of child development emerged that disparage the young mind as full of irrational, magical thinking.

But what if the religious imagination is, in fact, not delusional, not something to overcome for the sake of reality? What if the religious imagination, built upon wonder, is more conscious of reality? What if children—to whom the kingdom belongs—are indeed more porous, open to the abundance of life? Perhaps then children can help us see the universe not simply as lifeless matter to exploit and manipulate, but instead, as a realm full of aliveness, glowing with the sacred. Maybe the glow can even rub off on adults, helping us appreciate that, as Rabbi Abraham Heschel puts it, "Under the running sea of our theories and scientific explanations lies the aboriginal abyss of radical amazement."[23]

2

Origins

"I LIKE SCIENCE," eleven-year-old Hannah told Jane. "And I like finding out about the world, but I think some things are meant to remain a mystery. Like sometimes I wonder if God knows what animals are thinking, like how animals are feeling."

Such a simple little musing but one that illustrates how the imagination can work, how the religious imagination can work. Like Elly's feeding of Curious George, Hannah's wondering was spontaneous. Nobody had asked her to consider whether God, who knows in extraordinary ways, can know what's going on in the minds and hearts of animals. Hannah cannot directly experience either God's mind or an animal's, but in her imagination she can consider the possibilities based upon what she knows of both.

* * *

Maria Dias and Paul Harris conducted a revealing set of logic experiments with young children.[1] They presented syllogisms, for example: All cats bark; Rex is a cat; does Rex bark? Most kids before about ten or eleven will say: "No, cats don't bark." They don't buy the premise, or they think it's a trick question. But, as Dias and Harris discovered, if you pose the question in a way that evokes the imagination, you get a different result. "Let's pretend that I am on another planet . . . and on this planet all cats bark." When invoking this "make-believe mode," especially with some playful drama in the voice, children as young as four were able to follow the logic and answer that, yes, Rex barks. In other words, children's imaginations help them consider realities in an as-if mode, ones that they have not directly experienced. In that mode they can work out logical puzzles at a much younger age than anyone thought.

When our granddaughter, Elly, was five years old, she wanted me to join her and her brother, Jacob, in our tree house to "have an adventure, Granddad." I could barely wait to see what would happen. In the tree house, three-year-old Jacob began to draw chalk figures on the walls. Elly, on the other hand, pretended she was holding a book. "The wind started to blow," she said. "The tree house started to spin. It spun faster and faster. Then everything was still. Absolutely still." I recognized the lines from the Magic Tree House books she loves, written by Mary Pope Osborne. Each book takes the children in the tree house to another time and place for an adventure. And at the beginning of each trip, "The wind started to blow. . . ."

Elly put the pretend book down, came next to me by the entrance of the tree house, and looked out. "Where are we?" I asked.

"In the mountains," she said. "In India."

Jacob put down his chalk and came to take a look.

"Wow," I said. "It's beautiful."

"Wow," said Jacob.

"It's cold, so here's a blanket." Elly wrapped an invisible blanket over my shoulders and our adventures began. As we were hiking through the mountains, some dragons showed up.

"Oh no," I said. "Should we go back?"

"No, no, Granddad," Elly said. "They're friendly dragons. They'll help us." From that point on, with some help from Jacob, we traded lines on our mission to find the lost treasure.

On the one hand, Elly took us on a wonderfully wild ride in a magic tree house where we could see the cold mountains of India in the backyard of our house on a hot Louisville summer day—with invisible books and blankets, along with friendly dragons. In the imagination, the ordinary laws of physics can be suspended or transformed for the sake of an adventure. In this way the imagination works like hands on Play-Doh to bend, roll, and shape one reality into another. The imagination plays with what we already know and explores possibilities. On the other hand, within this framework of a magic tree house and dragon-loving universe, everything was quite logical. The tree house takes you to a faraway place; a pretend blanket keeps you warm in the cold pretend mountains; friendly dragons will scare away mean monsters. The point is that the imagination is not simply a realm in which ordinary assumptions about the world are suspended; it is also a realm in which logical relationships are practiced based upon given premises.

This ability becomes an important aspect not only of the imagination but of the religious imagination that considers the realms of invisible gods, angels, or saints, as well as places such as heaven or Eden, not to mention the origins of the universe.

* * *

"Speaking of animals," Jane said, posing another question to Hannah, one that pressed her imagination, "where do you think everything came from—animals, you—all of it?" In light of her interest in science, Jane was particularly interested in how Hannah would answer.

"I think I believe in both of the theories," Hannah said, "like in evolution and that God created the world. What my mom says, and I agree with this, is that everything is so perfect because God created it. So, like a solar eclipse. It's called nature's greatest coincidence because the sun is four hundred times larger than the moon, but it's four hundred times farther away. So that is why the moon is able to come right in front of the sun and block it out." She continued, "Like God set it up so that it goes in perfect order. Like he set up the world just right so that it could evolve. He set up the world just right so that Pangea could separate. So, I think it's both things. Yeah."

Here was a girl who understood the logic of why eclipses are possible and understood that the earth once had a supercontinent (Pangea) that began drifting apart some 300 million years ago. She had a scientific imagination. Yet, science did not threaten her faith. With the help of her mother, her religious imagination considered the premises of the question to solve the puzzle. God set up the world perfectly; the world has evolved; did God set up evolution? For Hannah the answer is clear.

I'm confident Hannah's religious community helped as well. I was able to listen to several Sunday school lessons from her church because one of the pastors created a podcast with the children. Not only did the children enjoy hearing themselves, their parents could hear what children were learning and saying in class. In one of the lessons, the pastor read the story of creation in Genesis 1. "Day One. When God began to create, nothing had formed and all was in the dark; God breathed over the surface of everything, and said: 'Let there be light,' and there was light. And it was good. The first day." But, instead of going straight to the second day, the pastor followed with a scientific account. "There was nothing. And then, there was a great big BANG! And our universe began. Clumps of matter formed, and gravity pulled more clumps together, until stars began to glow. And there was light. And it was so. Thirteen and a half billion years ago."

The lesson continued through each day of creation. Afterward, the pastor explained to the children that the Genesis version is a poem in contrast to science. "Can both be true?" he asked.[2] Immediately the children answered with a chorus of yeses.

As Dias and Harris discovered, so much depends upon context. Who or what does Hannah trust? What is the tone in which premises have been established? What kind of encouragement or discouragement has been given to imagine and consider possibilities? What is considered true? Or can truth take different forms? These are critical issues for reflecting upon the origins of the universe, but they are also critical to the origins of a robust religious imagination. And even as I value the voices of children and encourage adults to listen to them, even as I appreciate the ways in which children impact the spiritual lives of parents and adults, nonetheless, the religious imagination of children does not emerge in a vacuum.

* * *

As for Hannah, she is the oldest of four siblings, and her family belongs to a Presbyterian church (PCUSA) in an upper midwestern city. Her mother grew up in Michigan, in a cousin denomination of the Presbyterians, the Reformed Church of America, while Hannah's father grew up attending Episcopalian as well as indigenous churches in Nigeria as a missionary kid. They have been part of the same church since they first moved to town, when Hannah was six months old. According to Hannah's mother, they went to that church because of the bells. "We just heard the bells on a Saturday while we were looking at a house in the neighborhood and then tracked down what church it was." Both parents are musicians, and the bells were the melodic invitation to a congregation that values music—of all kinds. In fact, when I attended one of the services, Hannah's father was leading the congregation in a traditional Nigerian song while he played a djembe.

Hannah has been very active in the church her whole life. She described how much through her eleven years she has enjoyed the various Sunday school classes, choirs, youth group, and especially worship. Like her mother, she thoroughly enjoys the music. She added how much she appreciates the people, "how warm and friendly everybody is," she said. "You could have met that person once and they are like your close friends."

"When you grow up," Jane asked, "do you think you'll go to church?"

"Yes, definitely," Hannah answered immediately. "I think I want to stay at my church because I want to be a special-needs teacher when I grow up. It's so inclusive. It's so welcoming, and if I have kids, I want them to grow up in a positive environment. It's very awesome."

For the same reason Hannah likes science—"finding out about the world"—she likes learning in church. She mentioned youth group discussions, Sunday school lessons, the Bible, and sermons. "I like to pay attention and learn, learn things."

"So, I assume your church talks about God," Jane said, leading to another question. "So, what have you learned about God? What do you think God's like?"

"I've learned that God loves us no matter what, even if we sin. And I've learned that about Jesus and how he sacrificed and how Jesus sacrificed himself so that we could live and be free from sin. One of my favorite parts [in worship] is the assurance of pardon after we do the confession that goes 'Who is in a position to condemn us? Only Christ and Christ lived for us. He died for us, and he rose for us.' I really like that part." Hannah went on to say how she had also learned how "Jesus did many, many, many awesome things on earth. And how we should try to bring a little bit of heaven onto earth through our actions and deeds."

Jane was impressed and followed up. "Where'd you learn that? Where'd you get that idea?"

"Sometimes I read it in my devotions. Sometimes it's in the sermon. Sometimes it's in Scripture. Sometimes it's in youth group—what we talk about."

"So," Jane commented, "you get the idea that what Jesus was about has an effect on what you're about in this world."

"Yes."

Hannah's religious imagination was formed through a rich set of communal relationships at home and church that go back generations, offering worship, music, rituals, ideas, and opportunities for "finding out about the world."

"Why?" Jane asked Hannah. "Why do you think God created the world?"

Hannah thought a moment, then offered, "Because there was nothing, and he wanted there to be something."

Such an impressive response, and one that says something about the imagination, religious or otherwise. Conceiving of a time before time, a nothing before something, is a remarkable feat for a child, even a bright eleven-year-old like Hannah. Genesis provides a rich accounting of that something coming into being, the origins of the cosmos, but by doing so indirectly provokes reflection upon the *tohu va vohu*, as the first line of the Bible's Hebrew puts it, a formless void, an emptiness. Unless the cosmos itself is eternal, any account of its somethingness implies a nothingness. Even the idea of the big bang invites the question: What was before? Or, why is there something and not nothing? It may be the strangest accomplishment of the imagination—that we can think about nothingness. Or can we? Maybe we can only approach it, trace back existence until we find a limit to what we can know or even imagine. At that limit we find no-thing.

Hannah continued. "God wanted something to love. Because life on your own is just lonely." She began to reflect upon what life would be without her brothers and sister and parents and imagine how it might have been for God before there was a world, before there was something other than God. But as she spoke, the focus of her thought turned from loneliness back to love. "I guess he loved so much that he decided to create a world, a being, existence, the universe." For Hannah, on the other side of that no-thing, her religious imagination finds a loving God.

* * *

The way we typically asked children about origins was a version of this: *Have you ever thought about where everything outside comes from—the trees and clouds and sun, for example?* While a few, mostly younger, children said they didn't know or had never thought about it, most gave a version of "Yes, God made the whole world," or simply, "Jesus," or "God." These answers were not a surprise given that most of them grew up with Bible stories or Sunday school lessons that explicitly describe God as Creator. I came to think of these quick, immediate responses as something like "script" answers. That is, God making the world was such common talk in church that the kids would answer it automatically, without much thought. Yet sometimes, like eight-year-old Clara, the script answer was followed by comment that suggested thoughtfulness: "God. It's all his creation. I think it is his greatest masterpiece."

But most of the time we had to probe. To do so, the origins question was often followed with a version of: *What about houses and roads and cars?* (which Hannah was not asked). Here children had to think a bit, to get off the script in a way. Some of the youngest children still stuck to the script and said God made houses and cars too. But most fine-tuned their answers. Ten-year-old Bob made clear that God didn't actually build their house, that people did. But he speculated, "Maybe God talked to them. Then they found out how to create and make stuff like this." Like Bob, several children offered a version of this logic. "No, people make cars and houses, but God made people who make things." Or "God made people and the workers who made the buildings." Or, simply, houses and cars "come from factories." The children exercised a kind of logic within a set of premises—those scripts. They've learned that God created the world, but they've also learned that people make cars and houses—so how to hold these premises together?

Still other questions we asked, like the one Jane asked Hannah, were designed to push even further beyond the scripts and see what their imaginations would do. *Why do you think God created the world?* The question or an answer is not typically discussed in religious lessons. While there are plenty of Bible references or church doctrines that are suggestive—creation displays God's glory or handiwork, or that God saw it was good, or that one day there will be a new creation—even these answers don't directly address the question. An inference must be made about God's desire, for example, that God wanted a way to display the divine glory. When asked this question, some children said they didn't know why. Others made reference back to humanity. God created the world: "To listen to all the people talk," or God "wanted to love us," or "so we could have a happy life on Earth and not be just going around in space." Other children seemed to think about what it would be like to be God without a universe and, like Hannah, imagined loneliness or boredom. Eight-year-old Madison said, "He wanted to have something to look over. Maybe he was bored by himself. Like, we all want friends." Eleven-year-old Johnny: "Maybe he felt bored, and he didn't have anybody to help out or anything like that, so he had nothing to do really except look around and see nothing. Darkness and stuff." Twelve-year-old Adam: "I think God made a universe to un-bore himself. . . . It'd be boring to be an almighty and powerful God but sit there in a blank space of just nothing. You know what I mean? Wouldn't that be boring? Being an immortal, just sitting there all of your life in a blank space?"

Tohu va vohu. Nothing. Boring. Blank.

Some children emphasized the joy and beauty of creating something. Ten-year-old Toby said, "What I read in the Bible was he built this pretty beautiful earth to enjoy it." Then Toby went on to compare God's creation to his own Lego building. "When I read the first page of the Bible, there was this huge, blue ball floating in the middle of nowhere and he felt like he could do something with it. So, he made the solar system and Earth." Ten-year-old Jodie said, "I think he created the world because he thought that this earth needed more beauty." She stopped, thought some more, then added, "Yeah," as if she liked her answer.

Jodie attended an Episcopalian school (with religion classes and chapel) in a large US city in the Southeast. Her family is from Bolivia and Roman Catholic, but they had recently started attending an evangelical Protestant church through the invitation of a friend. I asked Jodie what the "more beauty" is. She answered, "The plants, the trees. Everything." She paused. "Because he knew that there could be more. There could be more things that are more beautiful and more." Like all the children who gave the question some consideration, you could almost hear the wheels of her religious imagination spinning, in this case, around a sense of the abundance of beauty.

If there was once nothing, the religious imagination of these children saw creation as something, something beautiful, more and more, abundant.

When asked why God created the world, eight-year-old Chloe answered: "I try to think back to the beginning of time and space. It just goes back and back and back. I ask my mom or dad how the world was created, and they say, 'by God.' But if God is Jesus Christ and there's a before Christ, then technically he wasn't alive. That's why I think of them [God and Jesus Christ] as two different people." In her answer we can overhear this young mind trying to journey back to the origins of everything, to sneak up on nothingness. Along the way she is trying to work out profound theological quandaries in light of the premises provided by her parents and community of faith. She hears that God created the world—God is on the other side of nothing. But the other premise is that there is a time "before Christ." We didn't get clarity on precisely what she meant. Perhaps it was simply the "BC" in dates, or maybe she was thinking about the birth of Christ and Christmas—which implies there was a "before Christ." Regardless of the source of the "before Christ" premise, her logic is sound: If there is a time before Christ in our world, and God created the world, then God and Jesus Christ must be different.

In contrast is the response from ten-year-old Dave, part of the Church of Jesus Christ of Latter-day Saints (LDS). I had asked him to tell me about Jesus, and the topic of creation came up in his response. "Jesus is Heavenly Father's son; he helped him to create the world." Dave started with a different premise, namely, that Jesus was around before there was a world. There was a Christ before the incarnation, not so different from what we read in the Gospel of John. "In the beginning was the Word, and the Word was with God. . . . He was in the beginning with God" (1:1–2). Similarly, I found most of the children of this LDS community to have a strong sense of, for lack of a better phrase, a time before time, or the preexistence of Jesus before his birth on Earth. Dave's twin brother, John, in fact showed me a chart he had of "God's Plan of Salvation" that makes more feasible not only Christ's premortal life but the premortal life of everyone and everything. The journey of "God's Plan of Salvation" is from premortal life, then to birth and mortal life via the veil of forgetfulness.

According to the LDS *Doctrine and Covenants*, one of the faith's authoritative texts along with the Bible and Book of Mormon, "Man was also in the beginning with God" (93:29).[3] Another text, *The Book of Moses*, from Joseph Smith, says that God made heaven and earth spiritually first: "every plant of the field before it was in the earth, and every herb of the field before it grew. For I, the Lord God, created all things, of which I have spoken, spiritually, before they were naturally upon the face of the earth" (3:5).[4]

This theme of premortal life came up frequently among the LDS parents, revealing that it was not simply an abstract doctrine but an idea integrated into daily, earthly family life. As one mother, Sharon, explained, "We believe that we all lived with Heavenly Father before, and we believe we all will after. It comes up in lessons all the time." She went on to explain that in our premortal life we actually choose our families: "I want my children to know it's not just an accident that they randomly came here, and that we're together, and that they wanted to come. They chose to come to Earth. I'm like [to her children] 'you agreed to this. You knew that I was going to be your mom, and you said okay before you came down here.' Just knowing that we had a life before this, you don't just feel like you're wandering aimlessly. . . . There is purpose to why you ended up in this current situation and that Heavenly Father knew you could do it, and that's why he stuck you with the people that you're with."

Whether this cosmology sounds odd to you or makes great sense, it is at least as old as Plato, who, in *The Republic*, tells the story of Er and how all the preexistent souls choose their "genius" that will be their destiny on Earth.[5] It also provides an orientation—a set of premises—upon which to move about in a life full of contingencies and ambiguities. This is one of the functions of a religious imagination. It could be Plato or Joseph Smith, it could be the opening chapter of Genesis, but reflecting upon origins leads to an empirical limit, a knowledge border, the beginning of time, the beginning of the universe. Yet it is difficult for humans *not* to wonder what or who was on the other side of that limit. Everything in our lives and experience has a source, an antecedent, a before. The limit does not prove—but it does imply—that there is something more.

The imagination, then, allows us to wonder and think about aspects of life that are beyond the world we can know directly with our senses. Not only God and germs, but origins and destinies, for example. The imagination plays out logical relationships based upon whatever premises have been accepted. In a religious imagination, the premises are formed through teachings and practices—for the children we interviewed, teachings and practices of a particular community of faith. God created the world, for example, or Jesus was born in Bethlehem—premises that can be about times and places as exotic as the mountains of India to someone in Kentucky. A major point here is that to speak of imagination is not necessarily to speak of a make-believe world, or a fantasy world, where anything can happen. There can be a scientific imagination as easily as a religious imagination. The difference lies in the premises. Of course, the premises themselves can be questioned or reexamined. Maybe the creation story in Genesis is a poem. Maybe space and time, as Einstein reimagined, are not separate.

For several children, like Hannah, the contrast between religious premises and scientific ones became explicit when we asked about origins. They openly wrestled with the relationship between religious and scientific approaches. Eight-year-old Sue was part of an interdenominational church of expats living in Germany. She said, "Christians think that God made the earth, but in my units that I just had in school, the earth was created by the sun. The earth was superhot." She went on to say, "I'm kind of getting confused, and I don't know which one to pick because I also like science very much, but I also believe in God." Twelve-year-old Adam, Presbyterian, also wrestled with the issue, saying, "I half believe in the big bang, but I like the seven days that God created the earth and the environment and the water—but I think I'm kind of more leaning toward the science one. . . . The science one makes kind of more sense for me because of all the other stars. [The Bible] doesn't talk about that. So, that's why I kind of think of it more in that way if I'm out in the real world. But if I'm thinking spiritually, I do understand how the other story could apply."

Adam was quite thoughtful throughout the interview—emphasizing the importance of serving others and understanding other points of view than your own. I found myself entering a conversation with him at this point, rather than simply posing questions. I asked him, "Do you think God could have used the big bang and evolution to create the world?"

Perhaps it was too much of a leading question, but he responded, "Mmm-hmm. That's kind of how I would think of it. God created the big bang, the two molecules that created the sun and then, I think he meant for the evolution to take place. And, also, because if you just plop two humans in the Garden of Eden, when they got kicked out, they wouldn't have any ecosystem to go to because it would just be the Garden of Eden."

"Good point," I said.

"Because the rest of the world would just be a giant ball of dirt and mud."

* * *

Paul Harris, half of the Dias and Harris team of developmental psychologists mentioned above in the "All cats bark" study, has more recently been studying the ways in which children learn by testimony, that is, by listening to others. As wonderful as hands-on learning and exploration are, "there is a profound limit to the role first-hand experience can play in cognitive development."[6] Why? Because in many realms of learning, children have no way to gather the information for themselves. The objects of learning—whether the mountains of India or the germs that can make you sick—are remote or invisible. Children depend on what others tell them.

The building blocks come early. When a preverbal child points to a box where Curious George is kept or to a kitchen cabinet where the cookies are, the child is navigating the world of "displaced objects," that is, objects that are not immediately present to the senses but are, at best, remembered. Even before children can speak, they can hunt for something not in view. If you ask, "Where's doggie?" a twelve-month-old can go look around the home or point outside. That is, they understand that objects or people or pets can be displaced, not in view. But by the time children can speak, they have learned that others have all kinds of information that is helpful to them. Where is Curious George? He's in your bed. Where are we going? We're going to the library. Children are aware of their own not-knowing, which in turn can initiate the cascade of *why* questions toddlers are famous for.

Even so, navigating the displaced world successfully does not happen all at once. In one study, Harris created a living room with several hiding places for a stuffed animal (for example, in a cabinet or a basket). Two groups of toddlers (twenty-three and thirty months, respectively) were instructed to hide a stuffed animal in one of the spots of their own choosing. Then the children were taken to an adjacent room with a window to the living room where the toy was hidden. In one condition (observation), children were lifted to the window and could see an adult move the toy from the original hiding spot to a different one. In the other condition (verbal) they did not see through the window. Instead, an adult—who was looking through the window—told them where the other adult moved the toy. The children returned to the living room and were asked to find the stuffed animal.

Harris found a difference between the twenty-three-month-olds and the thirty-month-olds. The thirty-month-olds nearly all found the toy, whether they saw the move or were told about it. Not so with the younger toddlers. If the younger children saw for themselves the adult moving the toy, they found it. That is, the new perceptual information could override their memory of hiding the stuffed animal. But if they only heard about the move, the younger children went back to where they themselves had hidden the toy. The new testimonial information from the adult was not strong enough to override their memory of hiding the stuffed animal.[7] (Explains a lot, doesn't it, for all you who live or work with young toddlers?)

Harris believes the difference is that older children have a more nimble system for assimilating new information based on testimony alone. The findings suggest a great deal about the power of hands-on learning and experience for the youngest children. But they also suggest the power of learning by testimony as they get older. Sometime during that third year of life, toddlers learn to relax their assumed knowledge and update it with information gathered only from the words of someone else.

Of course, life and learning get more complicated. Children learn that others have bad information. "Where's Curious George?" Dad tells Elly that Curious George is on the couch in the living room. Elly goes to the couch, and he's not there. Elly learns that Dad can be wrong. "Maybe he's in your bed." He's not there either. Elly learns that others sometimes guess because they are not sure. "Oh, I remember, he's in your backpack." And he is. Elly learns that others can forget information, then remember it. So, children eventually have to learn how to sort out all kinds of information they may get from others. People can be wrong; people guess, forget, remember, deceive, pretend, joke, and more. This is all part of learning the world of human information.

To get along in life, children must learn to navigate this world of displaced realities, good information and bad, in a process that never ends. To better understand how children do so, Harris has conducted multiple experiments testing how children discern what they are told. Trust is key.[8] For example, in one study, young children in a child-care facility were introduced to unfamiliar objects and taught their names and functions by an adult. If the adult was a known caregiver at their center, the children were much more likely to accept the descriptions compared to an adult unknown to the child.

But, as we've noted, even known and trusted people, like Elly's dad, can be wrong. So, it is not the case that trusting children naively accept anything a trusted informant says. Here, Harris draws upon attachment theory, that is, how securely or insecurely a child's attachment to a parent is. The punch line is that the securely attached child is able to exercise a more balanced approach to information, able to trust *and* able to be skeptical. The securely attached child is, yes, more likely to listen to and believe what a trusted figure says. But—and this just as important—the child is more likely to revise what they've been told based upon new information. "Secure children are flexible," says Harris.[9] These studies underline the deep connection between cognitive development, formation, and the emotional life.

Being loved deeply is like yoga for the mind, generating flexibility and the ability to learn!

Children indeed explore, probe, try things, take apart, and reconstruct the stuff of their environments. And this is a powerful, firsthand way of learning and why we can think of them as "little scientists." Yet Harris believes the little scientist idea is misleading, as it masks all the ways children rely upon relationships with others for learning. He sees children as behaving more like good anthropologists who "immerse themselves in the language, learn from participant observations, and rely on trusted informants."[10] In this way children can learn about stars they never see, great-grandparents they never knew, the origins of a country or the universe, organs in their bodies, microscopic germs, and, as Harris points out, God.

So, when we hear children attempting to hold together scientific accounts of the universe with religious accounts, we hear them weighing out the claims of trusted informants, the testimonies of others that provide the premises and possible logical conclusions in their imaginations. The work of Harris helps us see how important a secure base is for flexibly considering claims, and even, possibly, the ability to affirm the truth of science and poetry.

* * *

What is real? Philosophers throw around the term "ontology" in reflecting upon what is true or what is real. The root is from the Greek for "being" or "that which is," so it means the study of what is. Though a fancy term, it's what children are doing all the time. They are studying and sorting out what is real. They use their senses to observe the immediate world, but they are also able to conjure displaced objects and people in their imaginations. Children live in a world full of invisible entities, those not immediately available to the senses, whether atoms, first-century Bethlehem, oxygen, or the origins of the universe. These are all known via testimony. But children also may hear of fairies and dragons, read stories with talking animals and magic crayons, or see movies with mermaids and minions. The same capacity that allows children to imagine germs also allows them to imagine dragons and friends nobody else can see. That which is, that which is real, is not so simple.

How children sort these realities out has a lot to do with the words and behaviors of those around them. If people talk about washing hands to get the germs off, how germs make you sick, why doctors wear masks, why we get shots, or why we shouldn't touch a dead mouse—children are likely to think of germs as quite real. On the other hand, if dragons only show up in certain stories, are talked about in highly playful situations, don't seem to affect the behavior of adults, and perhaps are even said to be make-believe, then children begin to understand that dragons are game-like productions of people's minds—like being on a planet where all cats bark. Children understand the difference, in part, because they themselves know they can conjure up beings and situations that are "not real." They understand pretending.

Children are indeed little ontologists, figuring out different categories of reality, sorting out dragons, invisible germs, and God. Trusted informants and their testimony help. We can suppose that children who grow up in a home or community in which God, like a dragon, only shows up in certain stories, doesn't seem to affect the behavior of adults, and perhaps is even said to be make-believe would provide one set of premises. But for the children described in this book, God is a (mostly) invisible figure that people nonetheless bow to, praise, sing of, say is real, talk to, read about, and in whose name perform elaborate rituals of eating and washing. Though words may or may not always be involved, these are nonetheless forms of testimony and are likely a strong reason children may appreciate that the ontological status of God may differ from that of a dragon or imaginary friend.

* * *

Children's reflections upon the origins of the world have led down a winding path of syllogisms and imagination, somethingness and nothingness, displaced objects and testimony, science and poetry, dragons and imaginary friends, trustworthy informants and secure attachments, abundant beauty and the nature of what is. Even so, all this only scratches the surface of the complexity of children's religious imaginations.

When Hannah, whose words opened this chapter, reflected further upon why God created the world, she added another layer to the conversation. "Sometimes I wonder," she said, "is God the god of this universe or the god of all the universes—if there are even other universes, like in different dimensions?" She admitted that with such a thought her "head starts to hurt." But she went on anyway. "It's probably that he's the god of the entire universe, but sometimes I wonder if he's just

God on Earth, like he just takes care of the earth. If there are intelligent beings out there, I wonder if he's their god too."

Hannah's robust religious imagination is open and curious, flexible and thoughtful. It helps in her love of "finding out about the world." Deep premises about a loving Creator and a universe full of beauty and order, eclipses and supercontinents, music and love, cascade in her mind to generate new questions and possibilities and musings—from the minds of animals to multiverses. If the conditions are right, it seems the imagination builds upon itself toward the sense of more.

3

Faith Communities

"I'M TALKING TO MIGUEL," I said into the recorder. "Say hi, Miguel." He said hi. I explained that if I talk or write about our interview, I won't use his real name, so people won't know who he is. "Do you have a pretend name, or do you want me to make one up for you?"

He said, "Maybe Macaroni."

"Okay, I'm talking to Macaroni, Saturday May 26th."

Nine-year-old Macaroni—I'll call him Mac—is a "preacher's kid" living in a city in the US Southwest. (For the record, his real name is not Miguel either.) His father is pastor of a Presbyterian Church (USA) congregation that is relatively unique in the denomination because it is multiethnic—mostly Hispanic and Anglo variations—and conducts services bilingually, in English and Spanish, and has done so for decades. Mac's family is also multiethnic. His father is of European descent while his mother is from Guatemala (they met while he was living in the country). They conduct everyday family life bilingually as well, in English and Spanish.

I explained the research: "Mac, I'm talking to kids about church and God and things like that and trying to understand how young people think about these things. And the main thing to know is there are no wrong answers. I'm trying to understand how *you* think about it all, not what you're *supposed* to think, or what you think I think you should think about it." We both smiled at the loopiness of that statement. "If you're okay with that, I'm going to ask you to write your name right here." Mac was okay with it and signed his name. He wondered about other children I had interviewed. When I told him about interviewing children in Mexico, it led to a discussion about my Spanish skills. I explained that I had used a translator because my Spanish wasn't that good and the children there would never have understood me. Mac and I agreed to use English for our interview.

"My first question is: Would you be willing to talk to me about church and God?" He was. "Great. I know you go to church. Tell me about your church."

Without hesitation he answered, "I think it's amazing with all the people who are so kind to me. And listening to my dad preach." When Mac said this, I wondered if he was giving me what he thought I wanted to hear—despite my encouragement otherwise. Though, as he went on, it was clear that he had genuine affection and appreciation for the people. When I asked whether there were people at church who were particularly important, he mentioned his Sunday school teachers specifically and "adults" generally. "Adults," he said, "like so many people are so caring about me." As an example, he explained that his parents were about to make a trip to Spain. "A lot of people are volunteering to take me and let me go over to their house to live there for like a week." Mac showed no sign of trepidation or anxiety about this separation. The tone in his voice made it sound like he would be going to stay with beloved grandparents for a week.

The next day, Trinity Sunday in the church calendar, Jane and I attended the church, interviewed other children, and were welcomed to a potluck afterward. I noticed right away a mission statement in the bulletin that declared how their multigenerational, bilingual, and multicultural community reflects "the diversity of God's creation unified by God's hope and love." I had to agree with Mac—the people were so kind and welcoming, as well as curious and affirming about the research we were doing. The service was beautiful, including his dad's preaching that emphasized God as Trinity is God as Relationship, is God as Community. Jane and I were ready to join, if only we didn't live a thousand miles away.

* * *

As I was poring over transcripts from this and other interviews, a fellow investigator in the world of child development, Erin Smith, reached out by email to update me on the work she and a coresearcher had been up to. She and her colleague, Robert Crosby, were exploring the role of congregations in relation to "social support" for children. A week later we all met by Zoom to talk about their research.

"Social support" as a concept is self-evident.[1] It's a way of talking about the web of relationships that uphold us in our everyday lives. But over the last three decades the idea has become increasingly important in psychological, educational, and medical research. Generally, strong social support correlates with better mental/emotional well-being, learning, and physical health. Researchers have been exploring how and where people, particularly children, receive such support, for example, through families, neighborhoods, sports leagues, schools, and clubs. Typically, social support for children is measured by the extent to which relationships help children believe that they (1) are loved, (2) are esteemed and valued, and (3) feel part of a supportive community.

As Smith and Crosby explained to me, churches and religious organizations have been badly neglected in the research. Yet, for many children they are a rich source of loving and supporting relationships that help them know they are loved, valued, and part of a caring community. In addition, social support is ordinarily an explicit value in congregations, backed by theology and a worldview in which God loves and supports us and wants us to love one another. Preaching, teaching, rituals, creeds, and missions, for example, formally express the value of such caring relationships. And for some children, these relationships may endure for a lifetime. While favorite teachers and coaches may provide powerful support, the relationships often have a much shorter life span.

The focus upon social support through religious community

deepens the typical sociological research into people's faith lives. Most studies zero in on one or two measures, for example, religious affiliation or attendance. Such measures tell us something, of course, but they are so big and general as to be not that meaningful, especially to parents and church leaders. Smith and Crosby's work explores in a finer-grained way what specifically helps children know that the people at church love and support them. In one study, they asked children how they knew they were loved by an adult (nonfamily member) at church.[2] Most children named specific people—often someone in a leadership role like a pastor or Sunday school teacher. When asked for examples of how they knew they were loved by that person, the most common responses had to do with listening and attentiveness. "A nine-year-old boy said that his special adult 'will listen to everything I say,' . . . a fifth-grade boy described a special woman 'who used to be my kindergarten teacher, even when she sees me now, we say "hi" and we have a conversation.'" Smith and Crosby found that it was often the informal interactions (in the hallway, or at a nonchurch event) that communicated to the children the enduring nature of the relationships, even though these relationships may have started more formally (say, through the role of a Sunday school teacher).

Children were also asked how they felt supported and cared for by their peers at church. Often the response was a version of "just hanging out" together, though some children named specific events that communicated care, such as getting help when needed. But most spoke of playing or talking as ways of expressing care and support.

* * *

In our interviews with parents, one of the first questions we usually asked was: "Why do you take your child/children to church?" Mac's parents, Brian and Alana, both mentioned community. Brian said, "Some because of spiritual formation. Some big part of it is community and learning how to engage a community—support and be supported."

Alana agreed: "The same. I grew up in the church since I was little. I used to be Catholic, and I always attended Sunday mass. It's very important to me for them to know about their faith and have a community." She jokingly added, "Other than Brian's job, to support him, too. But mainly I would think if he weren't a pastor, we'd still–"

Brian finished, "We'd still go to church. Maybe not as much." They laughed.

Just as Brian and Alana mentioned both community and faith formation, nearly every parent responded with multifaceted, overlapping reasons for taking their children to church. That is, their motivations could not be boiled down into one simple response. However, frequently mentioned were knowing God's love; the structure and routine (including time together as a family); faith formation; and a moral foundation for their children. But a theme that nearly always emerged in the multiplicity of reasons was "being part of a larger worshiping community."

For example, according to Lena, mother of three children and also Presbyterian: "I think it's part of our family tradition, and it's part of the time that we spend together, and we all go happy, and we all come home happy, and that's part of being part of the community–and the grandparents and the friends and all those people that make up our extended family." Joe, her husband, added, "Yeah, being in the community that shares their faith."

Jane, who interviewed them, followed up. "You said 'we go happy,' is that the kids too?"

Lena explained, "Yeah, everybody's on board with it."

Joe added, "Once in a while, they're not excited. But compared to my experience as a kid, they do seem to enjoy it."

Lena illustrated by way of their ten-year-old. "Bob, every week–'Is there a potluck today? Is there a potluck? I want to eat.' He loves his eating together and playing with his friends, and he would have a potluck every week. So, he will really enjoy middle school youth group next year when he can eat every Sunday. It's painful for him that he can't go [like his older brother]."

When I asked Bob himself what the best part of church was, he answered: "Something that I like about church is how most people are super nice about everything you do. Like if you do something they're real nice about it."

The frequent naming of community—in the midst of multifaceted answers—is not overly surprising given that we recruited families primarily through pastors who identified those who were "actively engaged" in their congregations. But the question is why. Why were these parents and children engaged in church life? After all, many of the parents we interviewed had not found the church communities they grew up in to be so meaningful or supportive. Some chose to leave churches because they were too rigid or fear-based or shaming, while others left or drifted away at some point because going to church, in their experience, was *only* a social thing to do.

Teri was a member of a relatively new branch of Presbyterianism (PCA, or Presbyterian Church of America) and a mother of three children. She said, "I was raised in a very nominal Christian home. We went to church on Sundays but that was the only part of our life that had anything to do with the church." She explained going to church was just something people did where she grew up. "I remember asking [my parents] as a teenager why are we going to church? Why do we have to go? And the answer was that's just what you do. There was no personal belief behind it other than this is expected of us because we're good people." She gave up church in college, but a few years later found herself "kind of lost," and she connected to a church that offered not only social support but a community rooted in the conviction of God's love. "That's when the Lord really captured my heart."

Along the same lines, Annette, an Orthodox mother raised in a Protestant tradition, shared the shift in cultural, spiritual expectations when she converted at twenty. Growing up in her former church, she had low expectations. "You go to church and that's church and then you leave." Converting, she found both struggle and beauty when the expectations were upped. "In Orthodoxy, there is the expectation to make it to as many services as you can. There's the expectation of fasting. There's the expectation of—" Here she interrupted herself, then tried to summarize. "So, no matter where you are, you are constantly aware of your faith. It's a part of you. It's in every decision you make. 'Am I going to eat this hamburger or am I going to eat this salad? All right, I'm going to eat the salad.' You make a conscious choice to remain in the faith with every decision that you make. For me, there's beauty in the struggle. There's beauty in learning the lives of the saints." Her hope was that her children would learn this beauty in the struggle. "Part of me wants my kids to see a living example of somebody who chose to live the faith throughout their whole life, who struggled, who went through the ups and the downs, who just made that choice every day."

Stephen and Megan, parents of five boys, are part of an independent evangelical church. Stephen said: "I guess the reason we go is to hear good teaching and to worship with other people. I think there's something special that happens in corporately worshiping together that you can't quite replicate, at least on your own. I believe that the church was created, is God's body for us, to be connected together."

Megan agreed. She added how important it is for her boys to have other adults in their lives. "We talk to the boys about different things that are going on, and I think when they're hearing things from other people and not just their parents, that's really valuable."

Stephen described a time when he was younger, and he felt fine about not being part of a church even though his faith was important to him. "I thought, I can read the Bible by myself, I can pray by myself, I can do all these things. I didn't realize, until I stepped back in [to a church], to being connected in that body, that, 'Wow, I was missing out!' And so, as I crave it for myself and Megan, I crave that for my boys too, for them to see that God's design for us is not to be these isolated islands out there but to be joined together."

Claire, mother of three, discussed how important her Catholic upbringing has proven to be for her, now, as an adult, and how she wanted that for her children, though it's not always easy. They live in a large city in the southeast United States, and she mentioned how many people don't go to church. "And I will admit, it has been harder to go to church over the past couple years. [They had a child three years before the interview.] Every time you have a kid, you're on like a hiatus from church for a while. Then you get back in the groove again." Yet she said it was worth it. "But, yeah, I think just to be a part of that community and learn the goodness that it teaches, and just grow up in that environment. I feel like it's always something that you have for the rest of your life, and something to go to if you are in need. Or, you can always count on the church or people from the church."

Janet, mother of two (one of whom is Sue from the last chapter), was a member of the Reformed Church of America. But the family had been living in Germany and attended an international, nondenominational church of expats. Though it would have been easy to give up church for a while, they did not. "I think there are a number of reasons why we take our children to church. First, it's a good pattern and rhythm to bring them into a space where they hear about God." She explained that children in ordinary German schools have religious education as part of the curriculum. But her children attended an international school that did not have religious education. So, this was one reason she and her husband valued church. But she was particularly passionate about the intergenerational quality of church. "I think it's super important that they see all ages. I think our world is totally segregated by age, so I really love the family feel and interaction of generations at church." Perhaps this feel was intensified by being so far from home, separated from grandparents, aunts and uncles, or old family friends.

In reflecting upon the interviews with parents, it became clear that the connection to a larger community was important to parents not only for their children's sake but also for their own. Given the challenges of raising children—perhaps staying home with them full time, or juggling home and work, sleepless nights, sickness, exhaustion, school issues, screen-time battles, and so much more—on top of all the joys and concerns of life that have nothing to do with children, the relationships forged in congregations would indeed seem to underline the idea that, as Stephen put it, "God's design for us is not to be these isolated islands out there but to be joined together."

* * *

I asked Mac to walk me through a typical Sunday. He described worship and Sunday school and what happens in each—learning from the Bible, sermons, singing, prayer, crafts, and a fellowship time with "little snacks." I asked him what the best part was. Not too surprisingly, he said, "Just seeing a lot of people."

The particulars of church life for the children we interviewed varied somewhat from community to community: Orthodox children might talk of icons or chanting; Catholic children might emphasize communion; LDS children might describe the time of Testimony. But all their experience involved some form of worship, some form of learning, and some form of fellowship. Among the parents, whether or not they were professional church leaders like Mac's father, they often served on committees, taught classes, led projects, and helped organize various events and programs including service to a larger community (whether local or global). In short, church was important enough to them to bend their lives to the rhythms and responsibilities of their congregational communities. Church life was part of them, and they were part of church life.

As with Mac, after children described church to us, we asked, "What's the best part of church?" While it's tempting to imagine that children would gravitate to one or two activities—like snack time or crafts (which some children did say)—the responses to this question were highly varied between children. They reflected nearly every aspect of congregational life, from singing in choir and potlucks to Sunday school or play time. This variation itself disrupts any monolithic notions of who children are or what children's ministries should be. One strength of congregations is that they are typically communities providing multiple entry points for engagement for lots of different people with various interests and personalities.

Some children, when asked about the best part of church, claimed the whole experience: "The best part of church is all of it," or simply, "Everything." Most children named particular activities or moments like "singing," "kids' church," "Sunday school," or "Primary" (like Sunday school for LDS). One of the older children, at twelve, named the church's mission trips and service projects. One child in Mexico mentioned "processions" (that happen in the streets, between villages, during special holidays). Several children answered the question with the emotions they felt after going to church: "It feels good." (Sometimes this was in spite of not wanting to go in the first place.) A couple of children specifically named the good feeling of taking communion.

Even with all this variety, there were a few themes that came up more frequently, revolving around (1) food, (2) learning about God, and (3) people.

Eating was popular: potlucks, doughnut hour, Sunday school snacks, communion ("the bread is yummy"), or the "blessed bread" after an Orthodox service. (In the Orthodox community where we interviewed, everyone fasts on Sunday morning before communion, so the bread is the first food of the day, and the church holds a potluck after the service.)

Several children named learning: "I love learning about God," "talking about Jesus," "talk about God," "learning the Word," "the sermon." As one eight-year-old put it, "Sometimes I just get it, I know exactly what she [pastor] is saying, and I kind of figure out how it relates, and it is cool."

And many children said the best part of church was the people. As Mac said, "Just seeing a lot of people." Others: "seeing my friends," "our church is kind of small, but big in love," "being with my family," "spending time with family and friends," "just hanging out with friends and family before and after church," "I just like how the whole church is like a family and everyone cares about you."

"What's the worst part of church?" When I asked Mac, he hesitated. "Sometimes"—he stopped himself for a second—"I'm not sure." I waited a bit, then suggested that if he thought of something, he could tell me later. With that he offered, "Maybe one thing is when I'm so tired I have to wake up for church." He explained that he likes to stay up late on Saturday nights (though he never said how late that was). And Mac was not alone in saying that the sheer act of getting up and getting ready for church was the worst part. Though this was typically followed by a version of "once I'm there I'm glad I went." (More than one parent mentioned how just getting out the door with everyone could be a struggle.)

Some children named a particular aspect of worship as the worst part. "Sitting—it gets so long." "Having to sit, sit, sit on the pew, all morning." Conversely, "Standing for a long time." Then again, one child didn't "like being told when to sit and when to stand." And even as some children named music as the best part of church, a couple of children named "singing" and "the music" as the worst part of church. An answer unique among some of the Orthodox children was "fasting." And one child's answer was the flip side of her favorite part of church. "I just like learning about Jesus, and I don't like it when our Sunday school teacher comes late."

The most common answers children named as the worst part of church had to do with words and adults talking. *Sermon.* "Sometimes the sermon is long." "The sermon can be boring." *Prayer.* "The part where they name every joy and concern." "The litanies get long and repeat and are boring." *Testimony.* Among the LDS children, a few mentioned this time during the first hour of church when adults give their testimonies—personal experiences shaping their faith lives. "Testimony during sacrament." "During Testimony, I get sleepy."

Perhaps the most surprising answer to the question was "nothing." Despite the responses above, the majority of the children said something like "nothing," "I love church," or "I like it all."

* * *

"Mac, when you grow up, do you think you'll go to church?"

"Sure," he said, almost as if it were a silly question after all he had been saying. And maybe it was silly, given that all but two children answered with a definite yes. But I wanted to move the discussions away from present-day descriptions and experiences and more squarely into the realm of imagination, specifically how children imagined their future selves. Free from parental pressure to go to church, they would perhaps choose not to. Then again, that imagined future says a lot about present experience and feelings about church. One of the two who did not give a solid yes answer was Solis, a twelve-year-old girl with a lot of doubts about her faith. She answered, "Probably not." Her family had just dropped out of their Episcopal church over a leadership conflict. The other child was Nathan, a ten-year-old LDS boy, who simply said, "Maybe. I'm not sure." In talking with Nathan's mother, she said he had been the least engaged with church of their five children (one of whom is Nathan's identical twin), but she had no idea why beyond "It just doesn't click with him the same way."

After children told me whether they would go to church as adults, I asked them whether, if they had children, they would want their children to go. All the children, even Solis and Nathan, said they likely would. Nathan answered, "I would want my kids to go. It's the right thing to do." Solis said, "Probably, I would just let them explore all the different religions."

Some children pointed to a general feeling or atmosphere they find at church, such as "It's fun and I would want my children to go," or "Because it just makes me really happy. And I want them to feel how I feel," or "they need the experience."

When I asked Mac why he would want his children to go to church, I expected that he would say something like "the people." But he veered into different territory. "I think you learn a lot of different things that are very interesting. Like God, who created us." With this answer I asked Mac to tell me about God. "God created a lot of stuff. He created the whole earth, I guess, but then I think he went into Jesus, and he was actually playing the part of Jesus." So, I asked Mac to tell me about Jesus. "Jesus is somebody who surprises everyone, how he is kind, and he can heal people and has powers to walk on the water and inspires people to follow God." I eventually asked him whether his church talked about the Holy Spirit or Holy Ghost. He said they sing a song about it in church, but he couldn't remember the title or words. I asked him more directly what he knew about the Holy Spirit. "It's something that you can rely on. Something that's an incredible story." I wasn't sure what he meant at first, but when we started talking about Sunday school, it became clearer. "We learned about that story where everyone was speaking different languages, and they had the little flames on their head." I realized the week before had been Pentecost Sunday, celebrating the story from the book of Acts when the Holy Spirit filled the followers of Jesus, often considered the birth of the church.

Overall, I was fascinated by the circuitous route Mac had taken in our conversation—from the importance of people at church "who are so kind," to the Creator God becoming a person in Jesus who surprises everyone with kindness, to the reliability of the Holy Spirit, whose presence unites people so fully that they can understand different languages in the first multilingual church.

Mac was not alone. When asked why they would want their children to go to church, most children gave a version of: "So they can learn about God," or "I want them to learn about Jesus." What that meant was often connected to love. Nine-year-old Henry, who went to the same church as Mac, answered the question, saying, "Because I like church and I think they should experience the love of God too." Twelve-year-old Rafael, Orthodox, said he would want his children to "learn how to love people more, love God." Eight-year-old Pamela, LDS, said she would want her children to know that "He loves us all." She continued, "And I would teach them that they should go to church and their children should go to church and their children and their children."

In this way, children's reasons for wanting their imagined children—if not, like Pamela and her great-great-great-grandchildren—was not so different from their parents' actual reasons for taking their children to church. Phil and his family had recently moved from another city and joined Mac's church. They had previously been part of a nondenominational evangelical church but joined this church for two main reasons, he said. "Proximity to our house. It's not too far from where we live. We like the community here. It's multigenerational and multicultural, which we love." Phil was the father of a three-year-old, Brandon, whom we interviewed at the church, but also the father of a one-week-old. Still, he and Brandon made it to church this Trinity Sunday morning. When I asked why they take their children to church, he said, "It's important for us to have them grounded in a sense of who God is from an early age. . . . And you know, we just want to raise our kids so that they have an understanding of God's love. And I think church is a great way to do that."

Teri, the PCA mother mentioned above, admitted how hard it was to take little kids to church. "But I think it's so important—it's the most important thing we can do as parents." The reason: "We think it's important for them from the earliest age to know of God's tremendous love. And we hope that someday they'll look back and say they never knew a time when they didn't know the Lord."

* * *

Erin Smith and Robert Crosby, in their research into social support, conducted another major study (over eight hundred children, seven to twelve years old) exploring the ways in which children feel cared for by the people at their church in relation to self-esteem (one of their measures of social support).[3] They posed statements such as, "An adult from church makes me feel loved," and asked children to answer using a scale of 1 (never) to 4 (always). They also asked children questions about God, such as, "I feel like God is close to me" and "I feel God's love for me." In this case answers ranged from "never" to "many times a day." What they found may be particularly significant for social support through church, but also for the formation of children's religious imaginations. They indeed found a significant correlation between self-esteem and perceived adult support—but only for the younger children (seven- and eight-year-olds). Yet this is not the whole story. They found that children's sense of God's loving presence (they called it "God image") correlated significantly with self-esteem among children of all ages. In addition, they found a strong correlation between children's sense of adult support and God image. In other words, adult support seems to mediate God image. "Children who saw adults at their church being as supportive and responsive to their needs were more likely to view God in the same way, promoting self-esteem." Smith and Crosby go on to say how the finding highlights the importance of intergenerational church relationships.

Smith and Crosby also explored the relationship between family religious practices at home and children's sense of God. For example, "I pray with my family when it's time to eat." They found that children who engaged in such practices with their families not only were more likely to view God in loving, supportive ways but also were more likely to have closer, supportive relationships with people (adults and peers) at church. They conclude that everyday family religious routines help children establish an individual connection with God as well as supportive relationships in the faith community.

* * *

"It's in a little handbook for all the people that serve in a leadership position. All the instructions at the top say that it's about the home first, and we're supporting them." This is from Joy, who along with her husband was deeply involved in the leadership of their LDS community. "They always talk about the temple being the house of God, a holy, sacred place," Joy said. "They also say that the home is the other. It's the only other thing that could compare to the temple." She said that the message is for the home to be "a place where the gospel is, and where the Spirit is. I guess that's the biggest thing—we want all our kids to be able to feel the love of God and the Holy Spirit. So, you try to make your house like that." Though she immediately added that it doesn't always seem like that. "It's hard work. Being a mom is a dirty, dirty job, right?"

This was a theme that came up in nearly every interview with parents. They wanted their homes and family lives to be living expressions of their faith so that, as Teri (above) put it, they know from the earliest age of "God's tremendous love." But it's not easy. Competing interests and values of the larger culture combine with the stress and demands of raising children, to make commitment to family routines, let alone religious routines, challenging. Yet to the parents we interviewed, faith was so important that they were trying the best they could in various ways, depending upon the household—mealtime prayers together, bedtime blessings, singing sacred songs, devotions, and home altars, all woven together with kind words, in addition to Scripture reading and talk of God. And most parents spoke of not living up to their own expectations on this front.

In their research into "religious parenting," sociologists Christian Smith, Bridget Ritz, and Michael Rotolo interviewed over two hundred parents, who, like those in our project, were actively engaged in religious life.[4] Smith and company not only interviewed parents involved in various Christian traditions but also those from Jewish, Muslim, Hindu, and Buddhist traditions, across the United States. The research set out to identify major themes, similarities, and differences between parents or backgrounds.

One of the common themes across backgrounds was the importance of home and family as the primary influence upon children's religious lives. In fact, they found a general consensus that *congregations are secondary*. This finding surprised them. "We have all heard at religious education and youth ministry conferences many youth pastors complain that 'their' kids' parents often simply just hand over their children to them, saying, 'We don't know what we are doing, you do it.' We went into this research with those stereotypes and complaints in mind. But we were surprised to find something different." What they found was that the parents "unvaryingly believed it was their responsibility to pass on religion to their children." They hoped congregations reinforced the religion, but otherwise parents held "fairly low expectations for . . . their religious congregations."

This finding is indeed surprising and somewhat contrary to what our research found. However, we did not explicitly ask, like Smith's team, "Are parents or church more responsible for passing on religious faith to children?" Had we, perhaps we would have found the same responses as they did. But based on the conversations we had with parents, my hunch is that we would have found something less binary than this parents-or-church option. The parents we interviewed, by far, genuinely appreciated church, were often voluntarily involved in leadership roles, and, for all the reasons mentioned above (like social support), were grateful for the web of relationships fostered in their communities of faith. As Joy said, the temple is a "holy, sacred place," and "home is the other one." What I hear in this affirmation is a kind of braiding together of church and home life in a way that generates caring relationships. In this way both congregations and families are communities of faith.

"That's why God puts us in community or calls us into community," said Carol, mother of two. "Because we can't make it on our own. And our culture leads us to believe we can or should. So, we need to be in a community that we can depend on when we can't make it or when we're struggling. One of the things we love about our church—we feel like our children are experiencing that community, to know what that feels like, what a strong community feels like. . . . I guess I value that there's more than just me in the world. I know that I need to put my focus, not on me, but on us."

Laine and Frank, members of the same (PCA) church as Teri, met us in a public library to interview their two young children, Janelle and Michael, because they "hadn't had time to straighten up the house." Over the phone I told her I'd be the guy with white hair and a white beard. She said, "And when you see a Black woman and a White man walk in with two little kids, you'll know it's us." She laughed. We found each other easily enough. And when asked why they take their children to church, Laine said: "We take our kids to church, because it's the sweetest place for them to see community and to experience God and to have an opportunity for us to model what it's like to love God with our lives and how we spend our lives."

But it was the interview with their five-year-old daughter, Janelle, that provided a fuller sense of what it meant to them to "experience God." I asked Janelle whether she felt like God was ever very close to her, nearby. She told me about starting kindergarten. "On my first day of school my mom gave me this bracelet and then it had a feather on it." Trying to clarify, I asked whether that meant God was close to her. She said, "It meant that he will cover his wings over me." This did not make full sense until I heard Jane's interview with her parents. Laine, her mother, explained: "In the kids' playroom, we have this painting, that someone gave to us. It has a little bird, and it has Psalm 94, 'He will cover you with his feathers, under his wings you will find refuge.'" She didn't think the kids really knew what it was, beyond a piece of artwork. "But when Janelle started kindergarten, it was right after we moved here, and we didn't know anyone, and she was very nervous. A friend of mine who's a jeweler gave me this bracelet that has a feather on it. And so I let her wear it for her first day of school. I told her about that verse, 'He will cover you with his feathers, and under his wings you will find refuge.' So if you feel afraid, just remember that. We recited it over and over again and practiced it so that she could remember it. And she went to school and told me that that really helped her have confidence and to not be as afraid."

In this account we can see how the caring love of God made known in "the sweetest place for them to see community" intertwines with the love of parents—as well as the prayers of the psalmist and artwork and a playroom—to buoy a little girl on the first day of kindergarten. So much love packed into a feather.

* * *

"What did you draw?" I asked Mac. While I was interviewing his sister, Mac drew two pictures. One was of Earth—from the point of view of space—colored in with green and blue. "This is a picture about the earth that God created." The next was a drawing of his church. It was fascinating because he had managed to depict both the outside and the inside at the same time. In the upper right corner was a bright yellow sun, while in the upper left was a cross, roughly the same size, sitting on the roof of the church. Wavy lines connected the two—maybe a holy wind blowing between them as if an echo of this Trinitarian, relational God. At the same time, the drawing showed the inside of the sanctuary—carpet, stairs, steps to the chancel, and doors—but there was another section that I wasn't sure about.

"This is my church," Mac said. Pointing to the chancel, he said, "Here's the inside where my dad does communion." And pointing to the section in question, Mac said it was the place for "family promise." He explained, "It's where they get people who have families, and they situate them in homes." He pointed to the middle of the drawing and said, "Here's the fire that we do at Christmas." I couldn't imagine having a fire inside the sanctuary, but he quickly headed off my concern. "We would get a candle from here and go outside and light a fire and would just sing hymns about Christmas in that light."

Mac told me I could keep the drawings, and I thanked him. I found myself impressed at a young imagination moving fluidly between heaven and earth, inside and outside, communion and housing families. I could almost hear the congregation, this community of supportive and kind people, singing in the glow of that Christmas light.

4

We Need a Place

"DO YOU WANT TO SEE MY PRAYER CLOSET?" five-year-old Alexander asked me.

When Jane and I arrived, Alexander greeted us at the door, along with his parents and younger brothers. His mother told us how excited Alexander was to talk with us. She had explained to him that we were talking to children and asking questions about God and church. This family was part of a Russian Orthodox community in a small city in the US Northwest. An old friend was the priest and helped identify children and parents who might be interested in talking with us.

The evening before we had attended vespers at the church—a simple building with a large open space for services filled not with pews (because people stand) but with icons on the walls as well as an iconostasis, a wall of icons near the altar. While the number of people attending was small that evening, the room felt full, alive with figures from the Bible and church history. We noticed a young boy in a cassock (the robe of a priest) walking around swinging an empty censer (the container holding incense) roughly imitating the actions of the priest. Since Jane and I had been to only a couple of Orthodox services in our lives, we followed along in the service a bit awkwardly. But this young boy in a cassock with a censer clearly knew the rhythms and rituals of his community in worship.

That boy turned out to be Alexander.

* * *

Developmental psychologist Alison Gopnik makes a helpful observation about rituals in her book *The Gardener and the Carpenter*. She points out that rituals often make little practical sense, whether a Japanese tea service or a midnight mass. But their impracticality is what makes them powerful. The rituals are more elaborate than simply pouring a cup of tea to quench your thirst or offering you a piece of bread to feed you. "The whole point of rituals is that they don't make ordinary causal sense. They are potent precisely because they're divorced from ordinary principles of efficiency."[1] They signal something else is going on.

Gopnik knows because her whole career is filled with experiments and observations of children that demonstrate how gifted they are at understanding causal relationships and patterns in the world around them. One of her earliest books is aptly titled *The Scientist in the Crib*. So, for children, ritual behaviors that *do not* exhibit clear functional purposes stand out. If a young child, for example, senses you are trying to place a block in a box but keep dropping it, they'll typically pick up the block for you and either hand it back or go ahead and put it in the box. But if you hold the block in your palm and spin around three times, put the block in the box, and say, "your turn," they are likely to go get the block back out and start spinning. From their perspective, either something important is going on or perhaps it's a kind of game. The child is tuned into you and not the pragmatics of the situation. In other words, rituals signal something highly social going on. When they're repeated in a community, the child is learning something about the values and identity of the group.

* * *

As we entered Alexander's home, he was so eager to show us his prayer closet that he could barely contain himself. "Here it is," he said to me as he opened a door to a cubby in the wall. The cubby was about four feet above the floor, above Alexander's head. It was an older house, and I noticed the walls of the cubby were lined with cedar panels. Perhaps the closet had originally held wool clothing or blankets, but now it held the prayers of a five-year-old.

"Wow," I said. "How do you use it?"

He scooted a trunk over and used it as a stepstool to reach the opening and crawl in. "Here are some nails," he said pointing at the wall, "in case you need to hang an icon or two."

"I see an icon in there now. What one is that?"

"That's the Theotokos. I always put this up here."

Hanging on the wall was a six-inch square depicting the Mother of God in this tradition, Mary. She is holding the child Jesus to her cheek. Jesus is looking up with adoration at his mother while Mary appears to be looking up or away with sorrowful eyes, as if she knows what lies ahead for her child.

While there are many versions of the Theotokos, I immediately recognized this one from the cover of a book I use in a course, a memoir by the religion scholar Albert Raboteau called *A Sorrowful Joy*. Describing a particularly painful point in his life, Raboteau recalls visiting an icon exhibit at the Princeton Art Museum called *Gates of Mystery: The Sacred Art of Russia*. He says the exhibit astonished him so thoroughly he went back three times. "One icon attracted me with its spiritual power, an icon of the *Theotokos* with sad loving eyes. She seemed to hold all the hurt in the world with those eyes. I stood in front of her for a long time. I gazed at her and she gazed at me." He goes on to call this sad joyfulness "a sense that life in a minor key is life as it is."[2]

Here was a five-year-old drawn to the same image, and I wondered, in that instant, what troubles would inevitably come to Alexander's life and whether he might also find comfort from the sorrowful joy of those eyes keeping him company in his childhood prayer life.

Alexander went on to show me other important contents of his prayer closet—a bell, the censer, and candle holders, all implements of Orthodox worship services—the Divine Liturgy—that fill the senses with sights and sounds and smells to remind worshipers that their prayers are lifted to God. As he was showing me the contents, Alexander explained, "But, I'm too young to light candles or incense."

Jane joined us and admired the space as well. "So, this is where you say your prayers? Whose idea was that?"

"Mine," Alexander said. "One day me and my brother Samuel [two years old] were going to say prayers and then I just decided to go in here and make a prayer closet."

"That's wonderful," Jane said. "A special place to pray."

I noticed several books on a shelf inside the closet. "What do you keep up there?"

He showed me a prayer book and a Bible. Then he grabbed another book. "This is Winnie-the-Pooh."

I said, "Oh, I love Winnie-the-Pooh."

"We have the movie," he explained.

Alexander crawled back out of the closet, grabbed his stuffed dinosaur, Tryphon, which I assumed was short for some breed I didn't know, like Tryphonosaurus. But his mother explained the toy was named after an abbot of a monastery the family had once visited. Then Alexander, Tryphon, and I sat on the floor and talked while Jane interviewed his parents across the room.

As usual, I began with church and asked him to tell me about it, what he enjoyed ("the chanting and the meal afterward"), what the worst part was ("nothing"), before we turned to the subject of God. "Does your church talk about God?" ("Yes.") "What's God like?" I asked.

"Well, he's sort of like us, but not really."

"Where is God?"

"In heaven," Alexander said.

"Do you ever feel like God is nearby?" I asked.

"When I pray in the prayer closet."

I love the paradox, one I found in so many children, if not in theological history. God is "way up high," or "above the clouds," or "up high in heaven," or "beyond everything," while at the same time God is capable of being near, among us. "Right here," five-year-old Tracy told me, pointing to her chest, "in my heart." With Alexander, I became particularly aware of the spatial quality of this paradox. On the one hand God is in the huge open space of the heavens above; on the other, God is in the close space of a cubby in a wall.

When I asked Alexander specifically about Jesus, he went to another room and came back with an illustrated children's Bible that his mother often reads to him. He pointed to the cover. "There's Jesus," he said. In an iconographic style, Jesus is depicted as a boy next to his mother. Alexander pointed out that Mary wears red with a blue robe while Jesus wears blue with a red robe. They are in a boat with the disciples, who are hauling in a huge net full of fish. Alexander opened the book and began showing me the illustrations and telling the stories behind them.

"That's Moses because there's the burning bush," he said.

"What's that there?" I asked.

"His shoes are off."

"How come?"

"Because it was holy ground," Alexander answered.

We thumbed through the Bible for another ten minutes or so. He knew many of the stories, but whenever we came to an illustration that he wasn't sure about, he'd ask me, and I'd read the caption—making clear that Alexander wasn't yet reading.

At one point I asked him one of our standard questions: "Have you ever thought about where everything outside comes from?" He said Jesus made everything. I followed with, "*Why* do you think Jesus made everything?"

"Well," Alexander said while flipping pages, "let's go back to the beginning of time, to the beginning of the world." He went to the opening pages of the Bible, and we studied the illustration. Depicted were the sun and moon, land and sea and sky, animals and fish, and a man with his arms stretched out as if he's embracing it all.

"Who is that?" I asked.

He stared for a moment, as if a little unsure. The beard and hair could have suggested Jesus, especially since Alexander had just said that Jesus made everything. But then he seemed to realize something. "That's Adam," he offered, "because there's no halo."

I don't know exactly what prompted his next comment, perhaps all the water in the creation picture, but then Alexander said, "If you want to, we can talk about holy water." He found the story of the baptism of Jesus. He told me how John the Baptist (haloed) helped Jesus (haloed) down into the water and baptized him, and "now he's coming back up. . . . And that's the dove."

"And that's holy water?" I asked, still a little unsure of his thinking on the subject.

"Yes, that's holy water."

The remarkable aspect to his description was the narrative quality of it. Static, two-dimensional representations entered the imagination of a child and evoked a story, a sequence of events flowing through time like holy water from the Jordan River. Later, I found a copy of the same children's Bible, and in the introduction is a letter from the Department of Religious Education of the Greek Orthodox Archdiocese of America. "The primary reason for reading the Bible is to discover a loving God," the letter opens. It goes on to say that "God loves stories," and when we "sit and tell holy stories, God draws close and listens."[3] I could almost imagine an icon with a haloed boy Jesus sitting with Alexander and his mother and siblings as they read from this Bible.

When Alexander and I finished the interview, he asked his mother for a snack. She sent him to the kitchen for some grapes, but she added, "Remember to bless God." She explained to me that anytime they're about to eat or put something in their mouths, they give thanks, they bless God.

"I will," Alexander answered.

From the interview with Alexander's parents, it was clear that, indeed, the prayer closet was spontaneous and his love for the church and its rituals was genuine. "Alexander has been a surprising kid," said his father, a teacher at the Orthodox school connected with the church. "When your son is at the altar doing his prayer, I'm like, oh, I better do mine." Alexander's mother and Jane laughed.

Jane added, "Yeah, you normally think the kid is copying the parent."

Alexander's mother said, "Yeah, from the time he was, maybe, a year and a half, he was mimicking all these things he sees in church or at our home altar. Something I love about our church is that it is really welcoming of children. . . . It's been great for his younger brothers who see him loving church and they do too. But they're different too. Samuel really loves music and will go stand with my parents at church and sing, whereas Alexander really was into the priest swag."

Even so, Alexander's father wanted to make something clear, lest we place a halo around his head. He said there were plenty of times Alexander didn't want to go to church, especially when he was four. "We've had the full range of experiences," the father summarized.

In so many ways Alexander was a typical young child full of energy for play and love of Winnie-the-Pooh and snacks, if not dress-up. But there was also an intense spiritual energy at work in him as well as a rich religious imagination fed by the sights and sounds and smells of his community.

Back home, I listened again to the interview. While I did, I found myself staring out the window to the backyard and focusing on our tree house (the one Elly, Jacob, and I took an adventure in—see chapter 2). Inside, in paint, one wall reads, "kids club." I thought about Alexander's prayer closet and realized how his excitement for it, in another child, might be reserved for a such a clubhouse, a kid-sized space where children can play and dream.

* * *

When asked whether they had a favorite place to think about God, most children—across age and background—said church, or a specific location in church. A Sunday school room, a fountain outside the building, or, for one Orthodox child, "Behind the altar." Raphael, twelve, explained that he serves as an altar boy and helps the priests as they prepare the elements. In his church, this is done behind the iconostasis. "I mean, you're inside the royal doors. And the royal doors represent the doors being opened to heaven. Basically, it's the holiest place in the church." The next most favorite place—frequently in addition to church—was "home," often "my bed," or "my room," or "the table," though one child answered, "my bed, my room, and behind the couch." (She often played behind the couch too.) Only a couple of children said that they did not have a favorite place, or that they thought about God "everywhere, anywhere." And one child, ten-year-old Stella, went to an imagined place, a kind of peaceable kingdom. "I usually like to imagine big open fields where there's green grass and just wild animals everywhere and you can just be yourself and maybe God's there."

* * *

In the beautiful children's book by Katherine Paterson, *Bridge to Terabithia*, the two main characters, Jess and Leslie, fifth graders, are new neighbors at the beginning of the story and quickly become great friends. "We need a place," Leslie says, "just for us." She goes on to say it could be a whole country, and she and Jess would be its rulers. "It could be a magic country like Narnia, and the only way you can get in is by swinging across on this enchanted rope." They called the place Terabithia, and Leslie lent Jess her Narnia books so he could better share in the imaginative land full of strange creatures, talking animals, dangers, and adventures. "They dragged boards and other materials down from the scrap heap by Miss Bessie's pasture and built their castle stronghold in the place they found in the woods. . . . Like God in the Bible, they looked at what they had made and found it very good."[4]

In Alexander's case, the materials for his castle—a cubby, icons, candleholders—were gathered from the fields of his church and home. In this way, he is a reminder of what relentless model-makers children are—creating miniature versions of important dimensions of the world around them. From playing with doll houses to building Lego structures, toy cars, and rockets, if not drawing pictures and forming sand castles. In my part of the world, there are often props around that some children have access to, but even in humbler places where I have visited, places where I saw no toys or stuffed animals, children would create figures from mud or sticks to play with. Or in some cases, friends were created out of nothing but imagination. A three-year-old boy in Kenya described tending cattle with his invisible friend, an activity the local translator assured me is not something any three-year-old would be involved in. But the boy was imaginatively enacting both a friendship and an adult-world activity. The point is that children are constantly running simulations of their worlds. They gather key features from it like people (friends and family), activities (cooking and cattle tending), objects (cars and planes), and spaces (tree houses and castles). It's a fundamental way to learn that occurs across cultures, or better, a way to learn the ways of the culture a child is part of.

* * *

Alexander was not the only child we met who was into "priest swag," as his mother called it. The same day, when we arrived at the home of Daniel, three years old and the youngest child in the Orthodox community we interviewed, he greeted us in the front yard wearing a cassock. It was a warm summer day, and my initial thought was how hot he must be.

While I talked with his older brothers, Jane interviewed Daniel. "You're dressed like a priest, right?" she said. "Is that what this is? Is that what a priest would wear?"

"Yes," Daniel said. "And I have a cape too. And this is my black cassock. And this is my belt to hold my black cassock on. And this is my censer." Jane asked him whether he wanted to be a priest some day, and he said, "Yeah, because Father Jacob wears these clothes." He went on to talk about how his brothers dress up in costumes at school. We later found out that at the Orthodox school associated with the church the students indeed dress up in history class to reenact various events. Whether Daniel thought of his cassock as a costume, we'll never know, and it probably doesn't matter. But it reminded me that Gopnik's observations about rituals can extend to clothing. There is nothing particularly functional or efficient about wearing a long black robe over your clothes in the summertime, whether a priest at church or a boy at home. Something more social was going on, something about belonging, community, and identity.

Jane's interview with Daniel lasted about fifteen minutes, good for a three-year-old. With such young children, we generally would ask a couple of questions and let the conversation go where it will. *Tell me about your church.* Or, *Do you pray?* In Daniel's case, the conversation led to saints and his namesake. "I'm Saint Daniel," he said and talked about an icon of Saint Daniel he kept by his bed.

"What's it like to have the saints, your saint, right by your bed?" Jane asked.

But Daniel took things in his own direction. "I'm not really Saint Daniel," he said. "I always call myself Donny, it sounds like Ducky. I have a ducky in the bathroom. I can show you after we're done talking." Listening to the conversation later, I found the quicksilver movements between an icon and saint and ducky jarring, yet compelling at the same time—like a dream sequence transforming one scene into another.

* * *

When reflecting on Alexander and Daniel, prayer closets and dress-up, Winnie-the-Pooh and Ducky, it's tempting to think of it all as merely *play*. In other interviews, I met a child who loved to set up whole classrooms of stuffed animals and be their teacher, another who "baptized" her younger sister in the bathtub, another who conducted "meetings" with her invisible friends and even kept minutes of the meetings. Again, such play speaks to the model-making impulse in children, running simulations of the world around them and putting themselves in the middle of it.

But a question I have is whether calling a child's prayer closet or cassock play diminishes the sense that something spiritual and serious is going on. Is a five-year-old's enthusiasm for a prayer life the same as another child's play life? After all, we tend to associate play with lightheartedness or freedom from the gravity of life. Praying, on the other hand, is often about our deepest struggles, about relationship with God, about ultimate matters, the Really Real. Play, especially in young children, is a suspension of reality in the mode of *as if*—as if this tree house were a castle, as if I am tending cattle with a friend, as if Curious George eats, as if these woods are Narnia (itself an "as if" world), and so on. Playing is about magic and enchantment. Praying is about the spiritual.

But upon further reflection, I find myself resisting such a split between play and the spiritual. This sharp dichotomy is likely a sign that something has gone wrong. Theologian Wolfhart Pannenberg makes a similar observation concerning the dichotomy between play and work. Play, he says, is the beginning of freedom, and fundamental to people's ability to direct their own lives and resist manipulation from others (think of Leslie and Jess becoming the "rulers of Terabithia"). Play is built into life at the most fundamental, biological levels and is crucial to symbolic thinking, establishing identity, thriving relationships, art, and religion itself, according to Pannenberg. When play is segregated, say, from work, it easily becomes colonized by the alienating forces of modern industrial societies and manipulated to keep people from waking up to the madness.[5] Think gladiator fights or *The Hunger Games*. That is, play is uprooted from its soil and marketed back to us as entertainment, an opiate for the masses.

What if we thought of play a little differently, more like a posture, an orientation, or way of being in life, even in the tough times? To play is to be open to possibilities. To play with others is to engage and respond to them in a spirit that doesn't kill the joy. The more you're set on having your own way, the harder it is to play. Bodily play (say, throwing and catching a ball) generates a kind of nimbleness in relation to the activity, and in this case is closely related to practice (say, playing a ukulele), a fine-tuning of skills. I have a friend, Frank, who is a highly skilled opera singer. I once asked him how he gets himself to practice at the level he needs to maintain and develop his talent. He said, "Easy. When I practice, I get to sing, and I love to sing." What if this play posture—this open, relational, joyous love—is at the heart of prayer and worship? It seems to be so in the hearts of Daniel and Alexander.

In her lovely and powerful book *The Grace of Playing*, Courtney Goto makes the case that, theologically, play and love are indeed linked and rooted in the play of God's own creative activity. That is, "the play of creation has its being in God and God dwells in creation, much like the persons of the Trinity dwell in one another."[6] In this theology, love flows like a joyful dance between the persons of the Trinity, so much so that it overflows to create new settings for love to thrive. This is creation. In a sense, through creation, we could (playfully) say that God is running simulations of the infinite love known within the eternal life of God for the sake of a world of love. And even when this world distorts and denies such love, the grace of playing may yet be central to the possibility of "leaning into new creation,"[7] as Goto puts it. We are open to what is larger than ourselves, and "the spaces between human beings, humans and the world, and humans and God are charged with potential, creativity, and freedom."

I find helpful something Daniel's mother told us. While Daniel himself had known nothing but the Orthodox Church his whole three and a half years, his parents, Anne and Zach, were relatively new to the tradition, having converted as adults. Anne explained how she and her husband grew up in another church tradition but were never fully at home with it. They got away from church totally, explored Buddhist and other practices, but always felt they were still searching, until a friend from the local farmers' market invited them to the Orthodox Church. They went several times, but, as Anne said, "I actually didn't spend much time upstairs [in worship] because I had two nursing babies and I was downstairs a lot with the other women that were nursing babies too. We sat in the room and talked." But Anne recollected the feeling when she did join the service for the first time. "I remember walking in, and it was like, oh, this is what I want, this is it. I don't care what it is, this is what I want. I knew immediately that that was what I had been searching for. I remember that the people were so serious in church and so worshipful. It was a little bit scary because the people didn't really look at you and it was very focused in church but also it was very appealing." Anne's statement here would lend credence to the idea of separating the spiritual from play, that is, until she finished the description. "But when we went down to coffee hour [after the service], people were just so friendly and hospitable, and it was totally different than being upstairs. But it went together. It was real, very real."

Somehow the serious, worshipful, intensely focused church went together with the friendly, hospitable one to make something "very real." Rather than drawing sharp lines between playing and praying, between friendly coffee hours and intense worship, perhaps we can take our lead from those who hold them together—a child in a prayer closet or a community that welcomes children and nursing mothers as it focuses on worship.

* * *

While Jane was interviewing Daniel, I interviewed his older brother, eight-year-old Gabriel. Gabriel was particularly eager to show me and talk about the icons around their home. Like Daniel, he and his brothers had their own icons as well, each depicting the patron saint for whom they were named. The boys kept the icons by their beds to help them pray at night and to remind them that God, with the help of their saint, is watching out for them as they sleep. He took me to their altar—where the family prays together every night—and showed me the prayer books they use and how they use them. The wall was loaded with icons, and Gabriel began explaining some of his favorite ones. "This one is the icon of Pascha, the resurrection of Jesus Christ. He's trampling down on hell, or Hades, and he breaks the gates. He takes Adam and Eve out and all of these saints up to heaven."

"Wow, I see that."

Gabriel went on to explain about the two crucified with Jesus. "When Jesus was on the cross, he was in the middle. There were two robbers on the side. One robber repented—the one on the right. The one on the left didn't. And so he, Jesus, opened the gates of heaven and the first person he ever took up was the robber that repented. And then he took all the others."

Gabriel moved on to another icon, one of Adam and Eve in the garden with all the animals. Then to another icon, then another. The way he studied the icons reminded me of the way I used to study baseball cards as a kid, not only the pictures but the stats on the back—batting averages, earned run averages, home runs—and the story the numbers told. I could see how the icons were not only an instrument of prayer but a vehicle for learning, for religious education in the Bible and history of the church. It seems that icons do spatially what stories do linguistically—fund the religious imagination with characters, settings, and plots.

The contrast with my Protestant tradition was clear. Mine is a tradition of iconoclasm, of the suspicion of—if not the destruction of—images in favor of words. But in this community, in this child, I could see the power of an even older tradition in Christianity that teaches, prays, and worships through images. Here images fund religious imagination.

I think again of Princeton scholar Albert Raboteau. Not only does he describe the astonishing "spiritual power" of the Theotokos icon of the Russian exhibit he visited, but he describes another exhibit he went to at the Schomburg Library and Museum in Harlem. There Raboteau, African American, encountered a tradition even older than the Russian one, as he came face-to-face with Ethiopian icons. He says, "The African Zion exhibit, as it was called, graphically reminded everyone who saw it of how ancient Christianity was in Africa." He goes on to say, "I was excited to see an African face of orthodoxy."[8]

* * *

I find myself wondering how far back this "spiritual power" of images goes. Only a year before my visit to this Orthodox community, the archaeologist Adam Brumm and his team discovered what are so far the oldest cave paintings in the world, on the Indonesian island of Sulawesi. On a sixteen-foot wall are depicted figures over forty thousand years old. The figures "appear to be human, but they seem to have some features or characteristics of animals," Brumm says in an interview. "One appears to have a birdlike head, and another has a tail." He says that these "part-human, part-animal figures might signal early religious beliefs, because they indicate that ancient humans could imagine things they had never seen."[9]

Alison Gopnik might also want us to notice that the very act of drawing hybrid figures on a wall is anything but pragmatic or efficient. Something highly social was going on. Says Brumm, "We can't know if it has anything to do with spirituality, but at least we can say that those artists were capable of the sorts of conceptualizations that we need in order to believe in religion, to believe in the existence of the supernatural." Considering that an even older drawing—a more abstract set of crosshatched lines—was discovered in the Blombos Cave of South Africa that dates to seventy-three thousand years ago, we can only imagine how deep the use of images runs.

Of course, whether early humans prayed or worshiped in any way that we would recognize is an open question, one that may never be answered since we have no written history going back that far. Written language itself is a mere five thousand years old. But we do know that one of the earliest written texts—a cuneiform tablet—was a hymn of praise to the Sumerian goddess Ninkasi.[10] Praying is at least as old as writing.

* * *

Orthodox children certainly use words, chants, and songs to pray as well, but icons create something more through their images. When I interviewed Simon—Daniel and Gabriel's eleven-year-old brother—he also talked about the role of icons in his family's altar. But he wanted me to be clear that "we're not worshiping the icons." He said it was more like the "icons are a window into heaven, sort of. It's something making us focus more and actually know *who* we're worshiping." When I asked him whether he only prayed with icons or needed the icons to pray, he explained that he can pray anywhere, but even so, he described how he will often see an icon in his mind when he does.

Through the eyes of these and other children we spoke to in this community, I found it easier to see how icons can stoke a sacred imagination in the young. But in adults too. Like Albert Raboteau, many of the Orthodox parents we interviewed identified icons as an important feature of their prayer lives, if not faith lives more generally. In the home, they represent a connection to the larger faith community at church; they connect to the larger faith community in history; and, as one mother, Lily, put it, they contribute to a sense that "this faith is so rich. It's so living. It's in every part of our everyday." For her, it was a particular icon that drew her to Orthodoxy in the first place.

Lily was the friend from the farmers' market who had initially invited to church Anne and Zach (parents of Daniel and his brothers). Like them, Lily had bounced around other traditions, Christian and otherwise, but never felt at home. She said it didn't help that a high school boyfriend told her that she would never be as close to God as he was because he was male. After many years of struggling with her spiritual life, she ended up joining a friend at his church, an Orthodox one in another state. "Gosh, the first time I walked in, I was stunned by this icon of an old woman because I had never seen that in any Christ-centered faith that I had come across thus far—the picture of an elderly woman. I'd never seen that, never seen women involved at all, let alone old women. She was a very robust, gray haired, unattractive woman. And I was like, who is that? And I couldn't shake it, I couldn't shake her, I couldn't shake that whole thing. That was my first real introduction to Orthodoxy." She later found out the icon was of Saint Xenia of St. Petersburg, an eighteenth-century woman who lost her husband at a young age and eventually adopted a life of "foolishness for Christ," giving all her possessions to the poor and befriending and blessing children.

"It was like this window into something I had never seen before. I just couldn't get over her specifically." Lily eventually converted, but again, it was an experience with an icon that helped. "I started reading this book, *Christ the Eternal Tao*, and it really resonated with me in a way that I was surprised with and that helped open the door. And then I had this really like iconic experience with an icon of the Mother of God where she was just basically, 'What is your problem with my son?' I was like, 'You're right. It's the people that follow him that I have a problem with. He seems like a pretty cool guy.' She was very kind, but very firm with me. Like motherly. Almost mother to mother. 'What is your problem with my son? What is it specifically?' I had nothing. I could come up with nothing." For Lily, with the help of "iconic experiences" with Saint Xenia and the Theotokos, images became a window to something more, which for her led to a faith that is "so rich" and "so living."

When I interviewed Lily's daughter, Sal, I could not help but see how deeply this aliveness showed up in her four-year-old. Sal told me she had a dream of "the Panagia," another name for Mary (from the Greek, meaning all holy).

"What do you remember of it?" I asked.

"I can't remember all of it. Just that I was with the Panagia. That's all I want to tell."

"Okay, was it a good dream or a scary dream?"

"Very good!"

Next, our conversation turned to Mary's son. "So, what do you know about Jesus?"

Sal said, immediately, "That he was a refugee."

I thought that was quite a word for a four-year-old. I asked, "Do you know what a refugee is?"

"It's someone that had to run away from their home to be safe."

"You're right. How'd you learn about that?"

"Our mom told us."

I could feel the power of Lily's "mother to mother" conversation with the Panagia, the one who was looking out for her son, the one who eventually found a home in another mother's—Lily's—life.

* * *

One of the last Orthodox families we interviewed met us the day after they had moved across town into a new home. We arrived to see the typical chaos of half-opened boxes and pieces of furniture in odd places. By contrast, in the corner was an altar with a beautiful wall of icons, neatly arranged. "It was the first thing we did in our new place," the father, Jacob, said as the mother, Zera, nodded. Like Lily, like nearly all the parents we spoke to in the community, this couple had come to Orthodoxy by a long and labyrinthine route. For various reasons they found themselves refugees from their traditions or communities, never feeling quite at home religiously. Some parents felt their backgrounds too confining, so narrow and limiting that they had to get away. Others were raised with nothing or such a vague, dispersed spiritual sense that they were lost in the vastness of it all with nowhere to rest.

Abraham Heschel writes: "Even those who believe that God is everywhere set aside a place for a sanctuary. For the sacred to be sensed at all moments everywhere, it must also at this moment be somewhere."[11] *Everywhere* without the limits of a *somewhere* is too big to be meaningful. God's presence becomes a vague abstraction. On the other hand, *somewhere* without the sense of something more becomes smothering.

For those we spoke to, an Orthodox church in a small city has become a somewhere with a window to a sacred more. So too the family altars and bedsides filled with the company of saints. Also, a cubby in a wall. These places, these somewheres for prayer and worship, feed the imaginations of children and adults alike to sense the sacred everywhere.

"We need a place," young Leslie tells Jess in *Bridge to Terabithia*. "It could be a magic country like Narnia."

5

Capillaries of Presence

"WHAT'S THE BEST PART OF CHURCH?" I asked ten-year-old Natalia.

"The part I like the best is when they talk about Jesus." I asked what she'd learned about Jesus. "That Jesus brought us into the world the way we are, and he protects us, and it doesn't matter if you're ugly or bad or good or beautiful—he loves us all."

Sitting next to Natalia was eight-year-old Jorge. "I learned the same, but I also learned that God paid a very high price for us." I asked what that price was, but Jorge wasn't sure. Natalia, however, explained that Jesus paid with his life, that he was crucified on the cross, "but the Holy Spirit is so great that they defeated death."

"Where is Jesus now?" I asked.

Natalia answered, "Jesus is in heaven with his mother and all the angels."

Jorge added: "I think what Natalia said is right, but sometimes he comes down to help the people who are here and need him."

Natalia agreed. "Just as Jesus lives in heaven or as God lives in heaven, he also lives in our hearts."

"And where is the Holy Spirit?" I asked.

Jorge answered, "The Spirit of God is in our hearts, and it helps us be good people. And when we go to mass, the Spirit makes us very happy."

Natalia and Jorge were two of eighteen children we interviewed (with the help of a translator) in the Yucatan of Mexico. All were of Mayan descent, and all but one were Roman Catholic.[1] They lived either in the ancient city of Izamal or in smaller towns nearby. Despite popular notions of the "collapse of Mayan civilization" or the disappearance of its culture, Mayan peoples continue to live and thrive throughout the Yucatan and the regions to the south in Central America, especially Guatemala.

The city of Izamal itself was named for the Mayan deity Itzamna, a sky god associated with wisdom and agricultural fertility.[2] In 2001, Izamal was the first in Mexico to be named a *Pueblo Mágico*, a Magic Town, by the Mexican government. Now there are over a hundred across the country, but the program was designed to celebrate rich cultural heritages and traditions, natural beauty, and history. In the case of Izamal, its deep Mayan roots are an important aspect of its culture, evidenced by the partial remains of Mayan temples scattered throughout the city, the oldest going back some 2,500 years.

The children of Izamal call the temples "hills," presumably because the unexcavated ones simply look like hills. Natalia's home had an unexcavated one right out her back door. She wanted to take Jane and me up the hill to show us where she and her friends play. I was hesitant, thinking that two gringos traipsing up an ancient Mayan temple would be disrespectful. But Natalia insisted, as did her mother, and along the way my concern lessened. I still wasn't sure about the gringos angle, but I began to imagine how pleased her ancient ancestors might be for the company of playing children.

Izamal is also an important religious site in the Yucatan, with its grand monastery complex, San Antonio de Padua, nearly five hundred years old, where many of the children we interviewed attended mass and catechism classes. Natalia herself was in a communion preparation class at the monastery at the time of the interview; she would "receive Christ's body," as she put it, for the first time later that year, when she turned eleven. Jorge, at eight, would have to wait.

While the monastery is an important religious site now, Izamal had been an important pilgrimage location in the Yucatan for two thousand years even before the Spanish arrived. But after colonizing the Yucatan, the Spanish, in 1533, began construction of the monastery on top of what was the tallest Mayan pyramid, one dedicated to the god of rain, Pap-Hol-Chak, itself built on top of a temple platform likely built centuries earlier.[3] The colonizers destroyed the top of the temple, but they utilized its base to make the complex the tallest building in the area. The outside of the monastery is striking—two acres of an open-air atrium, or courtyard, surrounded by a colonnade of arches. The outsides of all the buildings, including the arches, were painted a bright, canary yellow in honor of a visit by Pope John Paul II, in 1992. On the facade of the main chapel, protected by the colonnade, are two frescoes. One dates to the sixteenth century and depicts two friars in a garden setting. The other, from the early seventeenth century, depicts Saint Barbara, a patron saint of mariners, who is also depicted in a garden. These frescoes (and probably others) had been whitewashed over for centuries, until they were discovered in the 1990s and partially restored.

Inside, the cathedral is filled with icons as well as three-dimensional statuary. Near the altar is a crucified, collapsing Jesus being held in the arms of a crowned king sitting on a thrown. Over the crown is a dove. Another striking figure is a crucifix with a Black Jesus Christ—Cristo Negro—who is yearly carried to the monastery in a procession from one of the nearby villages. The tradition may have been imported from Guatemala, and depending upon who you ask, is a celebration of "the worker" (labor class) or "healing."[4] However, another figure, by far, gets more attention than any of the others, Our Lady of Izamal, a Marion statue that is the patron saint, sometimes called "Queen," of the entire Yucatan. In 1992, during his visit, the pontiff brought with him a silver crown and placed it upon the head of the saint.

It was here—in this five-hundred-year-old complex with

whitewashed walls hiding colorful frescoes for centuries, in a monastery and cathedral built atop a temple to the Mayan rain god—that Natalia and Jorge worshiped and prayed and learned the traditions of their faith. Between the Spanish history and the deeper Mayan roots still so apparent, the border between past and present, not to mention the living and the dead, seemed less substantial than at home—more open, porous. The hills, monastery, icons, statuary, and silver crowns create what Catholic scholar Robert Orsi calls an "abundant history," filling and enlarging the imagination with "real presence."

But the religious imaginations of children were enlarged not only by the architecture and venerated figures of the community; homes themselves echoed this sense of spiritual abundance. In one house where we interviewed several children, the first thing to see inside was a four-by-four-foot poster of a Mayan temple on one side of the room; on the other side was an altar with several nativities, flowers, photos of ancestors, and statuary of angels and saints, including a five-foot Mary, as well as a colorful rendition of Da Vinci's *Last Supper*—except this one had a large version of the Guadalupe Virgin hovering over the head of Jesus. It was here that we heard about the near and protective presence of guardian angels, excitement over eating the body of Christ, and the near presence of God in hard times. Here children also talked about their imaginary friends, told stories of Mayan elf-like creatures (*aluxes*), and spoke of the love of Jesus, the resurrection, praying, as well as the memories of food shared with ancestors on the Day of the Dead. In the words of Robert Orsi, at work was "a capillary of presence, filling water, relics, images, stories, and memories."[5]

* * *

When asked the question, Where is God? most of the children we interviewed, not just in Mexico, located God "in heaven" or "in our hearts" (or both); others said, "everywhere" or "all around us" or "in us." These are not surprising answers given centuries of biblical and religious teachings. "Where can I go from your spirit? / Or where can I flee from your presence?" Psalm 139 asks.

> If I ascend to heaven, you are there;
>   if I make my bed in Sheol, you are there.
> If I take the wings of the morning
>   and settle at the farthest limits of the sea,
> even there your hand shall lead me,
>   and your right hand shall hold me fast.
> If I say, "Surely the darkness shall cover me,
>   and the light around me become night,"
> even the darkness is not dark to you;
>   the night is as bright as the day,
>   for darkness is as light to you. (Ps. 139:7–12)

In addition to the question of where God is, we also asked: "Have you ever felt like God was very close, especially near, to you?" Some children named the same specific locations where they liked to think about God—as previously mentioned, at church, or in in their beds. In contrast to places, other children named specific activities like praying or taking communion or singing hymns. Sometimes the question of God's nearness evoked descriptions of situational occasions. Jorge answered, "Yes sometimes [I feel God close] when I need somebody to help me and there's nobody there because they're busy. I feel like he is right next to me telling me how to do it so that I can do whatever I have to." Other children described God's nearness when they feel happy or when they are scared or when they "make good choices." In other words, these children named occasions for presence threaded through the joys and concerns of everyday living. All these responses seemed to reflect the ways in which the sense of God's presence moves out of the generic ether of "heaven" or "everywhere" and into particular places, actions, and occasions of their experiences, the bedrooms and prayers, as well as the ups and downs, of their daily lives.

Still other children described unique, specific situations. When I asked Natalia whether she ever felt God was very near, she talked about a very serious illness she'd had. "There was a time when I had to go to the hospital and I felt like he was right next to me," she told me. "And he said, 'everything was going to be okay.' And he was right there next to me."

"Could you see God?" I asked.

"I felt him," she answered. "I could feel that God was there, and he was telling me that even though it was very dangerous, and I could die, I had to be strong. I had to get better. I had to stand up and get better and recover. I would talk to my mom about it, and she would say 'God is with you through the good and the bad. He is always there with you.' Sometimes that made me feel"—she interrupted herself—"I would almost cry."

As I reflect upon Natalia's description of God's presence, I am impressed by the tender intimacy of the scene. The intimacy between Natalia and God that leads to a sense that everything will be okay. The intimacy between a daughter and a mother that leads to an overwhelming sense of assurance. They are surely related. A mother's deep and tangible presence and the securing sense of an invisible God in the face of danger. Here the God who can be as far away as the heavens, whose reach is to the farthest limits of the seas, can, at the same time, be at the side of a little girl who knows she could die, and hold her fast.

Within various Jewish rabbinical and mystical traditions is the notion of the Shekinah, from the Hebrew word for dwelling. God transcends creation yet dwells with it as Shekinah. As Jewish scholar Franz Rosenzweig explains, God "cuts himself off from himself, he gives himself away to his people, he suffers their sufferings, he goes with them into the misery of the foreign land, he wanders with their wanderings."[6] Similarly, Abraham Heschel in his work on the biblical prophets sees in them the revelation of the "pathos" of God, "the fact that God can actually suffer."[7] This is no Unmoved Mover or watchmaker deity or puppet master pulling the strings on the universe.

Christian theologian Jürgen Moltmann picks up on these traditions of Shekinah and God's pathos in his development of a theology of the cross, the passion and suffering of a "crucified God," as he puts it. God's power, in this case, does not come from controlling the universe but instead rests in God's passionate participation in life, even to the point of suffering. For Moltmann, this is ultimately a theology of love. "Love is the goodness that communicates itself from all eternity." He says that a "theology of love is a theology of the Shekinah."[8] Or, in Natalia's words, God "was right there next to me."

* * *

Eleven-year-old Rosa also went to mass and catechism classes at the San Antonio monastery. When I asked her whether she ever felt God particularly near, she said, "I feel like God is near when something good happens to me, or when something is protecting me from bad." Next to her was Juana, ten, and she said, "When people that I love or people that I'm very close to, when they pass away, I feel that God is next to me. He's telling me that the person is with him and that they're okay." She then went on to describe two specific instances involving her grandparents. "My grandfather died about two years ago, and when I went to bed, I felt like God was in my head, and my grandfather was in my head. And God said, 'your grandfather is with me.'"

Similarly, eight-year-old Marco answered the question, saying, "Yeah. When my uncle died, I felt like God was with me." I asked how that made him feel, and he answered, "I was sad because he was gone. But I was happy because I knew that my uncle was with God." Sitting with Marco was ten-year-old Rafael, and he too named a time of loss: "When my grandmother died, I felt like God was with me."

These responses led to a discussion with Marco and Rafael about *Día de los Muertos*, Day of the Dead, or in Mayan, *Hanal Pixan*. Elaborate *ofrendas* (altars) are set up in the home, and offerings are taken to the graves of loved ones. "It's in November," Marco explained. "The people here put out candles so that when the dead pass, their way is lit. They put up their altar and they put out water and they put out food and they put pictures, and we put our saints up." Other children mentioned flowers, candles, cloth, candies, and "a big bottle of beer."

Nine-year-old Miguel went into more detail. "I have a little cousin who died because he had a heart attack. So, we make an altar for him with his favorite food on the altar. We leave a little bit of food for him there and it's like even though he's not alive he was getting older—his birthday was passing." Miguel went on to say that if they didn't put food out or removed the altar, "it would be like taking his soul away."

A few days after this interview Jane and I visited the Centro Cultural y Artesanal Izamal, an arts and cultural museum in Izamal featuring the works of top regional and national artists. Though half a year away, the extent to which the Day of the Dead is expressed in the cultural imagination of the area was reflected in the multitude of paintings and sculptures associated with the celebration that were on display. Throughout the museum were *calveras* (skulls) and *calacas* (skeletons), often dressed or with hair, going about daily life. One of my favorites was a skeletal bread man riding a bicycle with a basket of loaves on his head for delivery. He is accompanied by a woman—also a skeleton—riding on the back of the bike, as well as by a fleshy angel with wings riding on the handlebars, leading the way. The museum was filled with dozens of such sculptural scenes as well as *alebrijes* (spirit animals), colorful dragon-like creatures with fantastical features who are said to assist in the journey between life and death.

Before the interviews in the Yucatan, I had interviewed Natalia's six-year-old cousin, Cristal, who was raised and lives in the United States. The subject of death came up. "I know what happens to people when they die," she declared. "They go over a huge bridge of flowers and become skeletons." Her mother explained that not only did Cristal know about *Día de los Muertos*, but they had also just seen the Pixar film *Coco*. The movie tells the story of a boy, Miguel, who accidentally journeys into the land of the dead during *Día de los Muertos*. He finds himself among his relatives who have indeed become skeletons. They had crossed over a bridge of marigolds, whose brightness and aroma are said to appeal to the dead.

Scholars debate whether the Day of the Dead traditions in Mexico emerged from indigenous practices celebrated long before colonization or from the influence of Roman Catholicism and All Saints' Day. Likely the traditions reflect some amalgamation of the two influences. Archaeological evidence reveals that ancient Mayan funerary practices varied from community to community, but most often the dead were buried at home—under a floor in the house, beneath an altar or shrine, or in the field where they farmed.[9] But the larger point is that the tradition of Day of the Dead keeps alive a deep sense that the ancestors are near, even in death.

This is not unique to Mayan or Mexican culture. For many peoples around the globe, presently and historically, the ancestors are nearby, populating one's home or land, offering advice and help to the living, and are to be respected, if not fed and celebrated.[10] While interviewing children in East Africa, I witnessed funerals in western Kenya and in southern Malawi. In these instances, both in Christian communities, the bodies were first visited by mourners in the home, then buried on the same property. And in both places, the sense that the ancestors were at hand was strong—to be consulted in family or property matters, for example, communicating through dreams or prayer, and not to be dishonored by one's behavior.

In relation to the subject of this book, we can notice how the sense of nearness of the dead animates the imagination. And we can notice the connection between the nearness of the invisible dead and the sense of an invisible God's presence in difficult times: "I felt like God was in my head, and my grandfather was in my head" (Juana). It's as if honoring the ancestors loosens the mind-set that draws hard lines between the visible and the invisible, the living and the dead. And what a wonderful paradox that material stuff—food and photos, skulls and flowers, altars and even beer—keeps the invisible sense of presence alive.

In her award-winning book *When God Talks Back*, Tanya Luhrmann describes the conversations she had with hundreds of evangelical Christians who are members of the Vineyard church in Chicago. Beneath the conversations was a research question, "How does God become real for people?"[11] That is, how does an invisible being come to be so important that one's whole life is affected—decisions made, behaviors directed, rituals enacted, beliefs adhered to? In short, how does an invisible being generate a way of life and belief?

Luhrmann points out how various studies and theories in psychology describe the ways humans have evolved to sense the presence of intentional beings where there may not actually be any. Our hominin ancestors may have sometimes mistakenly thought a stick was a poisonous snake or the wind rustling the bush was a lion. But better safe than sorry. Being wrong in these circumstances only leads to jumpiness. But being wrong in the other direction—assuming it's wind and not a lion—could mean the end. The theory is that our jumpy, quick-to-assume-a-presence ancestors, over millions of years, were the ones who survived. For some, especially committed atheists, this "explains" religion. Belief in invisible presences is a "by-product" of intuitive psychological features that had nothing to do with gods or angels. Sensing the gods is nothing but a misappropriated mental tool that kept the species alive. But Luhrmann finds such an explanation unsatisfactory. Primarily, as the book explores, it doesn't explain how God remains real to people, especially for those who have doubts. The "explanation" doesn't explain why people of faith struggle with the reality of God.

Luhrmann interviewed members of this evangelical community who also struggled with their own belief. While wrestling with nonbelief is nearly taboo in some Christian communities, this church addressed the issue quite directly. One of the important recommendations was to employ imaginative practices to help. Following C. S. Lewis's *Mere Christianity*, the church leadership suggested pretending, that is, acting "as if" God exists. Luhrmann, summarizing Lewis, writes: "he thinks that if you pretend that you are with God, God will become more real for you."[12] In this vein, the pastor of the church encourages, for example, when you're having coffee in the morning that you set out and pour a second cup for God, "to place it on an actual table, and to sit down at that table with your own mug to talk to God about the things on our minds." Other ways these Christians tried to cultivate a stronger sense of presence was by setting a chair or a plate at the dinner table, talking to God like a friend (even to the point of discussing haircuts), or having a "date night" with Jesus. The people who did this knew they were engaged in a kind of pretend play. Some felt silly about it, but nonetheless they were eager to find ways to experience the presence of God in stronger ways.

What Luhrmann carefully traces through her interviews is an interchange of knowing between the imagination and sense-based experience. She calls it an "epistemological double register" (epistemology being the study of knowing). At work is an externally oriented reality frame, based upon the power of the world we touch and smell and see. Also at work is an internally oriented reality frame, one full of images, memories, emotions, and dreams. In pretending or in play, these frames create a different kind of experience, a third way, that joins the inner and outer worlds in a kind of dance. Elly feeds Curious George invisible food from a plastic cup. An adult Christian has a real conversation with an invisible God over a cup of hot coffee.

Yet, compared to play with a stuffed animal, there is a uniqueness in the kind of sacred play of someone engaged with God. That is, "the distinction between belief and make-believe breaks down."[13] Luhrmann's epistemological double register means the experience is "real but not real, not real but more than real, absolutely real for all time but just not real in that moment." In other words, a different kind of knowing emerges. "When you sit on a park bench and imagine God's arm around your shoulders, God is real in a different way than either the park bench or a daydream."[14]

I believe this helps make sense of the distinctive ways material props are typically involved in religious experiences, in the distinctive ways in which God, angels, ancestors, or spirits are real to people. Statuary, temples, chapels, frescoes, icons, baptismal water, burial sites, silver crowns, relics, communion bread and wine, and so much more. These become, as Orsi suggests, capillaries of sacred presence.

* * *

For some children the sense of God's near presence is like Natalia's—direct, "like he was there next to me." For other children, the sense of God's proximity is mediated by angels.

Rosa, mentioned above with Juana, explained that angels "are wonderful beings and they protect us from evil because they are God's guardians." Juana agreed: "They are wonderful beings who have been dead a long time and sometimes when we're on our knees praying to God to ask him for help, he sends them to us to protect us." I asked whether either of them had ever seen an angel or had felt one. Rosa said she had. "I have felt them near me protecting me from danger. And I have seen them in my dreams where they'll tell me something powerful and they give me an idea to do things right." Juana jumped in: "About six or seven years ago, just before my grandfather died, I looked out and I saw in the backyard my great-grandmother." (Her great-grandmother had died before Juana was born.) "An angel was holding her [great-grandmother's] hand and walking with her."

Nine-year-old Carlos also described angels as people who had died, but now "they have white robes and wings." His friend Jesús, also nine, added: "There was a movie about an angel where the people needed help, so the angel came." Explaining further, he said, "The angel is the messenger of God, right, but you don't see them." But after he said this a little debate ensued. Carlos said, "Well of course you can see them." To which Jesús responded, "So here we enter our point of disagreement."

Natalia spoke not only of angels in general but of guardian angels. She explained that we each have a guardian angel who protects us from evil and cares for us when we're sick. When I asked whether she had ever seen her guardian angel, she said, "We can't see them, but we know they are there. And every night when we pray before we go to bed, after we go to sleep, our guardian angel takes our prayers up to heaven and gives them to God." That is, angels are not only messengers from God, in her thought, but messengers to God.

In her book about angels, New Testament scholar Susan Garrett points out that while there are hosts of references to angels in both Hebrew and Christian Scriptures, there is no clear reference to the notion of an individual guardian angel assigned to an individual person. The book of Deuteronomy does seem to imply that each nation has been assigned its own divine being from the heavenly court.

> When the Most High apportioned the nations,
>   when he divided humankind,
> he fixed the boundaries of the peoples
>   according to the number of the gods;
> the LORD'S own portion was his people,
>   Jacob his allotted share. (32:8–9)

Here, "the gods" are variously translated "heavenly assembly," "heavenly beings," "heavenly court," or "angels of God," while the Contemporary English Version renders the phrase as "guardian angels." But, as Garrett points out, there are no clear clues how the idea of a national guardian angel became a personal one. (The idea may have gained help from the Greek world. As mentioned previously, the idea was that a daimon, or individual genius, accompanies each person at birth.) Regardless of how the belief came about, there is evidence for widespread belief in guardian angels by the second century CE.[15] And the idea has flourished within both Roman and Orthodox churches ever since. However, with the Protestant Reformation came not only a general iconoclasm but also concerns specifically about idolatry—the worship of any thing or figure in place of God. For some reformers, the prayers to angels for protection, along with statuary, could creep into idolatrous territory, that is, displacing God's love and protection in favor of a lesser figure (an angel).

Natalia was the only child among the Mayan children who spoke of guardian angels, but I did not specifically ask about them. Among all the children I interviewed, the Orthodox were most likely to talk about guardian angels, figures who, as the children said, were there to guide or guard them, or were otherwise dedicated to them. They are generally invisible, unless, as eight-year-old Gabriel explained, "it appears to you and says its name," which had not occurred for Gabriel, but he had read stories about that happening for others.

Stephen, also eight and Orthodox, agreed that people don't see or know their guardian angels, but he added that "once you go to heaven you know them." He explained further, that "God sends them right when you're born—the second you were born you have a guardian angel and when you go to sleep the angels use their wings and they cover over you."

The only other children to talk about their guardian angels were from other Roman Catholic families interviewed in the United States. Three of the children were Hispanic Americans—seven-year-old Abril (whose parents were from Spain), ten-year-old Jodie (whose parents were from Bolivia), as well as her seven-year-old brother, Erick. The other child was an Anglo-American eleven-year-old, Ginger. Ginger attended a Catholic school and explained how they ended the school day with a prayer they all recited: "Angel of God, my guardian, dear, to whom God's love commenced me here; ever this day, be at my side, to light and guard, to rule and guide."

Abril, Jodie, and Erick would all agree that a guardian angel guides and protects, and is "someone that looks out for you," as Jodie put it. Jodie added, "and comes to you whenever you're sad." As we spoke, she revealed that her guardian angel was her Pawpaw, her great-grandfather (who had died). I asked whether there was a particular time she felt like her guardian angel Pawpaw was looking out for her. "Yes. When I did my end-of-the-year dance recital last year. I was super nervous. It was my first year dancing with my company, and I didn't know what to do. I was so lost. Yeah. And then [I knew], he was looking over me that day and he made me happy."

"How did you know he was looking out after you?" I asked. "What made you feel that?"

"Because I always feel him when I need him. . . . I just imagine him in my mind, and he makes me happy."

I gently pressed. "Do you try to imagine him, or does he just show up?"

"He just shows up like, 'Hi.'" She went on to say that she often talks to him whenever she feels like she needs him.

Jodie's guardian angel Pawpaw took me back to a young girl I interviewed several years earlier about her invisible friends. Sally, nearly eight then, described her invisible friends, Deen and Elisabeth, who had joined her many years earlier when the family had come back from a vacation. According to Sally's mother, that was when she was two and a half years old. Deen and Elisabeth had been part of the household ever since. Sally explained, "They live in an imaginary world," and they visited often "to play games like tag or hide and seek." But Deen and Elisabeth were not Sally's only invisible companions. Her Pawpaw John would show up on certain occasions. Pawpaw John was her grandfather who had died when Sally was a baby. When she gets sad, Sally explained, "He visits me from heaven and makes me feel better."[16]

Had Sally been Catholic or Orthodox rather than Presbyterian, perhaps she would have, like Jodie, called Pawpaw John her guardian angel.

* * *

Alux (ah-loosh): "Supernatural beings created by the will of the gods. They live for hundreds of years and help to protect the fields" (from *The Great Book of Mayan Legends*).[17]

"You have to ask them about *aluxes*," a friend told me over dinner. The friend, originally from a village outside of Izamal, had helped me coordinate the interviews in the Yucatan. He brought up *aluxes* because he knew about my interviews with children who had invisible friends. He didn't know whether the children would have imaginary friends (he had not had one), but he felt *aluxes* were in similar territory.

I ended up asking about both—invisible friends and the *alux*.

One of the notable findings of my previous research into invisible friends was the way in which they reflected an intersection between culture and individuality—social influences with uniqueness—just as the particularity of a child's Pawpaw combines with a religious-cultural idea of guardian angels. Four-year-old Amy's invisible friend was Cinderella, a little girl whose name clearly derived from the popular princess story. But, depending upon the occasion, Cinderella could be a blue dog. Some children identified their invisible friends with religious figures. A Korean boy, Hwan, said his invisible friend was the Holy Spirit. Hwan and the Spirit prayed and read the Bible together—very religious cultural activities. Even so, there was an individual intimacy to the relationship, pulling what could be simply a religious doctrine or idea (Holy Spirit) into an active personal relationship.

When I asked the children around Izamal about invisible friends, I approached the question this way: "Some children have friends that nobody else can see. Do you have any friends like that? Or did you when you were younger?" In all, ten of the eighteen children in the Izamal area said they did. The others did not but had siblings or friends who did. However, one child told me a story about a boy he knew who had one and ended up seeing a psychiatrist. Another told me about a movie in which a child had an imaginary friend, but it turned out to be the devil. These latter responses reflect a general suspicion or anxiety about the phenomenon—one I sometimes found in the United States and elsewhere—but they were very much the exception among these children.[18] Most children described their friends in relationship to play. For example, Natalia said, "When I was young, before I went to kindergarten, I would have my dolls and I would play with them. And I would have an imaginary friend who would play with the dolls with me. I would ask her, 'Would you be my friend?' 'What's your name?' and things like that." Natalia's friend turned out to also be called Natalia. Jorge, in the same interview, said he'd had one as well. "It was just like an identical twin."

While children were clear about the difference between an invisible friend and an invisible God ("God exists. Imaginary friends are your imagination. They do not exist"), I found myself in murkier territory when asking about the *alux*. *Aluxes* are not frequently seen but are not invisible as such; neither are they considered imaginary. They are small, like children, and hide from people, at least most of the time. They protect the crops of farmers by chasing away animals and insects, and by throwing rocks at potential thieves. But they can be tricksters and nuisances as well. You have to leave food for them, or they'll curse your fields or other projects.[19] Around the Yucatan you can find small stone shelters, like little temples, where people can leave food for *aluxes*. A regionally famous one can be found near the airport of Cancun, under a bridge built in the 1990s. After several setbacks in construction, a Mayan shaman was reportedly brought in to appease the *alux* and to ask permission for the bridge. Whether a shaman actually conducted a ceremony or not is unclear, but a stone shelter is there today where people leave food offerings.[20] According to anthropologist Bruce Love, there is still a strong and persistent practice of shamanism in the region. "Maya villagers throughout the peninsula of Yucatan rely on local shamans to mediate between them and the spirit world, where forces beyond ordinary control can bring sickness, cause accidents, and most important, damage the harvest." These shamans, or *j-meen*, are trained by older ones to conduct various ceremonies, from appeasing spirits and *aluxes* to healing the sick or praying for rain.

The shamans are also Catholic, often quite devout, according to Love, and the ceremonies will include prayers to traditional Mayan gods and Catholic saints alike. A harvest ceremony will incorporate candles, incense, and a crucifix along with chickens, breads, and cigarettes. While a Catholic priest would not likely conduct the ceremonies of the *j-meen*, the *j-meen* apparently hold both spiritual traditions together with ease.[21]

All but a couple of the children knew about *aluxes*, and several told stories about them. But the surprising factor was how animated the children became when talking to me about these elusive, fairy-like creatures. In the very first interview, with Rosa and Juana, I brought up the subject, unsure of the kind of reaction their mention might provoke, if any. Juana started talking a mile a minute and kept talking, even as the translator tried to catch me up. Juana began: "Okay, they [*aluxes*] are Mayan. And when the pyramids were built the *aluxes* would protect them because there were jewels inside or more valuable things. They would protect the things that were inside the pyramids from the Spanish, so that they wouldn't take them." Rosa jumped in: "They set traps."

I asked whether they had ever seen an *alux*. Rosa said, "Yes. I had an aunt who is eighty-seven years old, and I was at her house while my mama was shopping. I went into my aunt's room because the light was on in the bathroom. I saw something. I went into her room, and I saw something jumping on top of my aunt in her hammock. When the *alux* saw me, he jumped up and ran away and I chased him. The next day, while my grandmother and mother were out, I was there with my aunt. I heard something in the kitchen like dishes and things. I went to see what it was, and it was the *alux*, and he was there eating something." Rosa went on to explain, "They look for food. And even though they are very, very old—they are ancient—they look young and they're always looking for food." I asked what they like to eat, and Rosa said, "They like anything but prefer bones and fruits."

Food often came up in the stories. Eleven-year-old Patricia explained, "So if you're out, if you're drinking your *pozole* [soup] and you have your gourd with your drink in it, you have to leave them a little bit. Because if you gobbled it and you don't leave anything they're going to get everything from you. Including your clothes. They'll take everything away."

When I asked Santiago (twelve) and Martín (eleven) about the *alux*, they got very excited and both started talking over each other, almost leaping from their chairs. Finally, Santiago summarized. "Okay, *aluxes* are very small beings. They'll go to your house and eat your food. In fact, just this morning my sister asked my mother about the *aluxes*. She said, yes, they're little beings and they will eat all your candy. And if you're bad or mean to them, they will hide your shoes and other things. Then I said, 'But Mom, where do they live?' And she said 'They live in the hills [temples].' I asked my mother if she had ever seen one and she said, 'Yes, when I was a little girl and I was in my house one day and I was playing and I thought I saw something and I went into the room and there was this little person that only came up to my knees. He was running around, so I started chasing him and then he just disappeared.'"

Another child told of his uncle chasing one from their garden. Another described how *aluxes* live in deep wells and sound like children laughing. Another had a rock thrown at her by an *alux*. Another's brother threw rocks at them in a well. Another heard them call his name from a well. Another described how they'll knock you from your hammock. Another, how they'll protect your crops. And so it went.

* * *

After our last interviews in the area, Jane and I had lunch in a small *cocina* near San Antonio de Padua. We shared a plate of *salbutes*, a local favorite—corn flower tortillas, fried, topped with about anything you like, but always with layers of avocado, lettuce, and pickled onions. I couldn't stop thinking about the *aluxes*. My friend who told me to ask about them was on to something. Whether or not we should consider *aluxes* as part of a religious imagination, or the religious imagination of these particular children, I won't try to determine. But they were certainly part of the children's cultural imagination, like the temples, reaching back to an earlier era and persisting into the present.

As intriguing and even entertaining as the *alux* stories were, I found myself even more stirred by the intensity with which the children told them. I kept thinking about the monastery across the street, about the whitewash covering up the hundreds-of-years-old frescoes on its walls. I imagined the artists painstakingly removing the whitewash to restore the vivid, colorful world beneath. I thought about those walls built on top of the older Mayan temple, the layers of limestone beneath. Layers upon layers of material expressions of invisible powers—an "abundant history," as Orsi calls it, serving as "capillaries of presence." Layers upon layers of a people's religious imaginations. Then I saw them—in my mind's eye—the little trickster elves, hiding gemstones in the heart of a sacred place, protecting precious cultural memories for a bite of tortilla or sip of *pozole*.

6

The Way of Parenthood

JANE AND I SAT with three-year-old Jay and his mother, Hope, in their home near a small city along the East Coast. At this point, most of the conversation had been between Hope and me while Jane played with Jay on the floor. Jay's father, Willem, would soon take him for a swim lesson. Hope reminded Jay that he'd be leaving soon. "Brad might have a question for you."

"I don't know," I said to Jay. "Do you have any questions for me?" He did.

"Why does the church have a cross?" the three-year-old asked.

"Why does the church have a cross?" I repeated. Jay nodded. "It has something to do with Jesus. Do you know who Jesus is?" He did. "Yeah. Who is Jesus?"

"He was a nice man," Jay said, "and there was some people that were trying to kill him."

Jay's mother stepped in. "Do you know why? Do you know why they were trying to kill Jesus?" Jay wasn't sure. "That's kind of the hard part, right, to understand?" Hope said.

Jay responded, simply, "They put him on the cross." He then brought over the children's Bible his parents read to him from, called

I Wonder: Exploring God's Grand Story.[1] "I'm going to show you that one of Jesus," Jay said, flipping through the pages. He found the one depicting the crucifixion. "That's the cross," he said. "That's a sad picture. He died on this." Then he asked me to read. His mother nodded that it was okay.

I read: *When evening came, Jesus and his disciples left the upper room and walked to the Garden of Gethsemane. And there in the darkness, the soldiers came with torches and weapons and led Jesus away.* "You were right," I interjected. *The next day at three o'clock in the afternoon, the sun stopped shining. The sky turned dark, heavy clouds of sadness hung in the air. Thunder roared. Trees trembled. The whole earth began to shake. And high on a hillside, on the cross, Jesus said goodbye.* I paused for a moment. *Goodbye world. Goodbye trees. Goodbye sunsets. Goodbye seas. Goodbye friends. Goodbye Mom. Goodbye world. And everyone. "It's all finished," Jesus whispered, and he closed his eyes and died. Except—Jesus wasn't finished and neither was God.*

As the name of the Bible suggests, after each story there are a set of "I Wonder" questions. I read to Jay. *I wonder how God felt when Jesus died.* Jay didn't say anything, so I said, "I'm guessing sad." And his mother agreed. Then I asked, "You think anything else can make God sad?"

Jay looked confused, then offered, "God is Jesus." Though this three-year-old was tuned into the story of Jesus on the cross, he hadn't yet worked out the interrelationship of the persons of the Trinity. I didn't try to explain, nor did his mother. I went in another direction. "Okay," I said. "What makes Jesus happy, do you think?"

"When he came alive again." Jay turned the page to see a robed Jesus stepping out of the tomb. He asked me to read it, but it was time for swimming.

"I'll read this part," I told him, referring to the end. *Good morning, world. Good morning, trees. Good morning, sun. Good morning, seas. Good morning, friends. Good morning, Mom. Good morning, God. New life's begun.*

"I like when Jesus does that," Jay commented.

"Okay, Mr. Monkey," his father said. "Let's go." It was time for his swim lesson. But Jay wasn't quite finished.

"Look at this rope," Jay said. "What's the rope attached to? Do you know what it is?" As far as I could tell, the rope was attached to nothing. He finally revealed, "It's attached to a lion."

"Uh-oh," Jane said.

"Can that lion swim?" I asked Jay, thinking about his upcoming lesson.

"Actually, it's just plush," he said.

I was struck by the use of the word "plush" by a three-year-old. But I was even more impressed by the layers of imagination. The visible rope is attached to an invisible lion, yet the lion is itself a nonthreatening and nonswimming invisible stuffed toy.

"Oh, you were pretending," I said. "Do you know what pretending is?" While Jay could certainly pretend, he didn't know the word. It was time to go, and Jay gave Jane and me high fives as we thanked him for talking with us.

His mother was willing to talk some more. Hope explained that Jay had always been verbally gifted, talking early and creating complex sentences at a very young age. But, she admitted with some disappointment, it's been hard to get him to talk about church. "So, we come home, and he doesn't want to talk about church. You know, like, 'What did you learn?' He'll say, 'I don't know, whatever.' But then every once in a while, he'll say, 'So they were talking about the parable of the sower,' and he told me everything. He talked me through the entire parable, every seed. So, it's things like that I'm like, 'I know he's learning.'"

She went on to tell us about a time at the ocean. "Last year, we went to the beach. We weren't reading the Bible very much. He was still in the nursery at church, so he wasn't getting much. But we were at the beach and Willem was holding him in the waves. And he goes, 'Baptize me, Dad. I want to go under,' which at our church, they don't dip. But he had seen Jesus be baptized in the Bible." She told about another time when Jay was pulling bread apart at the table. "I asked, 'What are you doing?' He's like, 'I'm making it in pieces so we can go feed people.' So, it's in there. But that's what I've learned in parenting, that my role is to not push it, just to be open to when I get those glimpses."

Hope's wise attitude about being open is no doubt related to her professional role as a spiritual director, someone trained in methods aimed at cultivating a closer relationship with God. Hope has two theological master's degrees and offers individual as well as group spiritual direction. With Jay off to his lesson, I asked a kind of blank-slate, open-ended question. "Given your background and position and thoughtfulness, what else might be important for this project? What else, from a parent's perspective, do you think might be important for us to think about?"

Hope thought about the question for a few moments, then offered, "Becoming a mother, I'm wanting it to be a spiritual practice, seeing motherhood as my spiritual practice now." She added, "Also really realizing all my spiritual practices have to change because there's no more getting up in the morning to have good quiet time or to meditate or do centering prayer, because he's getting up. Everything's changed."

This was a theme throughout our interviews with parents. Many of them had robust spiritual practices before children—praying regularly, meditating, reading Scripture, and engaging with various ministries of their churches. Kids changed that. Some tried to get up earlier for devotions or use nap time for spiritual meditation or use a Bible or prayer app in the car. All good things, but at the same time they pile on more to do for the overworked. Here is the challenge: If we associate spirituality with discipline, order, peace, cleanliness, and clarity, then the messy, sticky, murky, wild, and loud world with children would seem to doom it. If the spiritual life is about the view from a mountaintop with its crisp, clear air, parenting lurks down in the humid valleys, if not the muddy river bottoms, of life.

Hope explained how she had recently started a spiritual direction group for young moms. "So, it's like half book club, half group spiritual direction. We meet once a month via Zoom." Hope said that many of the participants simply need a place "to cry and fall apart." Between becoming a new parent—several during the pandemic—and whatever other stresses were going on in their lives, spirituality seemed to be on shaky ground, and they were looking for help. As one in the group put it, "My Legos of faith are spread out all over the floor." Hope's attitude with the group is like her attitude about being a parent—not to push but to be open.

* * *

"How has being a parent affected your spiritual life?" Jane asked Corin. She too described the challenges of the busy, hectic life she leads as a mother of three and, in her case, holding down a less-than-ideal job while her husband is in graduate school. As a child of a pastor, she had always been thoroughly engaged in church and church-related groups. She also had developed a rich devotional life—daily prayer and Scripture reading, for example, as well as reading theological works. But, like Hope and others, she found that her practices changed after children. She summarized, "I probably don't take enough time to just feed my soul."

Corin was also seeing a spiritual director. "I keep asking her for homework and she says, 'Just sit and listen. Just sit and listen. You don't have to do anything, don't have to read anything, you don't have to study anything. Just sit and listen.' So that helps me clear my mind and just listen and not be so busy. Just to sit and listen."

Here is the good news we found. Even in the midst of the valleys, down low on the sticky floors where kids and Legos spread out, the parents we spoke to nonetheless testified to something deep and sacred going on. Not that they always felt "spiritual." But as they reflected with us, it was clear that they had a sense that something meaningful was happening, that there is a different kind of spirituality, an alternative form of soul-feeding, one rooted in relationships and love.

* * *

When we asked how being a parent has affected their spiritual lives, the question evoked some of the most robust, energetic, and longest answers compared to any other question.

"Wow!" said Letty. "I guess, for me, parenting encouraged me to come around to—I'll say—sing the praises of spirituality. Instead of just being like, 'Yeah, I believe in God, sure.' But now that I'm a parent, I want to really know more and be active and proclaim this. So that's when I started the education classes to become a Catholic. Because of parenting, it gave me the strength to move forward with my faith."

While many, like Hope and Corin, had to reimagine their spiritual lives when they had children and change their understanding of faith practices, others, like Letty, found their religious imaginations awakened in new ways as a parent. Letty, a mother of two children, grew up with no religion. "I had a happy home," she said. "There was nothing wrong with it. I would say we were very spiritual. We just didn't have a practicing religion." Yet, she fell in love with and eventually married a Catholic man, Colby. Going into the marriage they gave each other the freedom to continue in their respective spiritual ways. Letty did not expect Colby to stop practicing, and Colby did not expect Letty to become Catholic. They were married by a justice of the peace.

But after the birth of their first child, something deepened in Letty. "It was one of those things that I thought about for a long time," Letty explained. "I liked everybody in the parish that I'd met, but it was something I just wasn't used to." That is, she hadn't grown up with "that community feeling," as she put it, that Colby had experienced through church. Letty and Colby agreed to have their child baptized, in part, because Letty wanted her to have such a community. "Especially in a crazy world like today," Letty said, "to have that kind of thought, compassion, empathy." Then she realized she wanted it too. "And I was like, 'I'm on board! Let's do this!'" Letty took the necessary classes and subsequently joined the church. She was grateful for the whole experience, for herself and for their children. "All the lessons we are learning are just amazing."

Colby offered his own take on the relationship between parenting and faith. "As far as my faith goes, parenting has enhanced it, for sure. It's enhanced awareness of my faith, and understanding my faith, and living my faith. You have two little human beings who are looking up to you. They're trying to figure out how to be human. And we're the closest things to that example of what that means and what that is. So, parenting gives lots of cause for self-awareness, to peel back the layers of your own onion." He discussed the sense of responsibility that comes with being a parent, but, he said, "It's a welcome responsibility." Why is it welcome? "The kids—the best way I can describe that connection is, it's loving another human being so much that your heart physically hurts from it. My cholesterol issues aside."

Letty's initial "Wow!" when we asked the question was common among the parents we spoke to. Their responses were filled with words and phrases such as "where do I begin," "oh my," "man," and similar interjections. For these parents, children and faith seem to intensify one another in an infinite loop of overwhelming love. "Having a kid was pretty mind-blowing," Letty said. "Amazing. Just like, 'Wow, this is a person. I made this person! Holy macaroni!'"

Listening to Letty, I couldn't help but think again of Abraham Heschel's description of "radical amazement." For Heschel, radical amazement, or wonder, is the root of knowledge and the soil in which faith flourishes. With radical amazement, "each thing is a surprise; *being is unbelievable.* We are amazed at seeing anything at all; amazed not only at particular values and things but *at the unexpectedness of being as such*, at the fact that there is being at all."[2] As one parent put it, "There's nothing like holding a newborn baby to make you believe in God. Man, when you hold a baby, you have to believe in something."

Perhaps Corin's "just sit and listen" or Hope's "just to be open" or Letty's "Wow!" reflects the same spiritual territory as Rabbi Heschel's radical amazement.

* * *

Another mother, Jenny, from a Reformed Protestant tradition, describes a particularly poignant way in which the world of babies and the world of faith came together for her. She was attending a conference that met in a Catholic church. "There was a painting above the altar of Mary with Jesus. And Jesus was nursing." She said, "And that's the first time that I've seen Jesus nursing before. It struck me right away, and in a really powerful way. I thought, I wish I'd had this painting when I was a parent of young kids, because it was hard work for me, having newborns and toddlers."

Again, taking care of young ones may not always feel so amazing. However, Jenny went on to say of that moment with Mary and the nursing Jesus, "That's when I realized, I recognized that Jesus is close to you, even in those moments as a mother. And God is near you in those moments as a mother. So, yeah, definitely as a parent, it alters your understanding of who God is, and the powerful ways that God moves." Even if in retrospect, Jenny could see the movements of God in the intimacy of nursing her own children.

* * *

In retrospect. Reflection. Looking back. This was another theme running through interviews with parents. I was continually surprised by the gratitude parents shared about the interviews themselves, about being interviewed. From my perspective, these hardworking, sometimes exhausted, adults were taking time out from their busy lives to help out a researcher they never met just because their pastor passed along our request for help. We'd ask a few questions, inviting them to reflect upon their faith and their lives as parents, and an hour or more later they would be thanking us and saying how meaningful it was to participate. Again, this surprised me. I share this not to say what great interviewers we are or how brilliant our questions were. I share this because I've come to appreciate how opportunities for looking back, for reflection on faith and children, are themselves moments to sense something deep and powerful going on, "the powerful ways that God moves."

In her book *Our Share of Night, Our Share of Morning: Parenting as a Spiritual Journey*, Rabbi Nancy Fuchs shares conversations she had with parents from all kinds of backgrounds, religious or otherwise. She structures the chapters by times of day. Instead of beginning with sunrise, as you might expect, or sunset, she begins and ends the book with chapters called "Four A. M." Fuchs does so because she found that in those middle-of-the-night feedings, parents experience both the extraordinarily mundane and profound at the same time. Reflecting on the birth of her own first child, she writes, "When I was in the hospital after my first daughter was born, I loved the feeding time in the dark between midnight and dawn."[3] She says it seemed like the whole city was asleep except for the other mothers and babies in the hospital.

"Only hours ago, many of these tiny creatures were still in the womb. Now they were snuggling up to the freshly engorged breasts of their mothers. These newly-in-love couples finding each other in the midst of a silent, dark world were incredible." But the wonder of it, for her, was not restricted to lactating women. "I spoke to fathers, to mothers who adopted children, to parents who chose to bottle-feed." All of them, she says, spoke of the power of the experience, "and what they remember especially is the 4:00 a.m. feeding."

"In the beginning," the great theologian Martin Buber writes, "is relation."[4]

* * *

Without a doubt, there are multiple avenues that can lead to the deepening of faith—from an ascetic life of prayer to a radical commitment to God's justice, from experiences of suffering and loss to moments of spiritual awakening and joy. What I want to highlight here, based on these conversations with parents, could be called the Way of Parenthood. It's the way of those who have found themselves loving and caring for young ones in the most ordinary day-to-day living. It is a way of life full of ups and downs, delights and boredom, menial tasks and big decisions, sleeplessness and challenges, scheduling crunches and emotional intensity, messiness and unpredictability. It is not a spirituality that is added onto parenthood but happens through it.

An Orthodox mother of two says raising her children "makes it [the spiritual life] deeper." She went on, "I think the bonds that you create between your child and you—I mean, how does that happen? It's just through God's love. It deepens your faith. It deepens your desire for them to have that same connection." While addressing the challenges of being a parent, she said, "It makes the struggle easier in some ways, to be like, 'I'm not even just doing this for me anymore. I'm doing it for them.'"

A father from the same community also emphasized the theme of deepening. "Oh, man. For me, at least, over the years, I think it's deepened my spirituality. Not that it was, necessarily, shallow to begin with. I think we all don't know the depths until we're there, then it keeps going and going. It never stops; there's never a bottom to it."

Several parents emphasized the intense feeling of responsibility that comes with the role—sometimes to a near breaking point—and the corresponding sense of vulnerability, humility, and the need to rely upon God. As Jenny (above) put it, "Holy smokes. You pray a lot more, it's hilarious. Yeah. I recall one moment especially, when Esther was a baby, and I was traveling with my mom and my sister and the kids, but without Will [Jenny's husband]. I was on my own for nighttime duty with Esther, and I remember one point just being so tired, and thinking, who's going to help me here? Will's not here. What can I do? And then I remembered that in every circumstance, no matter what phase of life, you can always rely on God. I was like, 'Oh yeah, that's right. God, I'm really tired. Can you help, please?'" Jenny described how she had first learned the lesson as a teenager but rediscovered it with each phase of life—as a young adult, and now as a parent. "The lesson," she says, "comes around again in really unique ways."

Megan and Stephen (briefly mentioned in chapter 3) are parents of five boys. Stephen is also a leader in their nondenominational, evangelical church. He described how they struggle with the sense of responsibility they feel for their children, not only in general but for their "faith walk." Four of the boys were teenagers at this point, which seemed to intensify the struggle. "I believe," Stephen said, "my responsibility as their parent is to guide them and shepherd them." He went on, "You crave so much for your kids in their faith walk, in everything that they do, the choices they make." But, Stephen admitted, the choices are going to be their own. "And, to give them that freedom to—I don't even know if I'm saying this how I'm intending to say it—but even their salvation is not my responsibility. . . . That's a vulnerable place to be, as a parent."

Megan expanded. "There's this humbleness that you get. It's like, oh, I'm not just a puppet master that can make them whoever they are. When they're in preschool, you can maybe still have this illusion that you're a puppet master. And there's still some people that have middle school and high schoolers that think they're puppet masters. But you're not."

Stephen pointed out, "And yet there's a little bit that's freeing at the same time, too. That I don't bear all that weight." He paused to reflect, then added, "Ultimately, I'm called to love them, to point them to God." In the end, Megan and Stephen agreed—how much more being a parent had made them both depend upon God. As Stephen put it, they have to rest in the knowledge that "he's going to love them."

This kind of struggle—between parental puppeteering and childhood autonomy, between control and freedom—pervaded so many of our interviews with parents that it comes as close as anything to being a "universal." Similarly, Notre Dame sociologist Christian Smith found a similar dynamic in his research among religious parents. Parenting, according to the parents his team interviewed, is made complicated by the tension between control and self-determination. Too much control can trigger "rebellion." But some structure is necessary for grounding, safety, and security. Parents can be too lax, or they can be overbearing—navigating is difficult.[5]

On this issue I again turn to developmental psychologist Alison Gopnik. In *The Gardner and the Carpenter*, she describes a version of this basic parental dilemma and cultural responses to it. The most prevalent approach in contemporary US culture, Gopnik believes, is what she calls the "carpenter" approach to being a parent. She does not even like the word "parenting," because she sees it as a late twentieth-century invention contributing to a cultural mind-set that traps parents into false expectations for the role. "Parenting" never used to be a verb, any more than "childing" or "spousing." The carpenter approach—which is the same as "parenting" for Gopnik—seduces parents into believing they need "to shape that material into a final product that will fit the scheme [they] had in mind to begin with. . . . Messiness and variability are a carpenter's enemies; precision and control are her allies." Approaching parenthood as a carpenter is very much like Megan's use of "puppet master."

Whether or not most parents actually approach raising children like carpentry is hard to judge. However, I suspect that Gopnik is right that there is tremendous cultural pressure to do so. From social media and television ads to parenting manuals and op-ed pieces, there is no lack of advice and prescriptions for parents. But as a scientist, Gopnik finds little evidence that the variations in parental techniques have any predictable long-term effects. From whether or not to co-sleep, let babies cry it out, or provide opportunities for more free play, she says, "from an empirical perspective, parenting is a mug's game . . . in fact, parenting is a terrible invention. It hasn't improved the lives of children and parents, and in some ways it's arguably made them worse, . . . the source of endless anxiety and guilt coupled with frustration." She adds, the consequences for children themselves are that "parenting leads to an oppressive cloud of hovering expectations."

Gopnik believes a better metaphor for being a parent is "gardener."[6] Gardening is still challenging work. "It takes hard labor and the sweat of our brows, with a lot of exhausted digging and wallowing in manure." Gardening demands tending, adjusting expectations, and a large measure of patience to create "a protected and nurturing space for plants to flourish." And to be clear, Gopnik imagines a particular type of gardening. The role is less like creating an orchid hothouse designed for specific blooms or like a bonsai gardener designing particular shapes—both are more carpenter-like approaches—and more in the vein of a meadow or a cottage garden. These are full of stubborn weeds and beautiful accidents; they rely less on one particular plant and more on a whole ecosystem. "And in the long run, that kind of varied flexible complex, dynamic system will be more robust and adaptable than the most carefully tended hothouse bloom." (Gopnik points out that in England the term "hothousing" refers to the same phenomenon as Americans call "helicoptering.")

In summary, Gopnik's alternative for parents does not involve less work. It is more of a mind-set—the intentions at work creating the conditions for children to grow and thrive. It's about parental imagination.

Children are highly tuned in to the intentions of those around them, often, more so than behaviors. For all the talk about setting examples, being role models, and practicing what you preach, it is the intentions behind behaviors that children are built to attend to. As in the example from chapter 4—of dropping a block as you put it into a basket—a child will typically assume that you intend for the block to go into the basket, not that you intend to drop it. But if you hold the block and spin around, then put the block in the box and say, "your turn," they are likely to go get the block back out and start spinning. The intent has shifted. The behavior is a kind of game. In short, the intentions—the imagination—at work in behaviors matter deeply.[7]

* * *

We would be hard pressed to categorize the parents we interviewed as either carpenters or gardeners. We could certainly feel the tension between these approaches at work in their parental imaginations. But in some ways the stakes are elevated when considering parents' spiritual imaginations in relation to the children in their lives. As we saw with Megan and Stephen, once the illusion of being a puppet master is shattered—parental or spiritual—parents are left in an intensely vulnerable position. They are left to rely upon God. "Having all these experiences with my kids," an LDS mother explains, "and having to rely so much on Heavenly Father because I'm like, I don't know what I'm doing. . . . Being a parent, I've seen Heavenly Father so much more in my life. I think because I've needed him more maybe."

Intensifying this sense of vulnerability is the world we send our kids into. I asked Lauren, a university professor and the mother of Hannah (chapter 2), how being a parent has affected her faith life. She said, "I think being a parent, you have to have so much faith because you're sending your child out into the world and not knowing. I remember before our first child [Hannah] was born having this moment of, 'is this really going to be okay having children,' and thinking, 'I can only do it with Jesus. I can't do this—there's no way to do this—without God.'" She went on to explain, "I think my prayers are more fervent because of the kids. Also, I can understand God's love differently as a parent myself, the way I love my kids—and forgiveness also, and grace." This was another common theme among parents—that the deep love felt for their children helped them better appreciate how God loves. Lauren continued, "When I mess up, when I see them mess up and I can forgive them because of my love for them and then think, 'Okay, this is likewise the way God forgives me.'" She summarized, "So, my understanding of my relationship to God—as his child—has changed because of my relationship with my kids."

Lauren's thoughts articulate well a major finding of our interviews generally. The Way of Parenthood is loaded with relationship from above, from below, and everywhere in between. Like turtles in the Zen proverb, it's relationships all the way up and down. These relationships are the pathway into the depths of faith by the way they intensify life—from sorrows, fears, and vulnerability to joy, love, and connection. These relationships, as muddy, entangled, and complicated as they tend to be, nonetheless have a way of clarifying purpose and what is important.

Richard, a Quaker turned Presbyterian and father of three, described this kind of clarification through being a parent. "It has helped me to recognize that what I would like to have in my life is meaning rather than pleasure." He went on to explain, "It's complicated and it's uncomfortable and it's over the long haul rather than the short term. It's not always gratifying and it's certainly not always easy, but having children has brought to the forefront what I am aiming for." That is, his relationship with his children affected his own religious imagination, including his place in the larger community. "I'm more deeply connected in community and the church that we're in right now than I was [before children]."

Abby, mother of three including Eve, whose IF was Moe the Taco (chapter 1), described how before children she thought of becoming a missionary. "But I missed that calling on my life," she said. "So, I think becoming a mom has made me realize that children are part of my mission field." Being a parent, she explained, has meant "broadening my perspective of what it means to preach the gospel."

The Orthodox couple, Anne and Zach (chapter 4), described how their family likes to take personal retreats at a particular monastery. With a new baby, however, this has become challenging on many levels. They described a conversation they had with an eldress at the monastery in light of the tension they felt between the demands of parenthood and the desire for the kind of spiritual renewal they experience on retreat. The eldress put it bluntly to them: "Your children are your salvation." Anne explained how she understood the message—that parenthood leads to struggle, and that struggle creates a deep sense of humility: "you learn to be more humble." She summarized, "You can only find Christ through being humble."

* * *

So, some parents had active religious lives before becoming parents while others were motivated to a more active faith because of their children. While some parents struggled to maintain the style of spirituality they practiced before children, most found themselves living their faith less like a carpenter, and in a way born of vulnerability and intense love. Nearly all the parents we spoke with affirmed that having children in some way has deepened their spirituality. And one of the striking features of these interviews is the way in which faith, for these parents, is not so much an add-on to their lives, but rests at the core of who they are. The spiritual life *is* life. No, they don't always feel particularly "spiritual" or "holy" or "faithful." But somehow the rhythms of the life of faith pulse beneath the challenges and struggles of this humbler way.

An Orthodox father, Jacob, shared a frustration related to his twelve-year-old son, Raphael. Jacob was a teacher, studying to become a lawyer, and a self-described "voracious reader." His son was not. "It's always been a little hard for me that he's just not all that into reading." Recently, with some outside help, they discovered that Raphael has dyslexia. In horror, Jacob realized that his disappointment about his son's lack of interest in reading would "be like someone who's mobilely disabled, like judging them for not running faster in a race. But the fact that they're running at all, is astonishing." Jacob became intensely worried about how his earlier disappointment may have affected Raphael, that Raphael may have interpreted his father's disappointment in his lack of reading as a general disappointment in him as a person. Jacob was sure his wife, Zera, had never made Raphael feel this way, but he was not so sure about himself. A couple of weeks before our interview, Jacob and Zera approached their son. Jacob explained, "In a delicate way—we didn't want to plant seeds in his mind—but we inquired as to whether I had ever made him feel like he was a disappointment." Jacob began to cry as he told the story. Through tears he said, "I apologized." Jacob went on to describe how he prostrated himself in front of his son. "And he just forgave us. And, not that it was even this huge thing—"

Zera interrupted, "It was a huge thing."

Jacob was trying not to make the act sound like he was some kind of Christian superhero, but Zera wouldn't let him dismiss it so easily. She saw profound implications. That her husband, Raphael's father, asked for forgiveness from his son out of a concern that Jacob may have diminished his son at some level, that he loved Raphael so much, and that Raphael in turn could offer forgiveness so easily—that indeed was a huge thing.

Jacob wiped his tears, adding, "It's been so much better in this really subtle way. It's so much clearer."

Reflecting now upon this event, I'm struck by the way in which the rituals of confession and forgiveness that happen in weekly worship—not to mention prostration—had been integrated into the household, deepening the everyday ways of being with one another. The father confesses, the son forgives. And the result was a deepening of relationship, even if in "this really subtle way." I'm touched that this deepening is a matter of subtleties, which, of course, constitute the everyday material of family life—a look, a tone, a laugh, a tear—all reflections of Jacob's intentions toward his son. Not that relationships can't be loud and dramatic. Still, underneath the boisterousness, millions of subtle signals pass between those in the same household. In this case the bold act of prostration led to clarity in the relationship, a sharpening of what matters.

* * *

Spirituality, faith, religious imagination, the Way of Parenthood—these are my clumsy ways of trying to describe the souls of the parents we interviewed. Again, spirituality is not so much an add-on to their lives as it is a way of being, a posture in life, an orientation to the world—including to their children as well as to themselves. This orientation is rooted in something larger than themselves and larger than their families and larger than their church. The posture is born from their knowledge of the love of God. This does not mean that loving is always easy or that relationships always flow smoothly. The Way of Parenthood is shot through with conflict, struggle, anxiety, and sleepless nights.

The temptation, in our technological society, is to believe we can fix everything hard about living—including family life and raising children—with the right set of techniques and carpentry tools. This is Gopnik's point. And, no doubt, some skills and tools are useful. But not everything is fixable, and approaching the world—our children—this way threatens to haunt them with "endless anxiety and guilt coupled with frustration," as Gopnik puts it. When Jacob sensed he was approaching his son, Raphael, in such a way, it led him to prostration. Jacob's faith created a larger, deeper context for his ways of being with Raphael. And it is no small finding of our interviews to say that even as parents raise children, children raise parents. Faith is not only passed on to children, but children can pass faith on to adults, even their own parents.

There is a mystery at work through these relationships, made known through the communion of family. Mystery, in this sense, is not the mystery of the technological approach to life—problems to be fixed. Mystery comes from the Greek root *mystos*, which has the meaning of "keeping silence." Mysteries evoke silence not because we cannot know anything but because we know more than our words can capture. "Just sit and listen." Here, mystery is the sense that something more, deeper, wider, is going on.

The twentieth-century philosopher Gabriel Marcel wrote as powerfully as anyone about this mystery. A mystery, for Marcel, lies in contrast to a problem. Problems can be solved or fixed with the right tools or information. A car's stalled engine. A murder mystery. But for Marcel, genuine mysteries are never solved or fixed. Why? They are irreducible; there is ever more to them than could be figured out. Mysteries present a surplus of meaning.

By contrast, to approach life, including our children, as a problem is a framework of controlling power—puppet mastering. Marcel uses the example of a sleeping child to illustrate the difference between problem and mystery and the different moral frameworks attending each. From the point of view of power, "the sleeping child is completely unprotected and appears to be utterly in our power; from that point of view, it is permissible for us to do what we like with the child." This is barbarism, according to Marcel. "But from the point of view of mystery, we might say that it is just because this being is completely unprotected, that it is utterly at our mercy, that it is also invulnerable or sacred."[8] To approach others as mysteries is to recognize their sacredness. They are not to be reduced, ridiculed, or manipulated. That is sin, if not evil. But to approach others as mysteries is to sense the breath of God in them—that which is irreducible, beyond words, or deeper than linear categories. Your children are mysteries. You are a mystery.

As mysteries, others are ever more than we could exhaust with our words, concepts, ideologies, or stereotypes. As Craig Dykstra, relying upon Marcel, puts it, "People are mysteries, and being moral means treating them as such. Our world is a mystery, and being moral means encountering it that way. At the depth of being there is an Ultimate Mystery, and being moral means being properly related to that Mystery."[9]

* * *

Over and over, we heard parents express this sense of mystery—in the sense of Marcel—through their lives as parents, through the relationships with their children. The relationships are irreducible. Love is larger, more meaningful, more abundant than either parent or child alone. As Richard, above, put it, "There's something bigger than me, than us." His hope for his children was that they would be "humble enough to recognize and to respect that, that it's a power for good, not evil, and that we should be church together in community."

Nearly all the parents identified this power for good as love. More than anything, the motivation for going to church, practicing faith, and tending their relationship to God expressed by these parents was love—the love they feel for their children, the love they find in God, and the hope that their children will know this love. "What we hear at church," as Lauren, above, put it, "is that 'you are a beloved child of God' and that would be one of the main things that we want them to believe—that they are a beloved child of God, and to have that as the rock-solid basis of their self and also that everyone is a beloved child of God and that we treat everyone that way." Patrick, a father of two, said it this way: "The biggest thing for me is that love is not conditional. You don't love people because of who they are, what they look like, or who they believe in, or what they're going to do for you. And to me, that's what loving God is about. That's what loving our neighbor is about."

Though expressed in a variety of ways, through different belief systems and theological doctrines, knowing love was consistently the intent behind the words and practices of the spiritual lives of the parents we interviewed.

Craig Dykstra tells a story that expresses this hope through an everyday analogy, taking us back to swim lessons.[10] Dykstra was a professor of Christian education at theological seminaries at Louisville and Princeton, and later served as the longtime head of the religion division at the Lilly Endowment. When he was a seminary student, he worked at the local YMCA, teaching preschoolers to swim. He describes how they would come from the locker room clutching their towels and gritting their teeth from both the excitement and nervousness of facing the deep waters. "Well, it is a law of nature that you cannot swim while cramping your body and gnashing your teeth," says Dykstra. "The first priority in teaching children to swim is to enable them to trust the water." As the children began to do so, they relaxed, and with a little time and practice, they came to understand something powerful that they can neither see nor understand—buoyancy. "In a deeply somatic, bodily way—and in a way that is in no small part existential, for it is a knowledge that must be strong enough to address their fears—they must come to know the buoyancy of the water. Buoyancy is not something you can teach children—or anyone else, for that matter—through a lesson in physics."

For Dykstra, this lesson in buoyancy provides a strong analogy for the life of faith. "At the heart of the Christian life there lies a deep, somatic, profoundly personal but very real knowledge. It is the knowledge of the buoyancy of God. It is the knowledge that in struggle and in joy, in conflict and in peace—indeed, in every possible circumstance and condition in life and in death—we are upheld by God's own everlasting arms."

Perhaps in addition to Gopnik's carpenter and gardener metaphors, we can add another—swim instructor. In faith, parents help children swim—to know and trust the buoyancy of God. "It is a deep, profound, existential knowledge that infuses not only our minds but also our hearts and even our bodies. It is knowledge that, as we come to know it more and more deeply over many years, will give form and substance to our entire imagination, to our whole way of being in the world, to our very existence. It is the knowledge of the overflowing abundance of the grace and mercy and love of God."

It is a powerful lesson. Yet one of the findings of our research is that not only can parents help children understand the buoyancy that is faith, but children are helping their parents know this overflowing abundance of God. To quote Colby again: "The kids—the best way I can describe that connection is, it's loving another human being so much that your heart physically hurts from it. My cholesterol issues aside."

7

Dreams

"HAVE YOU EVER DREAMED OF GOD?" I asked Kathy, who was nine years old.

"Actually, I used to dream about him all the time," she answered, "when I was younger. I used to think he had yellow hair. Like the banana man, a yellow hat."

I took a moment to assimilate this information. Then it hit me. "Like in Curious George?"

"Yes," she said. "And now I know that he doesn't really look like that. He's like a Holy Spirit."

* * *

Several children told me about their dreams of God, some spontaneously, but most because I asked. It was something of a bonus question that I posed if the child was still conversationally engaged and there was enough time. That turned out to be in about half the interviews. To be statistical for a moment, we asked 69 of 151 children. Of those 69, 34 children, nearly half, said they had dreamed of God and could describe at least part of the dream. The other half (35) answered no or said not in a dream they could remember. Even so, some of those who said no did describe a sense of God's presence at the edges of sleep. For example, eight-year-old Esther told me, "Once or twice, I felt God holding my hand in bed when I was falling asleep, and it was the most lovely feeling I've ever had."

Reflecting upon these dreams, as well as the one from our son, David, at three (see the introduction), I continue to be touched by the way God can show up in this liminal, intimate space of the night.

* * *

Six-year-old Liam, who lives in New York City, dreamed that God was on the subway with him. Liam and his three-year-old brother, Gabe, were being raised Catholic, after their mother, while their father was a practicing Quaker (who also attended mass with the family). The conversation had begun with Liam sharing everything he was learning about Pokémon. Liam's father confessed he couldn't follow the baroque details of each character and story, but he was trying. His mother agreed. But soon enough I was able to talk with Liam about matters other than Pokémon while his brother played with his plush animals—chiming in now and then.

I had asked Liam what he thought made God happy, and he told me, "Being nice to all the living creatures." The conversation turned to baptism: "It's when the priest blesses babies with holy water." He had been baptized as a baby, he explained, by a priest who was a longtime friend of his mother. Next, we talked about communion. He told me that he would be able to take communion next year, when he was in second grade and had learned more about it.

"Where is God?" I asked. Liam looked a little startled, and I realized how abrupt the transition from communion to this question was. I had earlier shown him, as I did the other children, my list of interview questions with several assurances, for example: (1) that we would see how many we can get to, (2) that we could stop at any time if they get tired or don't want to answer any more, and, as mentioned earlier, (3) there are no wrong answers—that I want to know what they actually think. I asked Liam again, "So where do you think God is?"

"In heaven," he answered.

I followed. "Do you know where heaven is?"

"In the sky?" he said, a little unsure.

"So, is God far away or is God nearby too?" Listening to the interview now, I can see that the question was too leading. But at this point in the research, I had interviewed over a hundred children, and again and again I listened to young minds wrestle with the paradox of God's transcendence and presence—not in those terms, of course—but with God being above or beyond this world yet with us at the same time. "So, is God far away or is God nearby too?"

Liam said, "Both. He's watching over us, but he's also right next to us."

"Oh wow, okay," I said, impressed again by the workings of a child's mind. "Have you ever felt like God was really, really close by?" Liam couldn't think of a particular moment. "Okay. Do you have a favorite place where you like to think about God?" He pointed to his bedroom. "Really? How come?" He said his room made him feel very comfortable. "Oh. And that helps you think about God?" Yeah, it did. "Have you ever dreamed about God?" I asked.

"I've dreamed about him being on the same subway with me." Liam explained that he and God were playing the guessing game I Spy.

"Really?" I said. "On the subway?"

"Uh-huh, and God kept saying, 'I spy with my little eye—nothing.' And guess what I guessed?"

"What?"

"Air! I was always right. You can't see it."

"Wow," I reacted. "That was kind of a tricky one, wasn't it? And you were doing that with God?" Yes, he was. "So, what did God look like in your dream?"

"Blue. He had a gold crown, blue hair—blue and white hair." Liam paused, thought for a little longer, then added, "and a red little cloak." Those were all the details he could remember.

At the time, a scene from a music video flashed through my thoughts. It was Joan Osbourne's 1995 hit "One of Us," in which she sings, "What if God's like one of us? . . . Just a stranger on a bus?" I later confirmed that when she sings that line in the music video, it's not a bus, but instead a subway train passes by. I could almost see Liam and God inside. Regardless, as I reflect now upon the conversation, I'm impressed by the way in which this six-year-old's religious imagination puts him in touch with a subway-riding blue God who likes to play games. The I Spy riddle even speaks to the paradox of the presence of something—air—that is unseen, invisible, and nearby all at the same time. Air. Wind. Spirit. On the one hand, God is in heaven, in the sky way above us. On the other hand, God is as close as a dream in our comforting bedroom.

* * *

It may be the case that dreams themselves, if not the imagination, help hold together what could be the incongruence of a God who is both near and far, invisible yet riding a subway with a gold crown and red cloak—something like: "On this planet, all cats bark."

In his book *An Evolutionary Psychology of Sleep and Dreams*, Patrick McNamara, a neuroscientist, explores the potential purposes of dreaming in human cognition.[1] Sleep and dreaming, from an evolutionary point of view, are potentially very costly activities and put us in an extremely vulnerable position in relation to a world full of predators. Think of it—in sleep our awareness of our surroundings shuts down for the most part, and on top of that, dreams lead us to believe we're awake in a different time and place. Yet we need sleep to survive. Our active brains need time to rest and restore. In many species—birds and fish, for example—the resolution of this dilemma is a brain that can rest and watch out at the same time. Half the brain sleeps while the other pays attention. But not so much for humans. Instead, dreams heighten the dilemma and intensify the vulnerability. We feel like we're awake and doing things like riding subways when we're actually lying unprotected. So why?

At the experiential level, dreaming may feel simply like the leftover flotsam and jetsam from the day's events. I forgot my wallet at the store yesterday, and then I dream that night that I can't find my ID at the airport security line. But McNamara, by approaching dreams from an evolutionary perspective, invites us to consider why our minds would trick us every night not only with memories from the day but also with fantastical situations that we never experience. Flying, traveling to other worlds, breathing underwater, or (for most of us) hanging out with movie stars. Dreams, as McNamara points out, not only pick up fragments from waking consciousness but they "are creative, productive, generative, and fecund." Dreams are more than simply the "froth" of cognition, he says.

Instead, dreams help us with a cognitive skill fundamental to humans: counterfactual thinking. Counterfactual thinking is the ability to imagine alternative possibilities. Why is this helpful? When we encounter a frustrating situation in life, we begin to imagine alternatives, what could have gone differently or what we could have done or could do to produce different outcomes. We "cognitively generate simulations of imaginative scenarios that would allow or promote the alternative outcome." We are learning from our mistakes and frustrations and find future workarounds.

The point is, whether we remember our dreams or not, they are working on us, loosening up the mind and creating flexibility. Without counterfactual thinking, we are stuck in what simply is, what we already know. Dreams not only reflect but help generate the plasticity of our minds, which is at the heart of learning. Dreams open our minds. This flexibility in our thinking helped our hominin ancestors adapt to all kinds of new environments around the globe.

McNamara sees a deep connection between dreams and play, especially pretend play. Dreams and pretense run simulations of the world injected with counterfactuals. Our research with children who had invisible friends would confirm this. Children pick up an idea here, a plot there, a character from this story, an obstacle from that one, and they combine them to create something new. Maybe an invisible friend. Maybe a tree house trip to India with dragons and treasure.

One of the earliest IF interviews we conducted was with three-year-old Sophia. Her friend was Lucy. Sophia's mother suspected the name had to do with the *I Love Lucy Show*. Some days, Lucy was "a mom," according to Sophia, who had a daughter, Alice. But on other days, Lucy could be a rabbit. On other days still, Lucy was a lion, tiger, mouse, or zebra. In another IF interview, six-year-old Sasha told us about Bob and Jeff, her invisible friends. Bob was "a five-year-old boy who is really good at karate." And her friend Jeff was a year older, at seven, and, she said, "sometimes is a girl, Jeffette, who likes to wear diamond jewelry."

These are only a couple of examples of the way pretend play demonstrates the flexibility of the young imagination. But as Elly's and my magic tree house trip to India suggests, creative play is not limited to characters like Lucy or Jeffette but can generate settings and plots as well. In other words, the dreaming mind of the night has a daytime version in play. And just as our bodies tend to lose flexibility as we age, listening to children reminds us that our minds can lose flexibility as well, especially as we forget the world of play, if not dreams.

* * *

Six-year-old Cassie and I were discussing prayer, but the discussion turned to dreams in general. She shared that she sometimes has nightmares and described one in which a giant bird came out of her bedroom closet to attack her. But her mom came in and rescued her. Cassie explained that she often prays at night in bed, before going to sleep, and God tells her "to think good thoughts" as a way of warding off such bad dreams. She didn't share any dreams of God particularly, but she got excited to tell me about one involving a trip to the local grocery store. "One time I had the best dream ever about friendly dinosaurs at Albertsons. They were outside moving the car so we would get home faster!"

"I love that," I told her. Rather than a giant, threatening bird, there were friendly, helpful dinosaurs.

"And they moved the car before we were even in it, so we had to run on a scooter!"

"So, you had to chase after them?"

Cassie said, "They were being silly and ran away from us!"

Not only friendly and helpful, but silly—which I took to mean the dinosaurs were being playful, like running away in a game of tag. The point is that dreams, sometimes scary, sometimes funny, present counterfactual events that potentially loosen the imagination. Dinosaurs at the grocery store, giant birds in a closet.

As mentioned earlier, I found similarly strange juxtapositions in the world of imaginary friends—vivid examples of this counterfactual, flexible thinking. Shape-shifting Lucy. Gender-bending Jeff/Jeffette. Cinderella, who was a little girl one day, a blue dog the next. Coda, who died from "too big a bite" one week and was alive the next. Hee-tome and Boo-gong were in Florida one moment, then under the table in Louisville, Kentucky, the next. Form and substance, space and time are as flexible and full of possibilities as a science fiction novel or fantasy film. Dreams and pretending, among other things, are a kind of mental stretching, expanding our sense of what could be and filled with surprises. Think theater of the absurd or even simple improvisational "yes-and" exercises:

"Your cat, Rex, was barking at me."

"Yes, in Louisville, all cats bark. It's a sign of affection."

"Rex must love me."

"Yes, and that mouse on your head."

In their research among preschoolers, Marjorie Taylor and Stephanie Carlson found that four-year-olds who engage in pretend play with imaginary companions performed significantly better on theory-of-mind tasks (see chapter 1) than other children.[2] While it could be that a robust theory of mind in children leads to more fantasy play, Taylor and Carlson suspect the reverse, that fantasy play helps children better understand minds in general. It makes sense. In such play, children are imagining the perspectives of others (of the IF, of the friends you share the IF with, of the parents as the child tells them about IF, and so on). They are "becoming practiced in negotiating interactions between imaginary companions and real people."[3] The payoff of this counterfactual play seems to be a form of social flexibility, that is, not being stuck in one's own point of view, perhaps even enhancing the capacity for empathy—central to communal life, whether among friends, classmates, or family members.

* * *

When I asked eight-year-old Thomas, Orthodox, whether he had ever dreamed of God, his answer presented an intriguing ambiguity. Thomas and I were sitting in the living room of his home, on a sofa across from a wall of icons. Thomas showed me some of his favorite icons and could go into detail about the stories behind them. He had a sharp eye for the images, if not the spirituality, at work through them. When I asked whether he had dreamed of God, at first he said, "not really," but then he qualified his answer. "I have"—he paused—"I have had some dreams where there's *icons* of him," he said, emphasizing the "icons." He was making clear the difference between God and an icon of God. In the dream, "There are floating things that you can kind of see through. It kind of looks like God, the mother of God. I'm seeing, basically, people that are like floating, floating people, that you can kind of see like ghosts."

"Do you mean like transparent?" I asked, trying to clarify. He wasn't sure about the word "transparent." "I mean like see-through, like glass."

"Yeah," he affirmed. "It's like that you can partially see. So, you can see the body, but you can partially see through it." I asked what he saw on the other side of the floating figures. "You're seeing where the heart is," Thomas said, "and seeing the icon and you're seeing like kind of the person that you're seeing through. I'm looking at the icon and looking up and they look exactly like the same."

I was a bit confused, so I asked, "You're seeing the figure but you're seeing the icon?"

"Behind it [the figure]. You can see the icon behind it, but you can also see the spirits."

I didn't push for any further clarification. It can be hard enough to describe the soft-edged world of a dream at any age, let alone when you're an eight-year-old talking to an adult you just met. But I did find this notion of seeing through the icons fascinating. I think of Simon, from the same community, who said "icons are a window into heaven." So, when eight-year-old Thomas dreams of transparent figures from icons, his religious imagination is depicting the very act of seeing through them like windows.

I did ask Thomas if his seeing through the figures ever happened when he was not dreaming, when he was awake, maybe praying, for example. "Not really," he said, but added, "sometimes I look at an icon and I see this blink, like it blinks kind of."

"And what do you think that means?" I asked.

"I only see that sometimes during church. And I look over at the icons and I see in the corner of my eye it blinks and I look over and I see the mother of God or Jesus blinks over there." Thomas had no further explanation, and again, I did not press the issue. But the comment did lead to a playful conversation about Harry Potter movies and the ways that the figures in the paintings at Hogwarts talk.

Like Cassie's mother chasing away a threatening giant bird, a few children told me about dreams in which God plays a rescuer role. Twelve-year-old Drew shared a particularly dramatic one. When I asked if he'd ever dreamed of God, he told me how in a dream he saw a light that, at first, he thought was something good, but he then realized he was being abducted by aliens. "I was like, 'No! I was tricked!' But then God came through somehow and busted me out of the alien ship. I was like, 'Yay!' And then I woke up and I had to go to school."

Some fifteen hundred miles to the south of Drew, in the Yucatan, another child, ten-year-old Miguel, told me of a dream in which he was alone, walking somewhere in the dark, when he encountered a stranger that scared him. In the dream, "I said a prayer for God to be with me, so the other person wouldn't hurt me." God indeed showed up to help him.

Similarly, nine-year-old Javier told me, "I dreamed I was walking through town and God was with me. And nothing happened to me." His friend, Daniel, twelve, told me of a dream in which he was lost and all alone. "And then Jesus came, and he walked with me, and he helped me go home." I asked what Jesus looked like. "He had on white clothes, long hair, and with marks in his hands and his feet from when he was crucified."

Remarkably, while about half the children overall described dreams of God, among the Mayan children thirteen of eighteen (72 percent) did so. Most of the dreams were less dramatic or not so plot-driven as the ones above. The children described a feeling or a sense that God was with them or that they saw God with the saints or angels. For example, Rosa, eleven years old, said, "When I dreamed of God, I felt like he was talking to me, and he was telling me something good that I could do." She went on to tell me about angels. "I have seen them in my dreams where they'll tell me something powerful and they give me an idea to do things right." David, nine, dreamed he was in heaven. "I saw all the saints," and he named several. Patricia, nine and the only Pentecostal child among the Mayan children we interviewed, also found herself in heaven. "I'm walking in heaven and I'm walking down the road when I came to the mansion. And then I saw the golden gates open and a lot of angels come out."

I have no particular theory about the prevalence of these types of dreams among the Mayan children except perhaps that they live in an environment rich in religious imagery—statuary, icons, paintings, and impressive church buildings. Other children we interviewed may have been in churches or households full of such imagery; however, the Mexican children lived in towns and villages that were full of visual expressions of faith outside church and home.

* * *

In one of the few interviews with adolescents, I spoke with Rebecca, fifteen, and her sister, Eliana, fourteen. When they learned about the research from their youth minister in a Presbyterian church in the Northeast, they really wanted to participate. Before I learned their ages, I had already set up the interviews by email through their mother, Eva. She was eager to share the story of her husband, Mike, Jewish, who nonetheless was actively involved in their church—teaching Sunday school, for example—and supported the mother and daughters' Christianity. I explained that I wasn't really interviewing teens, but rather than cancel the interview, we decided it could be a good chance to listen to the girls reflect on their memories of church and faith as children. I interviewed the girls together, and a dream came up in an unexpected way.

"Can you think back to what your earliest memory of church is?"

Rebecca answered first. "Well, I guess when I was—I don't know if I was in kindergarten or some young age like that—but I had an ear infection. I had swimmer's ear, and I was sick for four or five days or more, and I was missing school. At the time I loved school, so I was sad. I was just upset, and obviously I was hurting. I think I had a fever because of it, and I was just sick. And we prayed and we prayed. And one night I had a dream that Jesus came down to our elementary school—"

"Wow," I interrupted, but she kept going.

"—and he was glowing. It was like on the playground. He came down to the playground at elementary school, and it was kind of orangey, hazy. He came down and he was just glowing. All the kids ran up to him. The next morning, I woke up and I turned my head and saw all this gunk come out of my ear, and I was pretty much better the next day. And that was the first time, that's my first memory of any, of any—" Rebecca paused, searching for the right phrase.

I offered, "Any religious memory."

"Yeah. So, it's not really being at church," she said, remembering that I had actually asked about a church memory.

"Actually," I reassured her, "it's one of my questions with kids, have you ever dreamed of God?"

"Yeah," Rebecca said. "I was completely better the next day, and my mom saw this gunk"—Rebecca began to rehearse the dream with me again—"I turned my head, and this actual stuff came out of my ear, and they were just like, what? It was just. Yeah, no—" She seemed at a loss for words. The experience clearly still held power in her adolescent religious imagination. She finally landed on "It was good."

I found myself imagining this glowing Jesus on a playground with excited children running to him. I thought about Jesus telling his disciples, "Let the children come to me." Yet in the case of Rebecca's dream, Jesus comes to the children. I remembered how in my son's dream, God also came to a playground, specifically to a sandbox on a preschool playground in our shared backyard.

I turned to Rebecca's sister, Eliana, and asked about her earliest memory of church or anything related. She confessed she never had any dreams like the one her sister just related, even though she wished that she had because, she said, "I thought it was so cool." She thought for a moment. "I think my first memory of church was actually not about Christianity. I don't know when it was or how old I was, but I remember being really young and being in a service, and my dad was holding the bulletin with the prayer that everyone was saying." She didn't remember the content of the prayer. But she said, "I remember I had recently learned that my dad was Jewish, and he was bar mitzvah-ed, and he was not raised Christian. I was wondering why he was at church and what made him do that? I mean, I think it was for my mom. I remember then thinking, well, what does he believe? I remember thinking about that, and I couldn't have been more than kindergarten age."

"Oh, wow," I said, impressed by such a complex thought from a kindergartener.

Rebecca commented too. "Some deep thoughts."

Eliana resumed. "I remember thinking about this, and I think now, reflecting on that moment, I realized that my dad, going to church for my mom and raising his kids in a religion that he was not familiar with. It was really just an act of love."

Rebecca responded. "And that in itself is Jesus's message, right? To love your neighbor. And him [Dad] doing that, I think is a good example of what love is. And a good example of how you can love, especially when it might be hard to, or when it means sacrificing something of your own to help someone else or to make something better for someone else."

This comment moved Eliana to tell a story about her mother and grandmother during the pandemic. "In the beginning of the pandemic my grandma got sick. They lived two hours away, so my mom was there seven days a week basically. And she would sleep over there and so for three months, it was a lot of—"

Rebecca interrupted. "Oh my gosh, look at the butterfly. Sorry." Outside was a beautiful yellow swallowtail dancing around their back porch.

"I love them too," I said.

Rebecca explained, "We always say that our grandma—sorry—whenever we see a butterfly, we think of our grandmother. She passed away and we were just talking about her. So, it's just every time we see a butterfly, we're like, Tati is near us. Tati is what we call our grandmother."

Eliana resumed her train of thought, explaining how their father had come to appreciate the sense of community he felt both at a previous Presbyterian church (in New York City, before they moved to their present location) and the one they are currently involved in—how accepting the churches have been of him. I felt obliged to point out that in some churches, Presbyterian or otherwise, it could go the other way. Eliana and Rebecca understood that, but it only made them more grateful for their congregations.

Their mother, Eva, was from an Armenian Orthodox family, but, with no such congregation where she grew up, they worshiped at a Baptist church and sent Eva to an Armenian camp in the summers to learn more about her religious heritage. Over time and through several moves, she had worshiped with those from many different denominations. "I felt comfortable in a lot of different churches. Wherever you really feel a sense of community and the Holy Spirit and just God's presence, I felt comfortable." Their father, Mike, indeed was raised in an Orthodox Jewish household but was only nominally practicing when he met Eva. He began accompanying her to a Presbyterian church in New York City that was meeting in a synagogue during a renovation. The church and synagogue had a strong historical relationship devoted to service in the community—something Mike deeply appreciated about that church as well as their current one. "I think foremost," Eva said, "I feel that it's really important that they [Rebecca and Eliana] know how loved they are by God, by this amazing divine being that's beyond our comprehension, that loves them, and that they are so treasured and so special. And with that love, they can let it pass through them and out to others and be a light."

The comment made me think about the ways in which community, love, and faith itself—in addition to dreaming and pretend play—could potentially generate flexibility if not unusual juxtapositions like Presbyterians in a synagogue or a Jewish man in a Christian congregation.

* * *

Later, I found myself thinking more about the butterfly, not only the synchronicity of the appearance when they were talking about Tati, but also the paradoxical, even counterfactual, thinking at work. The girls missed and grieved the loss of their grandmother. Yet at the same time, they felt a sense of her presence when a butterfly was near.

Freud would see a form of animism. Piaget might see residual magical thinking left over from early childhood. But I believe something more complex is going on. As I found with children with imaginary friends, they were clear that they understood the figures were "pretend friends" or "imagination friends." Children knew IFs were of a different reality status, known in a unique way compared to their neighborhood or school friends. Though I didn't, I'm sure if I had pressed Rebecca and Eliana about the reality status of the butterfly—is that really Tati?—they would have admitted that it was just a butterfly. But that would have been like pressing a young child to give up the "illusion" of their imaginary friend. It would be the equivalent of watching a great movie with a friend and saying, "you know, these characters are just made up."

Instead, I would call the Tati-as-butterfly mind-set a form of "as if" thinking. It's as if that butterfly is our grandmother—she's beautiful, inspiring, free, and nearby. This as-if thinking creates an imaginative space in which Tati can be dead but the love and attachment to her live on. The imagination is open to more than meets the eye. Or it has a sense that what meets the eye is more than the senses present. In the religious imagination of this family, love stretches not only beyond the limits of religious identity but beyond life and death.

* * *

As described above, a few of the children's dreams began with fear or dread but ended with God as the rescuer. But more often than not, God was simply a source of comfort or well-being without the drama. God walks alongside children, keeps them company, tells them something good, or in one dream, God is very happy, and this makes the child happy.

Eight-year-old Pamela was part of the LDS church in her community.

She was the last of eleven children I spoke with in this setting, over two days, and going into the interview I was flagging a bit. But Pamela was quite engaged and seemed to be gaining energy from our conversation, which in turn perked me up. We were nearing the end of my questions, but she was still going strong, so I asked her whether she had ever dreamed of God.

"I had a dream that Heavenly Father and Jesus were sitting by me reading me stories," she said. This happened when she was five or six, she thought. I asked her to describe the dream. "Well, I jumped. I was awake and looking at Heavenly Father, and he was sitting there on my bed, on the corner of my bed, reading me stories from my bookshelf."

I was a little unsure whether she thought of this as a dream or that she really had awakened to see God on her bed. But she clarified that it was a dream, and it was in the dream that she jumped and was awake. I asked if she could remember what Heavenly Father was reading. "He was reading to me scriptures because I had those on my bookshelf."

"And you said Jesus was in the dream too?" I asked. Turns out Jesus was sitting on the edge of her bed as well, though she didn't remember what he looked like. "All right. How did the dream make you feel?"

"It made me feel happy. I'm pretty sure I smiled in my sleep."

* * *

In his poem "Manifesto: The Mad Farmer Liberation Front,"[4] Wendell Berry confronts the many ways our modern world dehumanizes our life together and desacralizes the environment. He does so through a series of counterfactuals. "Every day do something that won't compute." Instead of cash crops, "plant sequoias." Or in one of my favorite counterfactuals, "Laugh. Laughter is immeasurable. Be joyful though you have considered all the facts." And in the final line holding together multiple subversive directions, "Practice resurrection."

If dream and play are as crucial to creativity and counterfactual thinking as the dream researcher Patrick McNamara suggests, I find myself wondering what kind of role dreams of God play in the young imagination. Among the children of this chapter, we've seen the God of their dreams comfort and protect, guide them home and rescue from threat, ride the subway playing games, save from alien abduction, wear a big yellow hat, read Scripture on the edge of a bed, and come to a school playground glowing and healing. We've also seen dream icons generate their own theological lesson as windows to heaven, transparent to more than themselves.

When taken together, these dreams present a wildness at work in these religious dreamers. The children we interviewed have been immersed in Bible lessons, catechisms, worship, theologies, and loving communities. Yet something not so neat and consistent as a Sunday school curriculum or systematic theology is at work as well. At Pentecost, Peter quotes the prophet Joel, favorably, that as the Spirit is poured out on all flesh, the young will prophesy and see visions while the old shall dream dreams. Perhaps the wildness of dreams has something to do with the wildness of the Spirit that blows where it will, turning expectations around and stretching our understanding of the world, if not children themselves.

8

Stretching Religious Imaginations

"YOU KNOW," River said, "not enough people talk to kids about imagination." We were discussing Zoe, River's imaginary friend from early childhood. "I mean, imagination is the source of everything. Creation comes with creativity and with creativity comes imagination. So there has to be imagination." This was the first time, in all the interviews I've conducted, that a child emphasized to me the importance of imagination as well as tied imagination to God's creation. I was impressed and said so.

I interviewed eleven-year-old River in a small apartment in Washington Heights, New York. The family had recently migrated from their previous church to a large interdenominational congregation, a move that River found difficult at first but had come to appreciate, especially with the help of the youth minister, Pastor Alicia.

River's mother, Lily, had come to New York to do musical theater, but now was a health-care worker. She was raised Christian Scientist—the daughter of a "First Reader," which she explained was the equivalent of a pastor. But the family's relationship with the church fell apart when Lily's sister was diagnosed with leukemia and the family had to choose between medical healing and faith healing. Neither worked.

The sister died, and at least some in the church blamed the death on the parents, for taking her to doctors.

Lily later spent some time in Baptist, then Pentecostal, churches in her young adult years, but it was not until she landed in a Presbyterian church that she felt at home. Her husband, Ian, had a less dramatic religious past, having been raised Methodist. When they started dating, Ian joined her at the Presbyterian church where they were both actively involved. They particularly appreciated the church's outreach ministries and commitment to social justice.

Yet, once River was born, Ian and Lily began to worry about the lack of children in the congregation as well as any kind of programming for them. The pandemic hit when River was seven, which delayed any church moves they were considering. Once COVID began to wane, they made the move to an interdenominational congregation that has a strong commitment to outreach and social justice as well. This church also had plenty of young people and ministries involving them. In fact, it was Pastor Alicia, the minister for children and youth, who put me in touch with the family.

In addition to our conversation about imagination, River and I had another rich discussion, this time not generated by one of my questions but by a T-shirt. The shirt said, "Ask me about my pronouns." So, I did. River said, "It's 'they, them,'" and went on to explain that they were gender-fluid, a term River had discovered a few years earlier and thought, "Oh, that's me." They explained, "Gender-fluid means I use all pronouns," and added, "I am every gender."

"How do you think God feels about gender fluidity?" I asked.

"I believe that God is okay with that because everyone should be accepting." They went quiet for a moment, thinking. Finally, River said, "Well, God, he isn't just a he, even though people say that a lot of the time." They concluded, "God is gender-fluid."

I shared with River an interview with six-year-old Joy. We had invited Joy to draw a picture of her church, but, to our surprise, she decided instead to draw a picture of God. The figure she drew, all in orange crayon, had long hair on one side and short on the other. The figure also had one shoe that was a high heel, while the other was, in

Joy's words, "a regular shoe." She emphasized that God was both male and female. "She was just six years old," I said to River.

"Yeah," River said, "it's like that."

When I later listened to Jane's interview with River's parents, I discovered that River had been thinking about these matters for a long time. Lily explained how she kept a notebook of things River had said or conversations they'd had together over the years, whenever Lily thought they were particularly interesting. "I was going back over things that I have written down or saved . . . now that they are nonbinary. When they were three, they asked about God's gender—and asked a lot of questions about God being a guy or a girl and why. Well, in what I wrote—it's at the end of the conversation—they had decided that God was gender-fluid. And they were like three and a half at the time." Lily went on to explain how her background had likely shaped the conversation. "I grew up with a Father-Mother God because Christian Science was started by a woman [Mary Baker Eddy] in the mid-eighteen hundreds, and she really did a lot to try to get women to be seen as equal people in her religion."

Expanding on the topic, Lily and Ian explained why the church move had been hard for River at first, as well as how it got better. When they made the move, River was already identifying as nonbinary or gender-fluid. But not all kids at the new church were comfortable or accepting. "And so that meant that the kids were getting it from their parents," Lily said, "because they would go tell their parents and their parents would say, 'Well, that's really weird.'" But when the church hired a new youth pastor, the situation improved. "Pastor Alicia came in and was saying, 'Okay, I'm going to be the youth group person and I'm nonbinary.' I was like, 'Fabulous. Could you explain that that's a real thing? Because my child has been here for a year and people are telling them that they're not a human being or that they're not real in some way.'" In addition, a child of one of the other pastors also began identifying as nonbinary. "So, there's more of that showing up. And we're getting more of an acceptance of it from a lot of people."

The more River and I spoke, the clearer it was that River's identity and imagination did not sit separately from their religious beliefs, from

River's sense of who God is—from the gender-fluid, accepting creator of life. Their religious imagination revealed a deep appreciation for the community they feel through the church and the acceptance they feel from a loving God. When I asked River what makes God happy, they emphasized the importance of kindness, courage, patience, and love, and made a point of including self-love. "You should definitely have pride," they said, but at the same time warned, "not so much pride as to make you a narcissist!" Sin, for River, was a way of not loving, either not loving others or not loving yourself. Clearly, River had given all this a lot of thought long before I came along asking questions.

River's father shared that one of the values he hoped to pass along to River was "trying to encourage them to see God in other people no matter what their sort of social status may or may not be." Ian explained that when he and River see someone asking for help, they try to give a dollar or two or some food if they have it. But he went on, "If possible, you can connect sometimes with folks that you see on a regular basis. When River and I were going to piano lessons there was a guy near that subway stop, his name was John, and we would regularly stop and chat with him. And if I had cash in my pocket, I'd share. And if I didn't, I'd say that. And River was there of course because it was their piano lesson."

Jane asked how explicit they were with River talking about faith. Lily explained, "New York has some interesting examples of when you can explicitly talk about your faith and that is because there's a lot of street preaching on the subway." She went on to tell about a guy who, on a daily basis, goes from car to car yelling about Jesus. "'Repeat after me,'" Lilly said, quoting the man, "'Jesus Christ, I'm going to accept you into my heart.'" Lily continued, "He's really very fervent, but he's also really yelling. And River is not okay with super loud, what they perceive as being angry tones of voice. But they got used to him doing this yelling." But one day the man wasn't paying careful attention and almost ran over River when everyone was getting off the car. "He was getting out to go to the next car and was really yelling and sort of almost ran into them and they just yelled back. 'I don't know why you have to be so angry about it. Jesus Christ is about love. You've got the whole wrong idea here.'" Lily said, "I'm just like, uh, could we move on, please? Because I don't want to have a theological argument with this guy on the subway system." To bring the conversation back around to the question, she added, "So we do actually end up having these kinds of conversations because it's in our faces."

As I reflect now, I can see how the religious imaginations of this family have generated redemptive possibilities in their lives. In Lily's case, her early experience of a deathly fallout with her church could easily have left her out in the religious cold for the rest of her life. Yet she persisted in looking for a church home that could support her faith. At the same time, she still drew upon her early lessons about a Mother-Father God to navigate a theological discussion with her three-year-old, a discussion that has deeper meaning knowing now that her child is "all genders." The religious imagination of Ian helps him encourage River "to see God in other people" no matter the circumstances. Such a message, and the intentions beneath it, have helped River see God not only as accepting and loving of others but as accepting and loving of oneself—a consequence of being made in the image of a gender-fluid God.

* * *

In another borough of the city, Jane and I were invited to "Puppet Church," taking place on Sunday morning in a relatively small Episcopal congregation served by two priests sharing the leadership, Mother Elisabeth and Mother Eve. I had learned through a mutual friend that the church had been working hard to welcome young parents and kids. I'd had a good phone conversation with Mother Elisabeth, and though she was going to be out of town that Sunday, Mother Eve would be there, and we would be in for a treat.

As we walked into the sanctuary, the first thing I noticed was a bright blue puppet stage set up in the chancel near the communion table. In front of the stage was a large piece of cardboard with hand lettering that read "Order of Service," with symbols next to words like: "Song" (musical notes), "Opening Prayer" (praying hands), and "The Peace" (peace symbol). This cardboard order was propped up on the floor below the chancel steps and was surrounded by colorful pillows arranged in a half circle.

We had arrived early to talk with Mother Eve, and she explained that the service, which was called "Let it Shine," was geared to young children and their parents. Most weeks it occurred before the "regular" or more "traditional" service. But the puppet service had become so popular that they decided to try replacing the traditional service with it once a month in the summers. This encouraged a better mixing of the young families—who were often new to the Episcopal Church or church in general—with those who were "cradle Episcopalians" like herself.

The service was part of a larger complex of educational and outreach efforts that the priests had initiated a few years earlier. "This is not only about serving the people who are here," Mother Eve said, "it's about welcoming the people who aren't here, and everything we do has to be outward-looking, and getting our people who wanted to come on board with us to stay." So, they began reimagining the church's ministry less in a "maintenance" mode, she said. "Our job is to figure out how to deepen our spiritual lives and how we are living as Christians in this world."

The other major component of this effort involved creating an after-school religious education program, modeled, as Mother Elisabeth had explained to me in our phone conversation, on Hebrew school. Many Jewish kids who are not in a Jewish private school still take classes to learn Hebrew and other aspects of Judaism. In that spirit, the priests began a once-a-week after-school program with the children of the church so they could learn more about their own tradition. Parents would join them for dinner (which provided a day of not cooking that turned out to be a popular feature).

Puppet Church had originally begun as a storytelling time. Mother Eve said this had worked reasonably well, but during the pandemic they hit upon a new idea. There was a parishioner who was into puppet theater, and he built them a puppet stage. The two priests animated the puppets talking with each other, and during the pandemic they recorded and posted the lessons for families to watch. Eventually, they switched formats a bit. They only used one puppet, Felicity—"a kind of

Sesame Street Muppet," as one parent described her. The other priest became something of a straight person to Felicity. Think Mister Rogers in the Land of Make-Believe talking to King Friday.

As Jane and I were talking with Mother Eve, people began to gather. Toddlers walked straight to the pillows up front, followed by their parents. Some older children walked up too. All were either sitting or wandering around the pillows on the floor waiting for the service to begin. Soon, songs were sung, prayers said, peace passed, and with each ritual act came a tiny bit of explanation to help the children participate. The brilliance and bonus of this approach is that it helps people who are new to the tradition participate too. Eventually there came a lesson from the beloved Felicity, followed by communion presided over by Mother Eve, then more short prayers, a benediction, and a final song. Each week a church member chooses a "fun song," as a transition into the larger world, and this week it was "YMCA" by the Village People, complete with hand motions. The fluid moves between the Eucharist and a '70s pop song with toddlers learning to make letters with their arms was as startling to my brain as a shape-shifting Cinderella.

* * *

Jane and I were invited to the picnic that followed the service. Only ten o'clock in the morning, but it was time for hot dogs and games. In the midst of it all, we were able to work in conversations with kids and parents alike about the church.

I sat down with Emma and Chloe, sisters who were twelve and nine, respectively. While they ate, I asked what they liked about the church. Emma responded immediately: "I like the community." Chloe added, "I like how everybody in this church is so nice." Emma then named Sunday school as something else she really liked. Chloe agreed but went on to name and describe the after-school program as well. The program started around three in the afternoon, when school let out, and lasted until six thirty or so. Parents and other siblings would come at five thirty, and they'd share a community meal. Originally it had been for elementary schoolers only, but it had gone so well the past year that they decided to expand to middle schoolers as well.

Emma, in middle school, was looking forward to participating in the fall, "because," she said, "I really liked last year how many friends my sister made and I liked what they did, it was really cool. . . . And I really liked all the community."

I asked Chloe whether she could add any more about the program. She described how in the past year they had made a *Book of Moses*. "We listened to stories about Moses and then after we heard the stories, some people wrote a chapter, and some people did some art to represent what was happening." That is, they would retell or depict the story in their own way, but, as Chloe added, "We added some jokes." When I asked if she remembered what she wrote, she said that not only could she remember, but they all had gotten their own copies of the book—something she was very proud of and grateful for. Later, Mother Eve showed me a copy, and she reiterated how engaged the kids had been with the project, how much they had learned, and how meaningful it was to receive their own copy.

Here was another example of the impulse to model making among children (see chapter 4). Taking the raw materials of the world, in this case religious materials, and making something, playing with them, sharing. For years I taught the preschool Sunday school class at our church. After a lesson we would always make something related, employing the tools of preschool—crayons and construction paper, glue and modeling clay. When parents came to pick up their kids, inevitably, I'd hear, "Look what I made!" The sheer joy of creating. "And God saw that it was good." Perhaps this is another dimension of what it means to be made in the image of God—we are reflections of the God who makes and delights in creation.

* * *

"What do you like about church?" I asked Ash, two and a half years old.

"Felicity!" Ash said with a big smile.

Ash is the son of Les and Jessica, who, along with Ash, were relatively new to the church. "We love it," Les said. "The repeat-after-me prayers, the singing, the songs that they've chosen, everything is just melodic and easy to follow. The way they've written out on the board the steps. It's brilliant. It's like the menu of the service." Les added, "But I also have ADHD and I can't remember the steps of anything. So, for me it's helpful. And Ash loves it. He loves church. He talks about it every week."

Les had actually been the straight man, or conversation partner, to Felicity that morning, and I thanked him for his role in the service. "It's so fun," he said. "I had told the Mothers months ago how obsessed with Felicity my child is. Felicity is a household name in our home. We talk about her regularly. So, I was just saying how excited Ash is about Felicity and then the Mothers were like, 'Oh, well, we have this service in the summer. Do you want to be Felicity's sidekick?' And I said, 'For sure.' So yeah, we have a two-and-a-half-year-old and we only started attending in January of this year. . . . It's only been six months."

Les and Jessica had learned about the church through parents from Ash's preschool. "And we started coming and it's been such a—and I don't use this word lightly, I've never used this word—but it's been a total blessing. It's been so fun. Let it Shine is extraordinary." He shared that he grew up going to church back in Michigan but hadn't attended regularly since he was eighteen. "Let it Shine is not just for toddlers, it is structured for families with young kids—it's really so thoughtful. And I'm crying just thinking about it. I'm deeply moved at how available it makes the experience of—" He paused. "If you want it to be worship, if you want it to be community, if you want it to be something else, it can be all of those things."

In addition to the Let it Shine service, Les went on to express his gratitude for the Wednesday night meals. Ash was too young to take part in the after-school program, but they loved coming to the meals afterward. They'd made good friends there and, though they don't have the meals in the summer, families had started getting together for shared meals in their homes. The fact that food, in the eyes of Les, could be such a binding source of community and friendship seemed to be no accident given that he runs a nonprofit that provides some four million meals a year to people around the city.

Ash's mother, Jessica, had her own appreciations for the church, especially the sense of welcome they felt as a family and connection to others. "I grew up with parents who are atheists and extended family who are extremely conservative. Extremely. So, not a great relationship to Christianity." But, she explained, around the time they were trying to get pregnant (which was full of struggles), Les had expressed to Jessica that he was feeling the desire to reconnect with his spirituality. When the friend from preschool mentioned the church and its service for kids, she said, "My ears perked up because Les grew up Episcopalian. So, I was like, 'Oh, maybe that'll be nice for Les to have a sense of familiarity. And we know it'll be fun too.' Also, it was building relationship with people at day care."

As I listened to Jessica, I was touched and impressed that, despite her history with Christianity, she was sensitive to the spiritual stirrings happening in her husband. "It was like, 'Okay, yeah, let's go check this out.' I think for me it was like, 'let me try and facilitate this connection at best.' But it has been really, really nice."

As for her own stirrings, Jessica added, "I'm also in a process of reflecting on why I might be drawn to having spiritual practices. I'm very, very slowly converting to Judaism. And the Mothers have been really nice about that. I mean everybody is." She went on to explain how, during Lent, people were invited to explore a spiritual practice. To help with the process, folks were paired up to check in with one another. The Mothers paired her up with Gale. "And part of that was her husband is Jewish and they wanted me to be able to talk with someone else who was here and an active member of the church, and an interfaith family."

I responded, "So rather than resisting or trying to nudge you another way, they actually just said, 'Here you go.'"

"Yeah," Jessica said. "They have not tried to nudge me another way at all."

* * *

This spirit of welcome by the church and its members and Mothers was also apparent in my next conversations, with Maria and Leonard, who had moved to the neighborhood two years earlier when their son, Paul, was only six months old. "So, I am Catholic," Maria told me right off the bat. They had moved from the West Coast and found the local Catholic parish church. But it was while the pandemic was raging. "They just made masks optional. And they were encouraging congregational singing. And we had a six-month-old, and we were not feeling comfortable bringing him there before there was a vaccine for him, or anybody else." In addition, Maria was pregnant with a second child. But, as Maria explained, "I had a former coworker who told me about—who was friends with—Mother Elizabeth, no, Mother Eve, from college maybe. She was like, 'Oh, there's a church in your new neighborhood you should check out.'" They did. "It was local," Maria said. "It was catering to young kids. It was following very strict masking guidelines at the time. And it was perfect."

I followed up. "What else have you appreciated about this church?"

"There's a lot. I mean, the Mothers are wonderful, very kind, very active in the community. And my husband is not affiliated with any form of Christianity." Her husband, Leonard, was a thoroughgoing atheist, yet he had been behind the grill all morning cooking hot dogs and hamburgers for this God-loving, praying, puppet-showing congregation. "He really likes the community," Maria said. "They have hot dogs in the morning! But it's great. That's the kind of people that come here, right? They like to spend time together."

"Okay, let's get a huge round of applause for Leonard and Maria." It was the emcee for the picnic, who had been calling out Bingo, giving small prizes, and was now wrapping up the picnic. I paused our conversation as the congregation applauded. "Thanks for all the burgers and the hot dogs. Thanks everybody for bringing stuff—all the salads and sweets."

"Thank you for talking with me," I said to Maria. They were headed to a birthday party for a friend of their two-year-old, Paul. Paul and I spoke briefly. I asked what he liked about church, and we talked about Felicity and friends and birthday parties.

* * *

When everyone had cleared out, Jane and I sat with Mother Eve in the basement of the church. We never turned the lights on, but there was enough sun coming in through the windows to illumine the room and one another. That struck me as fitting somehow.

Mother Eve filled in the recent history of the church and its decision to work harder at welcoming children and parents and neighborhood folk in general. For people new to the tradition, she explained, "It's really hard to cross that threshold. It's really hard to come in the doors. Newcomers think, 'What does it mean to do that?'" The Let it Shine service helps, she explained, especially for new parents, and it engages the children.

But as she spoke, Mother Eve focused more upon the service itself—not as part of a welcoming strategy but as worship. "It gives me goosebumps," she said. "Because here's the thing, Felicity is great, but when I tell you—especially when we're doing communion down on the table on the floor—it's crazy. It's crazy! I just don't even know how to describe it to you. It's a moment; these kids are so enrapt. And we do the fraction [breaking of bread] and there are audible sighs. I'm just like, 'This is amazing because it means something so—'" She broke off at a loss for words.

Finally, she offered, "It was so real. It was really real. It wasn't just some ritual; it was really real."

As I listened to Mother Eve reflect upon the motivations and experiences of being this really real neighborhood church, reflect upon the commitment to Jesus, reflect upon the sighs, I had goosebumps myself. At the heart of the faith at work in the Mothers, at work in the church, I sensed a powerful freedom, one born of deep security. Rather than join the panic over losing members, a "declining" church, or loss of Christianity's influence on the larger culture, they were willing to try something new, to experiment, to rest in the knowledge of God's love. On the surface, it may seem paradoxical that such a radical commitment to Jesus would lead the church to be welcoming of those practicing other traditions—Maria, who's Catholic, and her atheist husband; Jessica, who's converting to Judaism—but it feels more like an extension of their trust in God.

Speaking of Maria, Mother Eve said, "She's a devout Catholic. She really is. . . . She's not a former Catholic. She's a Catholic who comes here. And those kids eventually will end up going to catechism and whatever in the Catholic Church, and that's okay. We don't get attached to that [being exclusively Episcopalian]. And I think that's what allows us to not be fearful of losing people. You know what? This is not for everyone. The messiness of today. I think we do good liturgy, but there's a messiness, and that's not for everyone." She summarized the point, saying, "There's something really valuable about a neighborhood church, and maybe we allow the mystery to do its work."

I thought about John Lennon's song "Imagine."[1] I only recently learned that the song was inspired in part by a Christian prayer book that was given to John and Yoko by the comedian and civil rights activist Dick Gregory about the positive power of prayer. Even so, the song is potentially upsetting to religious sensibilities in that one of the lyrics is "Imagine no religion." But in an interview, Lennon explained that "Imagine" is saying that "If you can *imagine* a world at peace, with no denominations of religion—not without religion but without this my-God-is-bigger-than-your-God thing—then it can be true."

* * *

As Jane and I left the church, I noticed the rainbow flag in front of the building that read, "Welcome. We're your neighbors." I thought about the conversation with Les, the one who had helped with the puppet show earlier. "The way this church is just affirming and welcoming," he said, "is beyond anything that I knew as a kid. You can see their rainbow flag out there and the way there are families of all types. I'm trans, we're queer. We've got our kid born from IVF, we're having another, but we as a family, we're welcomed and showing up."

Les summarized his sense of the church in a way that, for its power, I cannot get out of my mind. Les said, "I feel like this church is a giant hug when the world is really hard."

* * *

"My grandparents were farmers," Benjamin said, "and regarding church, they would work outside all week and then go and sit in a building to talk and think and address things. I sit inside all week and then to go to another building [church] and sit inside to think more, it was just like, 'this is not useful.'"

We were talking to young parents, Benjamin and Linette. It was a gentle summer morning outside a city in the US Southeast, so we sat in their front yard while their sons Leo (two and a half) and Mateo (one) played. Both Benjamin and Linette grew up in church, but for Benjamin the family's participation was nominal, and he pretty much gave up on it, he said, at around thirteen. For Linette, church had always been important and remained so into adulthood. As their relationship developed, Benjamin joined her as they searched for a place that could be meaningful to both of them. It took time but after some false starts, they finally found one that welcomed them to a form of church that was new to them, one in which they both felt at home. It was Garden Church.[2]

The idea for the church came from a dream. The founding pastor saw in a literal dream a group of people worshiping on a plot of farmland. With the help of friends and support from his denomination, Garden Church was born. The denomination had some start-up funds for congregations experimenting with different ways of being church. The vision was to combine a worshiping community with the issue of food insecurity. The church is a community garden, a plot in the middle of a city about the size of an average residential lot. People can pick freely, but usually the produce is harvested by the congregation and donated to local food banks.

Linette explained what Sunday mornings typically look like—a mixture of prayers, reflection, and tending the garden. "The way they frame it—very intentionally—is that the gardening is worship. It's not gardening and then church. The whole thing is church. So, they usually start with a little reflection, or something really brief, before people go and garden." After an hour or so, they would have a time of prayer or a short sermon. "We've had different leaders, and the format of that part has changed; sometimes it's been a little more traditional and sometimes a little less so, but it never looks like a mainline service."

Benjamin said, "Garden Church was the first place that was like,

'We're going to talk for fifteen minutes about religion and faith, do our sermon, and we're going to work for an hour, hour and a half, and we're going to produce something for people who need it.' And then, I was like, 'Great, that's good for me.'"

Linette added, "For us, it was fun. We both enjoyed being outside and having the more tangible aspect of being in church. I really liked it, and it was important to me to find a space that we were both comfortable in."

I asked Leo, their two-year-old, what he liked about the church.

"They have beans there," he said.

"Recently, we've had green bean harvests," Benjamin explained. "The green beans have been coming in. So, we teach these guys [Leo and Mateo] how to walk through the rows to find beans that are good or beans that are not good and skip those. And you can pick them and eat them straight from the vine, and so they'll sit and eat forty peas, which is also great."

Linette spoke about the simple lessons the kids are learning about food and gardening. After picking some tomatoes, "Leo asked, 'Oh, are we gonna take them home?' And we're like, 'No, this is for people who need food.' So, that community sense."

Benjamin mentioned how much the kids enjoy playing on the huge dirt pile in the garden. "So, Leo goes climbing to the top of the dirt pile and shovels—"

"There's nothing better," I interrupted smiling at Leo.

"And the sand," Leo said, "we dig in it."

"Yeah," Benjamin continued, "and it's funny because whenever we invite people or tell people about Garden Church, we're like, 'Don't go in your Sunday bests cause you're gonna get filthy.' By the end, Leo has arms, neck, legs—deep in dirt, just absolute mess. And this guy [Mateo] too."

Jane commented, "That's a wonderful image."

Linette added, "Our church clothes are our dirty clothes."

"This is a very different vibe," Benjamin said. "But as the food starts to come in, I really like it because we teach them what food looks like and where food comes from."

* * *

The idea of a community garden associated with church was not new to us. In fact, the church Jane served for nearly two decades has such a garden. In the summers, there are camps for kids that address everything from growing and cooking to nutrition education and food insecurity. In all, the camps help connect young people to the source of food, as well as the dirt of the earth itself.

We were also aware that my alma mater, Princeton Theological Seminary, has more recently established a Farminary, a farm operated by the school offering classes, degrees, and a concentration for its master's students. With courses such as "Communion with Creation in an Era of Eco-Crisis" and "Soil and Sabbath," students learn and work at the farm, presumably in their "dirty clothes." The vision, according to the website, is to "bring together the life of the mind and the practices of faith in anticipation of new life. As students study and tend the soil alongside one another, they experience a deep dimension of Christian community and learn to love God, creation, and one another in new ways."[3]

We learned from Linette that there is a whole confederation of ecological/agricultural/farming-related churches. It's called the Wild Church Network, a loose affiliation of congregations that desire to connect spirituality to the earth.[4] According to their website, it began first with individual pastors and leaders leaving buildings "to connect with the natural world to restore sacred relationship." But as these disparate communities began to discover each other, they "blossomed into an organic, spirit-led and collaborative movement." Some are connected to larger denominations while others are not. But despite diverse theologies, they "share a united sense of calling, purpose and rootedness in the earth as sacred and alive." The network sets up gatherings and provides resources for worship and learning in outdoor spaces. But it is more than just meeting outside; it is about connection. "The old paradigm of 'nature as other' is shifting. Wild Churches . . . gather to recognize and learn to participate in the kindred interconnection of all beings, elements, and places. It is a relationship, rooted in love, that the ancients described as Logos."

Between Garden Church, the Farminary, and the Wild Church Network, it is clear that for some, there is a hunger to expand the ways in which church can be as well as a thirst for forms of spirituality that press not only for connection with others but for connection with the larger environment.

* * *

This chapter has shared how some individuals and faith communities have found ways to stretch understandings of the sacred: from a gender-fluid God who affirms the identity of an eleven-year-old to Puppet Church and a "YMCA" postlude and morning barbeque; from flexible understandings of religious affiliation to the prayerful picking of green beans in dirty clothes and calling it worship.

Even so, most of the interviews in this book have revealed how powerful a variety of ways of being church have been to its participants, whether predictable and inside or wild and outside. But if there is a common denominator between the great variety of churches, personalities, theologies, and spiritual practices, it is the desire to connect. If there is an overriding theme for the motivations of parents to raise children in faith, it is to connect through love. Parents want their kids to know the love of God. They want their children—buoyed by this love—to share that love with others, if not with creation.

9

Countercultural Rhythms

"THIS CAN'T BE RIGHT," I said to Jane as we found ourselves at a dead end. We were outside a small city on the East Coast. It was mostly farm country. I stopped and studied our location in the GPS app. "It shows a dotted line from here to the church. I guess we're supposed to walk from here?" But there was nowhere to walk. We weren't even on the right road. We doubled back, found a main road—one of those that changes names midway—and drove up and down it for twenty minutes until we realized the church was in a small strip of three adjoining one-story, nondescript buildings—a Jewish community center, a preschool, and the church we were looking for.

The church is affiliated with the American Baptist denomination, but you have to dig deep into their website to know that. Inside, Pastor Soo greeted us warmly. She was born in Korea, and her family had come to the United States in the late 1970s when she was a child. They were practicing Buddhists at the time, but they would gather at a local Korean church for dinners and friendship with other Koreans (at a time when there were very few in the area). Eventually a neighbor started bringing young Soo with her to church on Sunday mornings, for "children's church." She loved it, and she's had a passion for cultivating a welcoming atmosphere for children ever since. As an extension of this spirit of hospitality, she and the church leadership work hard at creating a multiethnic and multicultural community of faith. As their mission statement says, "We embrace the diversity and differences in our heritage and culture, and celebrate our unity in Jesus Christ." In addition to Pastor Soo, one of the associates is also Korean American while others of the ministry team are African American, Southeast Asian American, and Nigerian American pastors. Church members come from various backgrounds as well, many as first- or second-generation immigrants to the United States. The church has also expanded to a location in a nearby city and is creating after-school programs as well as establishing missions in other countries, particularly in East Africa.

As Jane and I were talking with Pastor Soo, a young father, Peter, and his eight-year-old daughter, Jieun, entered the building. Jieun had just been through some kind of conflict at soccer practice—the details were unclear, but apparently she was made fun of or ridiculed in some way. So, she was a little more shy about meeting new people and talking than she likely otherwise would have been. But her father, very sweetly, gave her a hug and said, "I love you. God loves you." Pastor Soo also comforted her for a few moments before introducing us.

When she seemed ready, I assured Jieun that she didn't have to talk if she didn't want to, or she could stop at any point, or that she could draw pictures if she preferred. She nodded and we ended up having a delightful conversation. She loved "children's church" and Ms. Hana, the director. They meet at the same time as adult worship and go for about an hour and a half. They worship, have lessons, and do crafts. When there's communion, the kids join the adults. Jieun told me how God is "kind, thoughtful, and compassionate," and loves people, as well as animals and nature, "that make God happy." She told me how she prays not only with others at church but at home, usually at night before bed with her mother. They share gratitudes. When I asked whether she thought God hears her prayers, she assured me that "God knows what you are going to think and say, before you even say it, or think it." Jieun also mentioned how kind everyone is at church, "at least everyone I know," she said. I invited her to draw a picture of her church. She was excited and drew a beautiful purple building with a cross on top (that didn't look anything like the actual building) with her family entering. She labeled the people "Papoo, Mamoo, Booboo, and Noboo" (Father, Mother, herself, and her new baby sister).

Whatever challenge had tottered Jieun earlier, it was not hard to see how her church, her God, her pastor, and her family provided the comfort and support to steady her again.

"So, how'd you find this church," Jane asked Peter, Jieun's father. "And what drew you here?" She told him how we'd had a hard time finding it.

"My wife and I," Peter explained, "we were coming back from a wedding, and we ended up driving past this road over here just randomly. This is the middle of nowhere. But there was a sign that says there's church on Sundays. I'm like, 'Well, let's try this out.'" At the time, they were feeling restless about the church they had been attending. They found it too stiff and not particularly welcoming to newcomers. "So, we went here and went to a bunch of other places," Peter explained. "The other places didn't speak to us, but when we came here, it spoke to us. So here we are."

Jane commented, "Isn't that amazing? Just that simple thing, welcoming, that churches can do. I would think as a parent, that's probably appealing too. You want your child to be somewhere that they're welcome. I don't know that much about this church, but it seems like they have a real emphasis on children and youth. What's that look like here?"

Peter agreed. "The children's church is run by Hana. She's really cool—awesome. And then all children are welcome. There's a lot of activities for the kids, and they're always trying to spin up clubs and everything to get the kids interested."

After describing children's church, Peter, unprompted, began talking about how, in his experience, parents of his generation don't want to take the time to be involved in church. "It's at least an hour, two hours or so, and people don't want to spend that time. It's not about the church per se, but it's about the general mentality." He said the mentality had become worse after the pandemic, that people had gotten accustomed to staying home.

"Interesting," Jane said. "So, do you feel a little countercultural coming to church in this day and age?"

"Yes," Peter responded immediately. "Yes, I do. We try bringing friends here, and this [church] is better than what they expect, but it's still a time commitment. But I personally feel it's worth it. It's hard to convince people. . . . So, I don't know. It's hard raising a kid in church nowadays, to be honest." Peter went on to say how "worldly focused" so many in the larger community are. "They have this path that they want to get to and that's what they deem as success. That's what they deem as happiness. Career. 'I got to work hard at this, or my kid has to get into this school' or something like that. So, do all these activities on the weekend in order to boost whatever their résumé is."

"Do you mean like their college applications?" Jane asked.

"Exactly. The kids are so young. I'm like, what are you doing? Jieun has a really good friend whose mom—we've been trying to get her to come to church and she comes sometimes—but she's putting her daughter in competitive skating because she wants her to win competitions and do all this other stuff. I'm thinking, 'Most likely your kid is not going to be an Olympian. Don't push the kid like that.' But it's that kind of mentality. It's hard to change because that's what everyone sees on TV now, what they read, all the social media stuff with influencers, everyone. You don't see a Christian influencer."

Jane commented, "You have to come here for it."

Peter agreed, then went on to talk about his daughter, continuing the countercultural theme. "She will go against the grain of all her friends. The world teaches you to be one way, and then we try to teach her to be the other way. And they conflict all the time." He gave a simple example of kids being mean to others rather than kind. He seemed to have the day's soccer practice in mind.

"So, how does this church help you as a parent?"

"Well, it's like-minded people. And then people reinforce the message. And then it's the community. Everyone chats with you, and if you have any issues or concerns, you can talk to other people about it. They've most likely gone through it before, so you can actually speak to them."

Jane eventually asked Peter what beliefs he hoped to pass on to Jieun. He said, "It doesn't matter what the world thinks. As long as God loves you and you know God loves you, and obviously your parents love you. It doesn't matter what other people think."

"Which is the message you were telling her today," Jane said.

"Yeah, exactly. It's hard for kids."

* * *

Peter was not the first parent to talk with us about the challenges of raising a child in a world that often conflicts with their beliefs and values rooted in faith. Beyond the parents we interviewed, Christian Smith and his research team, mentioned previously, found a similar theme among the 215 parents they interviewed for the book *Religious Parenting*. Across the board, from Protestant Christian households to Buddhist, Hindu, Catholic, and Jewish ones, a major concern for raising children was "the culture." When asked what their biggest challenges are as parents, for "nearly all religious parents a powerful force made up of 'the culture,' 'messages,' 'technology,' and 'the media' exists 'out there' and makes their jobs very difficult." As one mother put it: "The biggest challenge is being heard over the din of the crazy culture." Or another, "I often think our culture as a whole is like the end of the Roman empire: decadence and waste and the center is gone, there's no value center." Or as one father put it, "There's not a lot out there to give you support. Especially when we have video games, the internet, garbage on TV, the media I don't think gives a lot of support."[1]

Like Peter, these parents feel like they are competing with a larger culture that devalues life and faith and community well-being. Yet, sadly, sometimes churches themselves fall prey to the temptations of "decadence and waste." Sometimes, "the culture" that has to be resisted is within the church itself. Sara, a mother from the same church Peter and Jieun attend, spoke of some previous occurrences in the churches she had belonged to. "I can't say that the entirety of my church experiences were healthy. I think that created a lot of questions or a lot of distrust. I've seen church leadership steal money. I've seen them sleep with people's wives. I've seen them do all kinds of things. And this is not even on TV. These are people that I know. It was definitely a breach of trust."

Sara is a first-generation North American, born in Canada to a Kenyan father and Rwandan mother who had come to Canada before Sara was born. Her parents were raised Anglican and Catholic and brought Sara and her brother up in a Pentecostal church where there were other immigrants. "So, we all kept the church, throughout my upbringing and my brother's upbringing, we've always been Christian." The early formation had been strong and positive. Her faith ran deep and made her determined to find a community worthy of her trust—which she found under Pastor Soo's leadership at this church.

When asked why it was important to her to find a church home for her six-year-old son, Thad, she said, "it was really important for me to have him *not* have that [negative] experience." She wanted her son to be in a community that loves Jesus, she said. "And I can tell that people in this church actually love Jesus. It's not like they're only acting to be good people. That's just who they are."

* * *

"So," Michael said, "I think that love is central to Christianity, and I want to love my children in a way that is a Christian way to love people."

Michael is a biblical scholar and professor, as well as a father of two young children, Jaylen (three years old) and Micah (almost one). In addition, he and his wife, Jasmine, have been helping to care for their eight-year-old nephew, Carter, since he was a baby. They now live in separate states, but Carter still comes to stay with them in the summer.

Jasmine and Michael are active in a Baptist church, majority African American, in a city in the mid-South, and they are involved in its ministries—Jasmine with the church's day-care ministry and Michael with Christian education. Michael, at the time of the interview, was undergoing teacher training to be part of the church's educational ministry (remarkable, given that, by all accounts, Michael is a gifted teacher already). "Eventually I will teach something that introduces [Sunday school] teachers to the Bible," Michael said. "That's what the head of Christian education wants me to do. And the pastor wants me to teach a class that's on critical race theory, so I'm going to do both of those."

While their one-year-old is usually in the nursery during worship, Michael explained that he often ends up walking the halls with Jaylen, their three-year-old, during the service. "Since I can't force him to pay attention, I want him to have the experience of adventure and exploration of the church. And so, if he's quiet, he can crawl around the pew. If he's not quiet, then we'll have to leave the pew and go around the church." In other words, they seem to have found a gracious middle ground between "sit still and be quiet" and "anything goes." Michael said, "I walk the halls with Jaylen during the service because I don't want him to get the idea that going places, especially church, is a time to plug out and watch a screen. And so we're inside going through the halls, and he's saying 'hi' to people and meeting people." Michael said that in addition to greeting people, he'll check out the physical building—play with the water fountain, then run down the hall, and so forth. "So, he feels comfortable with people and the building of the church because that's what we do." Michael emphasized, "He's engaged with what's around him and not in a different world of a screen."

On the topic of love and its centrality, Michael asked if I had ever read Eric Fromm's *The Art of Loving*.[2] (I had not but did after the interview.) Fromm was a psychoanalyst who practiced and wrote in the mid-twentieth century. Jewish, he fled Germany during the Nazi regime and taught for several years at Columbia University in New York City, influencing a generation of psychologists. Fromm begins the book by making the case that love is an art rather than simply a "pleasant sensation." Michael had stumbled across the book in a giveaway pile at his school. "I read that book," Michael said, "and his definition of love as an action is something that I have wholeheartedly taken on. I believe that that is a responsible and beautiful way to love."

As Michael explained, there are four aspects to love as an art: care, responsibility, respect, and knowledge. All these working together, according to Fromm, are critical to the ability to love others, love self, and love God. "So, you care about what happens to the other person, which I think plenty of us do. The next one is what Fromm calls responsibility, not as in an obligation, but the ability to respond to somebody's needs. Love as an action, not just an emotion." Respect means that you "respect the difference enough to treat the other person as independent enough that you're not attaching your goals in your love for them." Finally, as Fromm points out, respect is impossible without knowing. Michael summarized, "If you don't actually know the person, you can't do those other things well. You can't respond to them well if you don't know them well. You can't respect their difference if you don't understand what's different." Michael said, "Having this four-part concept of love helps me to have something more solid that I can point to and teach from and keep in mind as I'm parenting." In summary, "these are things that make those different types of love a real art form, real practice."

We discussed what love, in this complex sense, might mean in the everyday lives of parents and children, and soon our conversation turned toward the concrete realities of raising African American children in this culture—a challenge of self-knowledge, self-respect, and ultimately self-love. Speaking of his nephew Carter, Michael said, "I believe that it's important to recognize and name racial difference and celebrate being Black. That was an important part of my growing up. I wanted to do the same thing for him." He mentioned that "research shows that children from an extremely young age start to recognize the cues from the world, not just about seeing racial difference, but about its significance." He went on, "And so I helped Carter to recognize that we're Black and at an early age."

According to Michael, by the time his nephew was four or five, he indeed had a clear sense of being Black—Carter would say, "I am

Black." Still, something was off. "There were signs that the media he was consuming had completely eroded the value of Blackness." As an example, "He made an avatar of himself on a phone app, and in the avatar, he made all his features that could be racial, racially White. So, his eyes were some light color, his hair was blonde, his skin was white, and this was supposed to be himself. . . . Then another thing was, I told him that he looked like Miles Morales, the Spider-Man person. And his answer was, 'But he's Black.'"

* * *

Michael's description of Carter reminded me of something told by the renowned child psychiatrist Robert Coles, whose *Children of Crisis* series won the Pulitzer Prize for nonfiction in 1973. Much of his work occurred not in a therapist's office but in the field, so to speak—homes, streets, hospitals, schools, migrant camps—wherever children were facing challenging situations, from poverty and severe illness to racism and homelessness. Coles was working with Ruby Bridges and her family in 1960. Ruby was six years old when she was among the first Black students to integrate the New Orleans school district, doing so with an escort of federal marshals through angry segregationist mobs (famously depicted by a Norman Rockwell painting that hung outside the Obama Oval Office). Coles often invited children to draw pictures of themselves or their challenging situations. It was a practice he picked up early in his career working with children at the suggestion of two of his guides, Anna Freud (psychoanalyst and daughter of Sigmund) and William Carlos Williams (doctor and poet). Both had used crayons and paints when working with children to bypass the overreliance upon words—which can be intimidating to children, especially those under the weight of massive emotional upheaval.

Coles began inviting children to draw or paint in the late 1950s when he was working with children with polio (just before the Salk vaccine became widely available).[3] Coles went to Dr. Williams for advice concerning a particularly taciturn girl. "I talked with Dr. Williams on the phone, heard his strongly worded suggestion that I 'sit still' with the child and 'maybe, do some drawing with her.'" As Coles reports, he and Williams together had once watched children drawing. "Look at them looking," Williams told Coles, "their eyes meeting the world. . . . A youngster drawing is a youngster thinking, a youngster telling you a hell of a lot." This proved to be very helpful advice, and Coles began making connections with the girl, and other children, in ways words and attempts at more typical therapeutic conversations had not. Reflecting back, Coles writes, "Sometimes, as Dr. Williams had taught me, children paralyzed by fear as well as the polio virus (their lower limbs for example, useless) were quite willing to draw pictures, and thereby communicate what they were feeling and thinking, whereas they steadfastly avoided sustained back-and-forth talking."

Noteworthy is the fact that when Coles invited children to create such art, he joined them—he drew and painted and colored alongside them. Though he was sitting quietly, he was not sitting still. Instead, he was creating, through a form of play, a kind of space and time that relaxed the everyday rules of adult-child conversation, let alone psychiatry.

When Coles invited Ruby Bridges to draw, she often drew herself at school, or her classmates, or the angry mob she had to walk through. In one drawing, as Coles reports, she compared herself to a white girl in her class. "Ruby's feet are not so well constructed, many of her fingers are missing, her arms are more frail, her ears are missing ('I try not to listen to all the bad things those people say,' she once told me, referring to the mob), her hair is less prominent, her mouth is also missing. The sun shines over the white girl, even as a decisive brown line interrupts the grass, which grows differently on either side of that line: a child's vigorous, detailed assertion of *difference*, of apartness as it gives shape to self-concept, to notions about the world beyond one's own world."

* * *

While Carter was not daily facing angry segregationist mobs, Michael was nonetheless alarmed by what he heard from his nephew—and he took it as a sign of a more subtle, yet ubiquitous, form of racism undermining Carter's identity. "To me," Michael said, "that was a big signal that what he's been taking in, in terms of watching TV shows and video games, where, if there is Black representation, it's peripheral to the main character—where we invest all our emotions. That's teaching him what image he wants to have of himself and should. So, I wanted to push back on that." The form of this pushback was, at first, with toys from Michael's own childhood, action figures that he had held onto. Of some two hundred of them, he said, only ten or so were Black. But when they played with them together, Michael said, "I would always pick the Black figures, and he wouldn't ever." This, along with the earlier signs, worried Michael. At about the same time, his first son, Jaylen, was born, which intensified the issue as he imagined the world of toys and play his son would encounter. "I was like, 'I need to do some things to change this.'"

One of the things Michael did was to start collecting and making his own Black action figures—using pieces from his own toys combined with Lego parts and whatever else he could find on the market. He created groups of them according to themes—cowboys and pirates, for example—and gave individual characters back stories and personalities. He included some from other underrepresented groups, such as members of the Apsáalooke (Crow) Nation or Mexican warriors resisting White colonization.

Not only did he start sharing these with the children in his own and extended family, Michael created a blog describing the action figures and why it's so important to have robust representation for kids' play. The site is called Black Toys Matter (blacktoysmatter.org) and at the time of this writing depicts and describes over a hundred characters. As the website summarizes, "I want to be intentional about crafting the narratives that my loved ones learn as they play with toys and create new worlds in their imaginations and their real lives."

In addition, as important as sheer numbers and options are, Michael's motivations for the collection and site were multilayered. "I started to realize, as I was working on this, that it's not just representation that's important to me. Because when Carter picked these toys, his first two questions were always, 'What are their powers?' and, 'Is it a good guy or a bad guy?' And being that Jasmine's a defense attorney, I don't think of the world in terms of good guys and bad guys."

Michael wanted to bring complexity and nuance to the moral life of his children, and in a manner Robert Coles might affirm, he found an avenue to do so through play. "So, I would say [to Carter], 'Wait, have you ever done the wrong thing? It's not good guys and bad guys. Sometimes people do bad things.'" With that, according to Michael, Carter started asking, "Is this a good guy or someone who does bad things?" Michael said, "I started to try to encapsulate in the best way I can communicate this with a five-year-old or four-year-old, why in the Black Panther movie, for example, Black Panther fights with Killmonger [both portrayed by Black actors]—just getting across what is motivating someone and what motivates someone else for their ideologies to clash." As one of Michael's blog posts on the website puts it: "I want my little ones to play with toys in a way that allows them to see that conflicts arise because of clashing worldviews, not because the world is split between good and evil people."

This led to an energetic conversation between us about creativity and imagination in relation to consumption, one echoing his desire for Jaylen to connect with people at church and not escape via a screen. "So, for me," Michael told me, "I want so badly, in terms of just their engagement with the world, for Carter, Jaylen, and Micah to be creators—as opposed to just consumers. And I think that the major push for everything outside of school, and maybe in school too—I don't know—is to just consume."

I asked Michael what was at stake for him in this resistance to consumerism. In addition to the erosion of Black identity that Michael witnessed with his nephew through consuming popular media, Michael discussed the ways a consumer mind-set erodes agency generally and makes us passive to the power of others.

I shared with Michael how I used to make up stories with my kids. We would do it together, one on one, back and forth, first when our son, David, was five or so, then later with Cora.

"Once upon a time there was a boy named?"

"Ganshee," David said the first time we played this story game, making up a name.

"And Ganshee lives?"

"Way back in a cabin in the woods," he filled in.

"Well, one night–?"

"Ganshee was afraid," David said, surprising me.

"Why was he afraid?"

"Because the next day was the first day of school."

Of course, it was the night before David's first day in a new school. This led to a whole story about Ganshee not knowing what his new school or teacher would be like. As it turns out, when Ganshee got to school, he discovered that the teacher and the other kids "were good" (he said), and the first day of school went well for Ganshee, despite being nervous.

The story was not only creating a connection between us, but it was also providing insight into David's emotional life. It was also a creative act–imagining a protagonist (Ganshee) in a particular setting (first day of school) with a plot (finding a way through the obstacles of fear and the unknown). While this particular story was about something existentially immediate for him, most of the tales we made up were about wild and fun adventures–usually with some surprise that would make us smile or laugh.

Turns out Michael did something similar. He and Jasmine and his nephew, Carter, would make up stories together when they were, say, driving in a car. They would go around, popcorn style, generating lines and eventually creating a story. Other times, Michael and Carter would each make up stories and share them. Michael said, "Carter had some very fun storytelling." For example, "When Carter was three, we were telling scary stories, and we did it in the dark. And then a year later we did some illustrations together where I drew some pictures, and he colored them in. And we made that into a little video of the stories." Michael found it on his phone and shared it with me.

Carter starts, "Once upon a time, there was a little girl named–"

There was a long silence. Michael assured me, smiling, "This is not a glitch. This is suspense! It's a lot of suspense!"

The dramatic three-year-old finished the sentence. "—Nothing. Her name was Nothing. A little girl, a little kid who went to a weird well. There was a powerful witch . . ." There was also a giant and a green goblin "that ate everything except the people—he was allergic to them." The story went on in Carter's voice and was accompanied by delightful illustrations he and his uncle Michael had created together.

Commenting on the process, Michael said, "So, to me, this was huge for Carter. Up through that point, we had done a good job, I think, with engaging his imagination, getting him to think, you 'are someone who has things that you can make in different ways.' And this was a chance to get him excited about what he made without even really thinking about it, because he just told that story, but then together, I drew it, he colored it, we put it together, and he could be proud of it and share it. And we've done some other little stuff like that."

For Michael, it was clear that these acts of creation, or better, these shared acts of creation between a caregiver and child, deepen who we are. "I think something very human is our creativity. Our ability to literally create helps us to live into the fullness of what we can be," Michael said. But, he pointed out, we live in an economic system that erodes this fullness by diminishing agency and identity and pushes "a narrative of the need to consume." Sometimes the narrative emphasizes deficits, he said, sometimes social clout, sometimes competition. "And I think that those ways of thinking, in terms of what's at stake, cut off a huge part of your human potential, which is, 'You can create so much without being in service to money.'" In other words, these acts of creation potentially have deep moral stakes.

Creating is also inherently meaningful. "I get a lot of joy and inspiration out of being creative," Michael summarized. "It's part of how I have dealt with trauma in my life. I feel like the chaos of tragedy, when expressed in art, can put a rhythm to where it doesn't erase the tragedy, but it can put a rhythm to it where you can experience beauty along with lament."

As I reflect again on the use of drawing by Robert Coles in light of my conversation with Michael, I can see even more clearly how the strategy was a way of bringing agency and power to children who have been knocked down by illness or angry mobs. Each line, choice of color, placement of form contributes to a rhythm of beauty along with lament. Each stroke is an act of countercultural resistance to identity erosion and economic manipulation. Each drawing, a deepening of humanity, of being made in the image of God the creator.

* * *

"So, what have you learned at church?" I asked seven-year-old Layla. "What have you learned about God?"

"That he is an upstander and an activist and he helps people," she said.

"Okay. God's an activist," I repeated. "And I missed the first word that you said, an up–what?"

Layla said, "Upstander." I asked her to explain, and she said it means "standing up for people."

"That's great," I said. "That's a great word." It was genuinely new to me. "Anything else you've learned about God? Or what do you think makes God happy?"

She repeated the theme. "To see people, to see upstanders and activists and people who care for people who are getting treated unkindly."

"Okay. What do you think makes God sad?"

Layla answered, "To see people getting killed because of their skin color."

Layla's mother, Lauren, is one of several ministers of a large church in a northeast city associated with the Reformed Church of America. The congregation and its leadership are ethnically diverse–Lauren is White while the senior pastor as well as other associate ministers are Black. Jane and I attended a Sunday morning service, and the message, liturgy, and music all strongly reflected commitments to justice and antiracism. A large "Black Lives Matter/Las Vidas Negras Importan" banner hung in the sanctuary. Lauren was preaching this Sunday, and her sermon was about "joy," based on Isaiah 51:11:

> So the ransomed of the Lord shall return,
>   and come to Zion with rejoicing;

> everlasting joy shall be upon their heads;
> they shall obtain joy and gladness,
> and sorrow and sighing shall flee away.

From my notes on the sermon: "Joy is from God. Joy grows in community, in marvel for the mundane, is an eye for wonder. Joy is an act of resistance, is disruptive, a tool for liberation, a door for justice, manifests abundance, pushes scarcity politics away." Though I never heard the actual word "upstander" during the service, it was not hard to imagine how this seven-year-old came to add it to her vocabulary.

We interviewed the family a week after this service. Jane was interviewing Lauren and her husband, Daniel, while I spoke with Layla and with her two older twin brothers, Liam and Noah, who were eleven.

Jane, also a pastor, commented on Lauren's sermon. "I mean, just joy. I kept thinking of that all week and still do. I wanted you to know that because you never quite know—what does preaching do? And I always think, if something just stays with you, I think that's it." Lauren was grateful for the comment. She, herself, is not Reformed Church of America but Baptist. Yet her commitment and experience in community activism made her a good fit for her current position.

"So why do you take your children to church?" Jane asked.

Lauren answered first. "I think the community aspect is definitely important as one of the places that we can intentionally be in community. And we chose this church for a reason, because there is so much racial and ethnic diversity, and we are really intentional about exposing our kids to that." Lauren explained that they want their children to understand that this intentionality is rooted in a theological, moral perspective, that is, "how the world should be." Lauren quoted the senior pastor as saying that worship is "rehearsing the reign of God." Lauren continued, "And I think that's so beautiful because we don't have it perfect, and the world isn't perfect. But when you come to worship, it's an intentional act to rehearse the reign of God."

Daniel, the son of a Baptist minister, jumped in: "The only thing I'll add is that part of me is still very much Baptist. I want them to be able to make their own decision one day about God, and their belief or disbelief." He said he wants them to know a source of hope, especially given that the world is in so many ways a "dumpster fire," as he put it. "It's easy to think that there is no way out of this, there is no redemption for the place we're in. And yet I do think that through the Christian faith and tradition, as I've learned it, there is that hope and there is a reason to keep fighting the good fight, getting in good trouble and doing these things." Daniel's emphasis upon hope, to my ears, echoed the way Lauren preached about joy. Aligning ourselves with hope and joy is tied up with rehearsing the reign of God. Taking their children to church, Daniel said, "is introducing them to where I find hope."

He was clear, however, that he doesn't believe church or Christianity is the only way. Daniel made a point of saying that he believed there are many paths to God, and he respects those paths very much. But in his case, "[I want to] introduce the path that I found and the one that introduced me to this hope and joy that there is for the world. But if my child finds that through Islam or through Judaism, then fantastic."

* * *

Layla's twin brothers, Liam and Noah, had been to a church camp all week and had just gotten home when we spoke. Liam decided to be interviewed first, he said, because he was older. "How much older?" I asked. He wanted me to guess. "Six minutes?" He shook his head no. "Two minutes?"

"No, but you're getting closer," Liam said. "Forty-seven seconds!" He smiled.

Liam liked their church a lot—the people and the music particularly. He admitted, though, that sometimes the service goes on too long and "is kind of boring." Overall, though, Liam said, "I like how the church invites everyone, makes sure no one feels left out. And it does this thing called 'Message for All Ages' where all the kids come to the front and they talk. Like, yesterday, we were making a song. Joy feels like something. Joy looks like, feels like, makes me move like." It turns out the kids filled in the blanks and the leader composed a song on the spot with their answers.

I asked Liam whether—if he ever had children—he would want his kids to go to church. Like nearly every child we asked, he thought he would. "It's good for them to learn about that." I asked him to clarify what "that" was. He said, "God. Jesus. How to be respectful." He went on to say he would want his children to know what happened with Jesus and why that matters. When I asked whether there was anything else he had learned at church that was important, he answered, "I've learned that God doesn't have any pronouns. You can call God they/them, he/his, she/hers. I normally call God she or they/them." He made a point of saying that at the church camp (not at their church) the leaders called God "he."

When I asked him what makes God happy, Liam said, "Well, seeing people be respectful. Us sticking up for each other, not hurting each other or animals. Being nice. And that makes God happy because that's exactly what she wanted her people, or people to do. But being mean or hurting people isn't good." I asked him how God feels about people in general, and he said, "I think God feels good about most people, a majority of them, because they do what she wants. And so it does make her happy. But there are some people that don't—like people at war, maybe. And nobody likes war except for the people that are helping the war or in the war, because my family definitely does not like war."

Like his brother, Noah also likes church and particularly enjoys the energetic singing. He gave a mixed review of the sermons. "Sometimes it's kind of hard to understand when the preacher makes these twenty-five-minute-long speeches. And so sometimes I just tune out. But other times it's kind of interesting and so I listen, and I learn a lot of stuff."

Noah also emphasized the importance of activism and standing up. "We learned about God being an activist last year, but we're learning some about it this year. And God being an activist means we always know that God is with us and upstanding for us, standing up for us. And so God can be an activist, like everyone who needs help."

While Noah did not talk about God's pronouns, his mother mentioned how passionate he is about calling out various forms of injustice.

"Noah is really obsessed with this. He calls out the patriarchy and sexism and racism and anything that he sees now, just on his own. He'll be reading *The Diary of Wimpy Kid,* and he'll say, 'Dad, Dad, look at this. This is so sexist,' and this kind of stuff. I think those things are very connected to our faith." She continued, "I do think that having a faith in an ethical framework or a vocabulary that is somewhere in their minds, is a reason that we go to church as well." Lauren took the idea a step further, to their style of parenting. "We try really intentionally not to be authoritarian in our parenting but rather expose our children to the ideals that we think are ethical and just, and hope that they can come to their own understanding of that as well. So being in a place like [our church] that aligns with our values is important." Daniel agreed.

The couple talked about how the sheer act of going to church can be a countercultural move. "It's a very different thing to go and ask your children to sit and worship—just sit there. Right?" Lauren observed. "I mean that's a very different thing than they do 24/7. It's not a screen, it's not a park, it's not a playground, it's not a—fill-in-the-blank." The kids may complain at times, but overall, as Lauren put it, "I really value that it's different. One of the examples of joy is that joy is disruptive, right? And so of course you're going to remember it because it disrupts the status quo. And worship is the same to me. It disrupts the status quo of the week and of the regular kind of cycle." Lauren paused for a moment, then offered, "So I hope to pass along that joy piece, which is this beautiful thing, that each of us have something that is unique to us that we can add to this grand story of life and of humanity. I think the justice piece is really big. And again, justice comes in a lot of ways, but of course Jesus was all about justice and was a revolutionary and a table flipper and a good troublemaker and all those things."

* * *

As we left Lauren and Daniel's apartment, I realized I had a song playing in my mind, one by Nick Lowe in the 1970s and famously rerecorded by Elvis Costello a few years later. The song is "(What's So

Funny 'Bout) Peace, Love, and Understanding?" The lyrics are about searching for hope and trust in the midst of a hateful world.

To many, the counterculture suggests communes, hippies, drugs, and Woodstock. But listening to children and adults struggle with holding onto kindness, love, and respect, while resisting racism, sexist language, and consumerist manipulation, brings a finer texture to the notion. Rehearsing the reign of God by breaking up the status quo of screens and competition. Playing with toys that introduce moral complexity. Learning to become upstanders. Creating a story with others. Establishing trustworthy communities. Welcoming. A child's prayer of gratitude. All these moves flowing from faith itself and generating countercultural rhythms of joy and lament.

10

Endings

"TELL ME ABOUT BAPTISM," Jane said to the Sunday school class of seven- to ten-year-olds. It was an experiment in interviewing a group of children in the earliest days of the project. The church was Presbyterian (PCUSA) in the northern Midwest but drew families and children from more theologically diverse backgrounds around the neighborhood. The pastor was friendly, gregarious, and quite involved in the community. Many of the families were new to the church or new to church in general.

"Baptism is when you join the church," an eight-year-old answered.

"The pastor puts water on a baby," replied another. Nods of agreement around the room.

Have you been baptized? Jane followed.

"Yes, but I don't remember because I was a baby."

"Yes," another child said. "It was on Christmas Eve night, I was seven, and it was very special."

In the midst of these straightforward responses, Dakota, a ten-year-old girl, volunteered: "No, I have not been baptized because my father is not comfortable with baptism. But at my old church my sister got baptized." Dakota and her mother were new to this congregation and had come from a tradition of believer's baptism, rather than infant baptism. "But my father said I shouldn't get baptized because of what happened to my younger brother."

"What happened?" Jane asked.

"My younger brother had leukemia and passed away when he was five." The class quieted and Dakota continued. "He got leukemia when he was two."

"How old were you?" Jane asked.

"I was six when he died. It was hard for me back at school, in kindergarten. I've gotten over it considering that he is in a better place and no longer in pain."

Jane and the class eventually moved on to other subjects—prayer, communion, what makes God happy, and more. By the end the kids were getting rambunctious, and the Sunday school teacher said the class could go get a snack in the fellowship hall. Jane invited anyone who wanted to stay and talk some more to do so.

The class left, except for Dakota. She sat there quietly, and Jane asked whether she was willing to share more about her brother. She was. "My brother was born the year after me, and two years after he was born, he got leukemia. . . . When he passed away, I felt sick. I felt like it was my fault because it was after my birthday." (The relationship between her birthday and her guilt was never completely clear.) "My brother loved us all, but leukemia changed him, and he started to dislike me because he fought it most of the time. . . . I loved him. I felt like he was my only sibling because my [older] brother and sister were always together. Then after he passed, they started to be mean to me so that's when I kind of felt like it was my fault."

"Do you still think that?" Jane asked.

"No," Dakota said. "It was just siblings being siblings."

"So, your brother being sick and dying," Jane asked gently, "how did that make you feel about God?"

"When he was sick, I thought he just needed some medicine. But when he passed away, I went to God more to talk to him. Then my sister said it was good that he passed, and I just started yelling at her like 'How, how is it good?' She said he's in a better place and now he's feeling better. And over time I came to accept that. We have a picture and memorial on top of the TV set, so we never forget him."

As cliché as accepting that "he's in a better place now" may sound to highly trained theological ears, it did not come easily or through a cheap denial of the pain of loss for this ten-year-old.

Dakota's friend Maddie returned to the classroom. "It's too loud out there," she declared. The conversation between the three of them turned to prayer. Jane asked whether they thought God hears prayers. Both girls said yes.

"What about when you don't get what you asked for?" Jane asked. It had been a topic that had come up with the whole class. Maddie thought some things were out of God's control. Dakota agreed. "I know God can't fix everything," she said, and admitted being mad at God not only about her brother but also about the neck pain her mother had been going through. "I asked for my mom to be all right because she is always in pain. You can just see it in her face. Even when she smiles you can tell she's in pain." But Dakota was hopeful now because her mother was soon going to have surgery to help.

Jane commented, "You both pray by talking to God. Have you ever felt like God was talking to you?"

Maddie said, "I like hear it in my thoughts—like 'Don't do it.'" For Maddie, the sense of these God-thoughts was something like a conscience when she was tempted to do something wrong.

Dakota followed. "For me it's just that I talk in my head a lot and then sometimes I hear this voice saying, 'Everything will be all right.' So—when you hear a little message saying everything will be all right."

"I love that," Jane commented. "I'm going to remember that."

For Dakota, God could somehow be an object of her anger, Job-like, yet could also become a deep security below the fault lines of suffering and death shaking her world. This ten-year-old is a powerful reminder that children face and live in the same kinds of existential challenges and dilemmas that haunt adult reality: life and death, suffering and hope, joy and concern, love and loss, grandeur and misery.

* * *

The subject of death came up a lot in our discussions with children. Not only among the Mexican children describing the Day of the Dead, but in one way or another in most of our conversations. That may be surprising. But consider that a major story, arguably *the* main story told in church, involves the death of God's beloved. Through Scripture readings, children's Bibles, devotions, sermons, hymns, prayers, communion (last supper before death), funeral services, and more, children are not easily shielded from the subject of death even if they haven't had such an intimate experience with loss like Dakota. While this was the only instance in which the subject arose because of a question about baptism, in fact, in her church, as the pastor put it, death is considered "the completion of baptism."

The subject of death arose in our conversations primarily when we simply asked children about Jesus. What do you know about Jesus?

Terse descriptions summarizing the life of Christ were not uncommon. "He was a boy," twelve-year-old Daniel put it. "He was born. And he grew up and he did miracles. And then one day the people got angry, and they wanted to sacrifice him. And they crucified him." Most children expressed great admiration, especially for the love he showed: Jesus "helps people"; "takes care of people"; and "his heart is bigger than the entire world!"; "he prays for people"; "he is nice and does a lot of things for us." "He loves so much he forgives us even for 'bad things.'" Some children emphasized miracles: "He was a miracle-worker"; "he lived a long time ago and did miracles"; "I like the feeding of the five thousand. I like it because he had a couple of fish and a couple of loaves of bread, and with the power of God, he made it so that everyone could eat and there's still extra." Several children described the birth/manger story of Jesus. Orthodox children often emphasized the role of Mary, the Theotokos, who gave birth to him even though "she couldn't have children." But nearly all the children who were of school age (sixish or older) eventually got around to his death, as twelve-year-old Graham illustrates. "Jesus was an awesome guy. If I were to meet him—when I meet him—I think he's going to be like a really radical dude, a cool person to just hang out with. Because he seems more, you know, down to earth. Like an easier person to talk to and get to know. Because, you know, God—he's the father, the king. But Jesus is just like the person you could sit and have hot chocolate with and talk to. . . . Yeah, he's a cool dude. He came down to earth and he died on the cross for us. And now he's the Son of God."

This is all to say that most children at some point talked about the death of Jesus on the cross and how he rose from the dead. Most could tell the story of the crucifixion even when they could remember no other stories about him. This was usually described as "dying for us," "a sacrifice for us," or "dying for our sins." While many children went on to tell of the resurrection, it was also common for children to stop at the crucifixion. We often then prompted, "Is that the end of the story?" Only a couple of children answered yes, while most went on to describe his "coming back to life"; "resurrection"; "rising from the dead"; or "on the third day he rose from the dead." The point is that we found that death as well as resurrection are at the heart of the children's religious imaginations about Jesus.

Another way in which the subject came up was from the question "What do you think makes God sad?" One bright-smiled five-year-old answered, "grumpy people," and a couple of environmentally minded children said, "when we pollute and put garbage in the rivers"; and "cutting down the rainforest." Nonetheless, most children spoke of behaviors like "being mean to each other"; "when we sin"; "not being nice"; "when you do something wrong"; "when we're mean to ourselves or others"; "when we disobey his commands—drugs, smoking, robbing things, stuff like that"; or simply "not following Jesus." But several children took such misbehavior to another level. What makes God sad? "Things getting torn apart or people getting hurt"; "hate and war"; "hurting people"; "when Jesus died"; "when they nailed Jesus to the cross"; "when people do evil things to other people"; "when people die"; "when people shoot people and the world isn't peace and stuff"; "Fighting. Bad people. Shooting"; "we aren't in world peace right now"; "to see people getting killed"; and "mass shootings."

While Jane was talking with Dakota and the Sunday school class, I interviewed some of the younger children. I asked two six-year-olds,

Audrie and Amy, what makes God sad. "Fighting. Killing people," Audrie said. She looked at me, "I just ask you, why did God have to make guns?"

Before I could say anything, Amy said, "I think the devil made those." I stayed quiet. The school shooting at Marjory Stoneman Douglas High School in Parkland, Florida, had occurred only four days earlier, and I realized what was on the mind of even six-year-olds.

Audrie was convinced. "Yeah, the devil made guns."

* * *

When children themselves brought up the subject of death, we let that be a bridge to other questions probing their religious imaginations—specifically about what they believe happens when people die. With younger children, we often did not ask at all, but if we did, we would ask the parent whether it was okay to bring up the subject of death.

Typically, regardless of age, after a child mentioned God's sadness about death or Jesus dying, we would ask, "Have you ever known someone who died, maybe someone close to you?" Very few children said they did not. Many, especially younger kids, named a pet. That is, for a great swath of children the death of their dog, cat, toad, turtle, goldfish, or hamster was their first conscious and personal awareness of death as something enduring.

As one parent explained, the first "firsthand experience of death" her young children had was of their dog, Patches. They knew that their grandmother had died and was in heaven. But the grandmother had died before the younger child was even born and the older child was only one and a half. When Patches got sick, however, "it was completely unexpected, and he was in the hospital. Then we had to make the decision to put Patches down." She said, "We were all petting him, telling him how much we love him, and then he died. We told them, 'He's dead now.'" She said the older child (around six at the time) just stared at Patches. "He's like, 'When is Patches gonna take off to heaven?' He thought he was going to start going up or I don't know. Then we were trying to explain the concept of your soul, your spirit, and how that's what probably just goes. That's the image they have—well, that people have. We bury them, but their spirit or their soul goes to heaven." The death of a pet, in addition to being the first experience of such a loss, may also be the first time children wrestle with the concepts of soul or spirit.

While many children named pets, many more named pets along with grandparents, aunts, uncles, great-grandparents, or, perhaps, a friend of a parent or someone from church. Often the child would share a little more about the person, or how the death made them sad, or what the funeral was like. Only once did a child, eleven, not want to answer: "I don't want to talk about it because a lot of the people that were lost were very important to me." This was an interview that took place after the COVID pandemic. The child went on to talk about "the death that was probably the least bad for me, the one that didn't have me crying in bed for the next seven days." That was the death of a pet turtle during the pandemic.

Twelve-year-old Shawn had also lost loved ones during the pandemic, but he focused upon one person, his uncle, who lived with his family. "Some of my other family deaths are painful, but like this is my uncle's room, so when he died, it was too painful. We were very close. Because he would take me everywhere. He coached me in baseball—and soccer for a few years—but most of my childhood baseball. And, well, he used to let me use his PlayStation. And then he had a hilarious sense of humor." I told Shawn how sorry I was and how painful the loss sounded. "Yeah," he said. "I mean, it was three years ago, but well, since then, I'm okay with it now, but it's still painful sometimes." I asked whether he ever thought about where his uncle is now. "Probably beyond space, beyond earth, beyond the galaxy at least. He's beyond all of this, he's in heaven, and heaven is over everything."

As with Shawn, after exploring what deaths children may have experienced, we typically asked a version of "What do you think happens when people die?" Overwhelmingly children said that when people (or pets) die, they "go to heaven" or "go to God" or they "live with God" or, as one child put it, "They come to life again in heaven with other people who have died." Another child mentioned her grandfather, uncle, and dog who had died. After they died, "they went up there [pointing up]. They live a happy life and look down at us and remember us."

Most children did not elaborate much, yet some didn't mind wondering aloud with us. "Well, I think they go to heaven, but there's no way to tell if you actually go because nobody's come back to tell you. So, I'm not really sure what happens to them. I know that something happens to them. Like they maybe go somewhere. I'm not sure where." Or, "They go up to heaven and they stay there for the rest of their life, well, the rest of their dead life. But nobody really knows what happens up there."

Some children were quite literal with their answers. "They get put in a grave"; "they bury them"; or "they get cremated"; or "people are very sad, and they cry, and they say 'why did they have to go' because they should have lived longer. And everybody is very sad." But most differentiated the body from the soul or spirit. "Their soul's still alive but their body is dead"; or "their bodies stay on earth but then their spirits go up to heaven." Some kids imagined other possibilities. "The soul then goes to a different person"; "I think that they basically get regenerated into another life or maybe another form"; "I believe that they go to heaven and then they get re-created into a new body and come back to life as a baby"; or "when you die, you become an angel and watch over people."

For children who named heaven, we explored further by asking, "What do you think heaven is like?" Some children answered with great confidence: "It's big. Like a palace"; "it's the color of the sea and there's a throne. And a lot of people"; "it's like a place where God is. You get to meet him and it's always happy. And then you get to watch your grandchildren, and like everybody else you knew." One older child likened heaven to God: "I've always thought that it was just all around us."

Other children were not sure what heaven is like but enjoyed speculating. "I have no idea, but I know it's a very bright place, and I bet Maggie [dog who died] and my mom's dad, Grandpa Ralph, are having a very, very nice time together. But I always wonder, 'Are we going to have houses? Are we going to have money when we get there? Are we going to have all the stuff we need?'" Jenny, eight, said, "When I die, I die. Death is just another great adventure. I go to heaven. I get to do whatever I like for the rest of the world. Eternity."

Nine-year-old Max took the speculation in another direction. "Heaven, I thought of it like you just are in a blank room. Well, you can just imagine yourself in an empty room, and there's probably a place where your whole family is. And once you're in that room, you can just imagine anything, and it'll come to life." I asked what he might imagine. "I'd probably imagine a roller coaster—and stuff that people have never come up with, like, a burger fountain."

While an overwhelming majority of children talked of, or alluded to, heaven, a handful not only mentioned heaven but also mentioned hell. "They go to heaven. But if they do something wrong, they go to hell"; "it depends on how you behave or you act as to where you would go. You go to heaven, or you go to a hell, or you go to a place that's kind of like hell—purgatory." One child imagined a meeting with God: "[The dead] either go to heaven or hell, and God has to take a minute to decide. They kind of sit in a room and talk. [God would ask] 'so what have you done?' He decides if you're lying. He checks everything. And if he doesn't like what he hears, he sends you to the underworld, or I've heard of this place in the middle of both of them."

It was clear for these children that heaven, hell, or in-between—in light of God's judgment—had everything to do with moral behavior. "If they were worshiping God and stuff, and if they were good, not like criminals and with the devil—the ones with God would go up to heaven. And the ones with the devil would go down to Hades." Another child said, "They bury the person. And then two days later it's like they come back to life. And they walk down the road until they get to the house of God. Then God asks them, or he tells them, 'Look, you did this, and that was very bad, or you did this, and that was very good.' And then these people either go to hell, or they live in the mansion with God." Another child: "Either you go to heaven or hell, I guess. With the Second Coming, which is when the world ends, God will divide people into the sheep or the goats. The sheep are the good ones, and the goats are the ones that will go to hell."

These were the exceptions. To repeat, talk of hell was rare among the children we interviewed. Some, like twelve-year-old Joe, wanted to evade the issue. "I think they go up to heaven to live with God, and we're just going to ignore hell because I don't like to think about that." Whether others simply didn't want to think about hell is hard to say. But one boy, Alby, also twelve, addressed the issue directly. "I think even though people will talk about hell and stuff, I think everybody goes to heaven. Because everybody has that good part of them that they want to be a good person and perfect. So, I think that everybody goes up into heaven and God welcomes them."

The interview with hell-denying Alby had been rich and robust, lasting nearly an hour. It could have gone longer, but he needed to get to youth group. Near the end I asked whether there was anything else he thought would be important for people to know about how he thinks or his church. "One thing that's kind of philosophical—is that how you say it?—is like when you die, do you stay up in heaven or do you come back down as your spirit and go into another person and kind of restart and be like a different person but like the same spirit?"

"So that's something you think about?" I asked. His answer surprised me with the turn it took.

"Mmm-hmm [yes]. I also think about if I were—I don't know why—but sometimes I try to put myself in the actual point of view of others. So, for some reason if someone's sitting in the front of a class, I try to envision what they would be seeing. For example, if me and you are sitting here, I would try to imagine myself sitting there and seeing me. And then like seeing the windows and the blanket and the pillows."

"Have you done that for a long time, or is this something more recent?"

"I've done it since maybe second grade. I don't know why. I just love to do it. I think it's kind of fun to try to put myself in another person's perspective."

Though we needed to wrap up, I found myself telling Alby about the "theory of mind" studies I had done—the first time I had ever used those words with a young person. "I was trying to understand when children realize other people have a different perspective." He thought that was cool. But Alby had no idea how fascinating I thought his own point-of-view experiments were. I also couldn't help but connect his desire to see from someone else's perspective to his conviction that "everybody has that good part of them" and would be welcomed to heaven. It was as if he were trying to see from God's perspective.

* * *

Many parents reported that conversations about death were among the most difficult they have had with their children—from explaining that they will never be able to talk to Nana again to sorting out the relationship between body and spirit. Most thought that their faith and faith communities helped. Church, as we've noted, deals with death a lot—from Good Friday to funerals. The world of faith has language and stories, rites and rituals, if not potlucks and prayers that feed the religious imagination with comfort and companionship in the midst of loss.

Even so, some parents struggled. In a couple of cases, the struggle had to do with their convictions about life after death. When her grandmother died, one mother said that her younger daughter, a preschooler at the time, kept asking whether they could visit Great-Grandma. "I had to tell her that no, she's dead. 'Can we FaceTime her?' No. So trying to explain that there is a disconnect between us and the people who died." This was the more typical type of challenge for parents helping their children better understand death. But with her seven-year-old, she said, "The older one will ask more questions, like 'What does it mean to be with God?' or 'What happens to you when you die?' Or 'What about people who don't believe in God?' That's hard to answer. I want to share what we believe, but I want to be truthful about it. I don't want her to be afraid. But I mean we basically believe in a heaven and a hell."

Similarly, another mother from the same church (Presbyterian Church of America) said, "I think one of the hardest questions that they've asked me is breaching the topic of heaven and hell. And specifically, they ask really probing questions about like, what is hell? And I'm trying to explain, which, even for an adult, it's like, how do you explain that to someone who doesn't have that concept—let alone to a child?"

Among these parents, the beliefs funding their religious imaginations about death raise some deeply disturbing thoughts and conversations.

On the other end of the spectrum, I return to Michael, father of two who created Black Toys Matter. In thanking him for his time, I mentioned how rewarding it has been talking to parents and to kids themselves—and how existential it all is—that is, how beliefs, values, and practices all come to a head when we're talking about children. Michael nodded, and the comment stirred an example in him. It was from the book *That All Shall Be Saved*, by the Orthodox scholar David Bentley Hart.[1] "The book is where he makes the case for universal salvation. That is the only coherent Christian belief. The more popular alternative of eternal damnation is not coherent. That's what Hart's saying." Michael explained, "The reason I brought it up is because in the introduction to his book, the first thing he talks about is exactly what you just said. For a child, this idea of eternal hell is an existential crisis that comes to a real head. Whereas as adults, we just put it on the back burner. We don't really address the cognitive dissonance that comes with it." (Hart suspects that most people just don't think it through because they are "supposed" to believe in it.) "So," Michael continued, "he starts with a story of a little kid who hears for the first time this doctrine [of eternal hell] and is in horror and reacts viscerally and has this huge fear of God and paranoia for everyone, everyone around. Right. Because that's what you would do if you really believed everyone was going to be damned forever in eternal torture unless they said the right thing. So yeah, these existential things come to a head for kids in ways that we [adults] just somehow live with and don't deal with."

Hart's conviction is in line with Alby's (above), that it is impossible to justify how a God who loves could condemn even the worst-behaving people not simply to a punishment or purgation of some sort but for ever and ever without end. That is, if we are to love, how in heaven's name could we enjoy the bliss of eternity knowing that a soul—maybe someone dear to us—is being mercilessly tortured forever? It would be in direct contradiction to the gospel itself. Hart draws from streams of universalist thought in early church history as well as biblical scholarship. (Hart has translated the entire New Testament.) He makes clear that any biblical case for eternal punishment is very thin, if nonexistent. Instead, the gospel, in its dawn, "announced itself truly as the 'good tidings' of a rescue on the part of a loving God . . . a way into the kingdom of heaven in which all of creation would be glorified by the direct presence of God." Or, in the apostle Paul's words, God will be "all in all" (1 Cor. 15:28).

* * *

"When she finally died, that was the hardest thing. It was like going through hell." These words are from Anthony, a former Orthodox priest, discussing the death of his wife, Judith, from cancer a few years earlier. Whether or not someone believes in eternal damnation, there is little doubt that the death of a loved one can bring the torments of hell with it.

Jane asked, "When your wife, the kids' mother, was dying, how did you talk to the kids about death in relation to faith?" Anthony was a father of four at the time of Judith's death. He was now remarried to Jewell, and they'd recently had a baby. Jane, Jewell, and Anthony had been talking about the impact of faith on them, as parents, when Anthony began talking about the experience of Judith's dying.

"Well, for the first year or two, I guess, we were just expecting a miracle," Anthony said. "We're like, 'There's no way.' Everybody that I knew was like, 'She's not gonna die. She's gonna make it. She's gonna get through it. She's too young. She's strong, she'll fight through it.' Then when she wasn't able to do that, it was like, 'God will give you a miracle. You're gonna have a miracle. You're gonna witness a miracle.'" People began to bring holy relics—a special cross, icons, myrrh—that had been attributed with miracles in the church. During this period, according to Anthony, "Death didn't even come up [with the kids] until finally one day it became apparent. I don't remember who I talked with it about, but I talked with somebody and they're like, 'Yeah, you should really have a talk with the kids. Because you understand what's gonna happen, but your kids don't know what's gonna happen.' Then sitting down with them, that was one of the most difficult conversations I think I've ever had, honestly. It was that horrible. I don't even wanna think about it too much. Because just telling them what was imminent and then watching their reactions and then not being able to not react myself." He apologized for tearing up.

"Yeah, it was really horrible. It was really bad. They really cried, I really cried. Honestly, I think we dealt with it horribly. I'm not gonna pretend. I think—it's not like we lost our faith in God, any of us, at all. I just think that they really can't teach you how to grieve properly. When she finally died, that was the hardest thing. It was like going through hell."

Complicating the situation was Anthony's role of being a priest at the time (in a different state). "It was this marathon," he said. "On top of everything, being the priest with all eyes focused on me all the time, and everyone wanted me to give this word, this encouragement. By the time it was over, I just collapsed, I think, spiritually, mentally, physically." He left the priesthood, they eventually moved, and Anthony began a new vocation as a creator of icons.

"To answer your question, I think that I did a horrible job talking about death with my kids—allowing them to grieve and showing them healthy grieving." At the same time, with the move, with the new marriage and child, "things started settling down finally," and he was making up for the lost conversations with his children and opportunities for grieving. This settling down has been hard won, with lots of time and grief and emotionally, if not spiritually, difficult conversations, and the help of a new Orthodox community (including a therapist-priest). He has even found some grace for himself, as a parent. Based on how the kids were doing, he said, "Maybe I didn't screw up too bad."

* * *

"So, have you ever discussed death with your children?" Jane asked Ada, Catholic, and mother of three.

"Oh, yes," she said. "That's very close to home, because when I was nine, I lost my parents, both of my parents." Ada was living in the Dominican Republic at the time.

"At once?"

"At once in an accident." She and her siblings were passed around to various relatives—grandparents for a while, then an aunt, then the siblings were split up among other relatives. Ada said it was like this until she went to college and "they shut the door behind us."

But that was not the only intense experience of death. "And then when my oldest child was three months old, I lost my husband. So, he's dead. It's been—" she interrupted herself. "Yes," she said, returning to the original question, "even my little one handles very well the conversation. He knows very well that his brother's biological father passed away, and he's very clear."

"I guess your oldest son wouldn't have known his father?"

"The first time that he asked me where his dad was, he was two years old. And I took him to therapy. And for many years, we went to therapy. It was hand in hand, the therapist and I, helping him understand. He had a couple ups and downs. But now he understands that, generally speaking, we're supposed to grow old and see maybe your grandkids and then go. But you just never know. So, we just have to be grateful, and it's okay to be sad, and it's okay to miss, and it's okay to cry, especially for boys [who may be discouraged from crying]."

Ada discussed how important her faith has been through it all. "When my parents passed away, being that I was in a very Catholic culture, we kept going to mass and we kept doing the prayers and all of that. I never questioned it. And I went to college, and I never questioned it. And then my husband passed away, and I got even closer to God."

"So, all this didn't push you away from God?"

"No. I did question why? Why me? I did go through that. But then, I understand that God is not going to have an answer. Why did he send his son, and then all of a sudden he got crucified. He went through so much torture and pain, and why him? Why his son? So again, that was what gave me a little bit of peace, I guess, in the middle of all this tumultuous state of shock and pain."

"Because God went through it too?"

"Correct," Ada concluded. For her, God is a fellow sufferer.

* * *

"Do you have any brothers or sisters?" That was my question to seven-year-old Logan, part of the LDS community. That's all it took to turn to the subject to death.

"So, I have Carter and Dylan. Carter is a baby. And we did have another baby named Hunter. But he died because he put a"—he paused—"put a blanket on his face and he couldn't breathe." Carter was almost four at the time and didn't remember all the details.

"I'm sorry. I'm guessing that made you pretty sad." He agreed. I asked about a funeral. He shared what he could remember.

"When Hunter died we went to the graveyard that's closest to us and, before they buried him, we each put one toy on the little thing that you put people in when you die. We both chose cars. I think Dylan chose a truck and I chose a motorcycle."

"Okay. How come you chose that?"

"Well, once Hunter saw a motorcycle and I thought his favorite color might have been red. So, I put a red motorcycle down and Dylan put a red truck or maybe a car."

"So, what do you think happens to people when they die? After they die?"

"Their spirit goes to heaven," Logan answered matter-of-factly.

In the interview with Logan's mother, Grace, we learned more. "So, my kids know about death because they had a little brother that died. Yeah. So, they do, they know about it firsthand and it's very—" She didn't finish the sentence. "Dylan had just turned two, and Logan was almost four—so he can still remember it, though he doesn't remember much. Hunter was two months old when he died. And it was a SIDS [sudden infant death syndrome] thing, so it was just an accident. So, they experienced it. They do know about death, firsthand. We've had discussion about death. It is hard, but at the same time it's been a blessing." She explained that though it was difficult, she appreciated that her children know at their young ages about death and dying. She said that her husband, for example, never knew anyone personally who died until he was in college, which made it very challenging for him. In addition, she said, their discussions of death have helped her children not be afraid of the subject or of death itself.

Like Ada through the loss of her parents and husband, Grace too found solace in the knowledge that God understands death and suffering. She mentioned specifically the atonement. "A lot of people think of the atonement like it's just for repentance, like I can be forgiven. And, the atonement is for so much more than that. It's for—he died for our sins and our pain. So he's already felt all that pain that I was feeling when I lost Hunter. He had already felt all that. So, I had a completely different relationship with Jesus Christ after that, because I felt like he's already felt this, and he is helping me cope with this. I know that someone has already felt this pain." She said that this is what she wants her children to know. "I want them to have that kind of relationship with Jesus Christ. I want them to have that foundation so that if something bad does happen, they're going to cling to the atonement and to Jesus Christ."

* * *

Reflecting upon these conversations, I think again of Eric Fromm's *The Art of Loving.*[2] That is, for him, the art of loving addresses a fundamental situation in being human, namely, the fundamental sense of separation and alienation that knocks on the door of existence. Just as we had no say in being born, we have no say in the fact that we will one day die. We will die before some of our loved ones, and some of our loved ones will die before us. Death is the ultimate form of separation. And this awareness arouses anxiety and is, according to Fromm, "the source of all anxiety." Eating from the tree of this knowledge, we, like Adam and Eve, know we are naked and will die one day, and this awareness leads to separation from the paradise of not knowing. Sadly, some children are kicked out of this paradise very early.

In Fromm's understanding, our deepest need as human beings is to overcome our separateness, "to leave the prison of [human] aloneness." This is universal, characteristic "of all ages and cultures," that we are "confronted with the solution of one and the same question: the question of how to overcome separateness, how to achieve union, how to transcend one's own individual life and find at-onement." Love, as an art, is about the knowledge and effort to overcome disconnection and existential alienation.

* * *

"We come from God, and we return to God." This is what one mother told her girls when their grandfather died. She'd picked up the line from a Jewish rabbi at a funeral service for a loved one. She found it so simple, straightforward, and beautiful that she repeated it to her children. "We come from God, and we return to God." At-onement.

11

Grandparents

"I GREW UP in a very strange Christian journey," sixty-something Sarah said of her childhood in the upper Midwest. "It was just very strange, and so I was kind of resistant to church." She explained, "I was baptized in the Presbyterian church, and then I became a Christian Scientist, and then I became an evangelical nondenomination Christian, member of Church of the Covenant, and then we were Methodist, and then we were Baptist, and then we were Swedish Covenant, and then I quit going to church. It's ridiculous." Sarah, now a Presbyterian again, had brought her grandson, nine-year-old Robbie, to church, and she was willing to talk with us as well.

In the religious life, or in family life, for that matter, form without flexibility can, of course, lead to morbid rigidity or stifling strictness. However, as Sarah illustrates, there is a flip side. Flexibility without structure can lead to "ridiculous" chaos. It was not until later life that Sarah discovered a spiritual home that could honor both form and flexibility. When her own children were growing up, their father was a "staunch atheist," according to Sarah, "so there wasn't a whole lot of church going on." But when her daughter and future son-in-law (Robbie's future parents) were looking for a wedding venue, the son-in-law remembered that his grandfather had been very active in a particular nearby church. Sarah spoke to the pastor, who said she was open to presiding over the service but encouraged them to first come to church to check it out. That made sense to Sarah, and the following Sunday they all visited.

Sarah confessed that, at that point in her life, the whole Christian message was "total gibberish." In light of the shambolic nature of her childhood experience of church, Christianity made no sense; it was like a foreign language. But, when she came back to help scout out a potential wedding venue, she said she realized, "I didn't really know what I was missing. It was like the Bible verse, 'When you have eyes to see, ears to hear.' I cannot say what it was, but a supernatural thing happened and suddenly it was like the heavens opened up and said, 'Hey, here we are, now we're not speaking Russian anymore or Chinese, we are speaking your language, whatever language that may be.'" It was a Pentecost experience, when everyone heard in their own native language.

Thirteen years later Sarah was still attending the church and bringing her grandchildren as well—Robbie and his younger sister. The church, or church in general, did not stick for her daughter and son-in-law, but they are happy for Sarah to bring their children, her grandchildren.

Sarah is one of several grandparents we spoke with who are actively involved in their grandchildren's lives on either a daily or weekly basis. Some were actively raising their grandchildren in light of challenges going on in the family. Others, like Sarah, were functioning something like spiritual parents, that is, taking responsibility for providing some sort of religious practice for their grandchildren, from getting them to worship and Sunday school, to teaching them to pray.

When asked why she brought her grandchildren to church, Sarah said, "I really think it's to give them a solid foundation. I mean there is going to be a time in life when they are both going to go out there, like we all do, and feel completely alone. I want them to know that they are never ever alone, and that God has them no matter what, in the palm of his hand." For Sarah, this knowledge was not simply intellectual but something experienced more deeply through community. "I think that a lot of that foundation is reinforced through church. . . . It's important for me that they see the beautiful, wonderful, loving people that are here so that they know that this is an example of what a Christian is."

Sarah, a self-identified left-leaning activist, spoke about her frustration with a certain brand of Christianity, one that, in her words, "is really confusing a lot of people—like a lot of behavior that has nothing to do with Christianity, in the name of Christianity." But she feels like this church gives her grandchildren an alternative, "by being in it and interacting with people who are walking with Christ and living a good Christian life." She goes on, "I think that's a powerful example."

Through the conversation, it was clear how deep Sarah's love for her grandchildren runs, and how much she wants them to know not only her love and their parents' love but a love that can hold them even when parental or grandparental love is not enough, a love larger than life and death. Even so, Sarah was a realist about her spiritual hopes for her grandchildren. "Who knows, who knows if any of this will do anything?" she confessed. Yet, she was sanguine at the same time. "I know from my own experience, for all the pushing that my father did, and for my rebellion, I always knew I was loved, I always knew God was there, and when it was time to come back, I went, 'Gee, Dad, thanks, thanks for giving me that.' Because I had the foundation, and I hope that's what I can pass on to the kids."

* * *

Social biologist E. O. Wilson coined a term for those who take care of the young who are not their immediate, biologically born, children: *alloparenting*.[1] "Allo" derives from the Greek for "other," that is, the nurturers are "other" than the child's parents. While several species show some evidence of such caregiving practices, alloparenting tends to occur most frequently among those with highly social forms of organization—from elephants and porpoises to certain ant colonies as well as some sixty species of birds, according to Wilson.

Among humans, alloparents include not only grandparents, aunts, and uncles (like Michael and Jasmine in chapter 9) but nursemaids, babysitters, and day-care workers, for example, foster-, step-, and adoptive parents, as well as teachers and coaches. When others can help with nurturing roles, the society can better handle challenging social or environmental conditions, historically for example, dealing with food shortages, habitat change, or the threat of hostile groups.

I believe alloparenting highlights the sweet spot of form-giving structure with flexibility. The structure of caring for the next generation can be taken on by a variety of parents and nonparents. For the grandparents we spoke with, religious nurture was fundamental to this care.

* * *

"We really needed the church," Marco explained. "It takes a village and St. Peter's [United Methodist] was that for us. They really rose up; they supported us." Marco was raised in New York City and attended a church and school serving his Italian neighborhood. He is married to Mimi, raised in the same tradition, but from the midwestern city where we spoke. They had moved to Mimi's hometown some two decades earlier, attended her home church, but eventually became frustrated with the leadership. At that same point they were at a very vulnerable point in their lives. They had started a new career together by opening a restaurant; they had two young children; and they had a sense of estrangement from their own spiritual tradition. The couple eventually discovered and joined a United Methodist church in the neighborhood. It became a spiritual home. Marco said the power of the community lay in "just being there for us, supporting us emotionally. And then, small groups and Sunday school classes and things like that, which we didn't ever take part in at our other church—we didn't even know it was available." In addition to the emotional support, Mimi explained, the church provided business support in the form of bringing whole groups of people to their restaurant. Emotionally, spiritually, financially, the family eventually found solid ground for themselves and their family.

Mimi and Marco are now grandparents. Their daughter, Angela, and her husband, Randal, have two boys, Derick and Henry, four and seven years old, respectively. A critical point in the family had come a few years earlier, when the young parents moved in with Marco and Mimi.

Angela and Randal had gone to the same Methodist college, got married, and had been working for a Methodist church about a hundred miles away. They had their first baby, Henry, but during childbirth, Angela suffered an abruption (when the placenta tears away from the uterus), putting Henry and mother in grave danger—Henry from a lack of oxygen and Angela from internal bleeding. They survived, but the fallout for Angela was deep and intense—grief, postpartum depression, and an accompanying spiritual crisis.

At their church (where they worked) Angela said, "There were a few people that knew how to—" she cut herself off. "But, no one really came to visit me. No one checked on me. People didn't really know how to handle grief or—I don't know." Her halting description made clear how painful a time it was, yet she was trying to not simply trash-talk the congregation. She resumed, "That's when I started to really step away from the church, because I went through this really traumatic event and no one was really there for me. I felt really far from God at that time too."

The event and the fallout led Angela and Randal to rethink their vocation with the church, to rethink church itself, and even to rethink God. They knew they needed to regroup, and helping them to do so were Marco and Mimi, Angela's parents. They invited the young family—daughter, son-in-law, and new grandson—to move in until they could find steadier ground. They lived with Marco and Mimi several months until they found new work and their own place. Soon after, Angela began searching for emotional and spiritual support. "I got to a place where I was, like, I could walk away from faith because I'd been hurt by the church, and I felt abandoned in my time of need. And I started to wonder if God had abandoned me too? I was suicidal after almost dying. I had really bad postpartum depression, postpartum anxiety, OCD, all of that stuff. I'd never experienced mental health crisis before until that time."

Eventually, after several false starts with different therapists, Angela found a therapist she trusted, one who was also a relatively new grandmother and was particularly sensitive to the tribulations of new parenthood. The therapist was also a trained spiritual director, and though they did not focus upon spiritual practices, according to Angela, those sensibilities allowed Angela to voice her theological pain. "She helped me have multiplicative thinking," Angela said. I asked what she meant by that. "I think everything was so binary for me. And so, [the therapist facilitated] a more expansive view of God and church and the religious experience, the faith experience." For example, Angela said, "I started to pray to God the Mother, and I'd never done that before. I'd never thought of God like that." Recognizing Angela's intense reflective nature, the therapist eventually gave her resources and books that contributed to this theological expansiveness. "That helped me not walk away. She provided me with resources and a space to really examine all those parts of myself. And it was a very safe, gentle space."

As Angela spoke, I could see the parallels between the safe, gentle therapeutic space she found and the safe, gentle home of Marco and Mimi, if not the safe, gentle love of God the Mother. Multiplicative alloparenting perhaps, nurture from multiple directions.

During this time of spiritual turmoil, Mimi and Marco took the grandchildren to their church, the one that was so supportive and welcoming of them when they moved to town. Angela and Randal went sometimes, but they were not completely satisfied with the church. Part of their less binary theological thinking included reimagining God's relationship to those who identify as queer, according to Angela. The church, as of the time of the interview, was more ambivalent about its acceptance and inclusion policies. But Angela and Randal treasured the consistency for their children that Marco and Mimi provided by taking them while Angela and Randal scouted out other possible church homes. Besides, Angela said, "the kids love it."

"And how does that feel to be worshiping with your grandchildren?" Jane asked Mimi.

"It's wonderful," Mimi said.

Clearly alloparenting—whether at home or at church—is not only for the benefit of the next generation but brings its own joys to the caregivers.

* * *

Over the course of the research for this book, we spoke formally and casually with multiple grandparents who play some kind of role in the religious lives of their grandchildren. Often the situation was like Sarah's above, in which the parents are not very involved in church (for various reasons) but are happy to let grandparents take their kids to church. But as we can see from the lives of Angela and Randal, the role and potential support of grandparents can be particularly visible when something goes wrong. In these cases, we can see how homes, congregations, and therapist offices can have tremendous power in people's lives. This power can be used to intensify or reinscribe the suffering that people are going through, even if unintentional. But this power can also be used to create supportive, gentle, safe spaces for life-affirming love.

* * *

"It's very important as a parent, especially in the Black community, to bring your child and raise them up in the church, to give them that spiritual nurture, to give them God's word—just not to be street-taught, but to be taught in the church and a Christian family."

These comments are from Allison, a member of a historically Black Presbyterian church in a city in the mid-South. In our interview, she described how her own mother had been part of this church before Allison was born and reflected upon the importance of growing up in such a community of faith. "My mother was a strong, strong woman of the Lord, and being in her household, you were in church. I don't care what age you were." Allison not only brought up her son in the same way, but she was now bringing her grandson, Jordan, to church. It began when he started staying with her on weekends, when he was around seven, but it continued even when he stayed at home. "In my household," Allison continued, "as my mother's, if you're in my house, you're going to church."

Jordan's parents didn't like the church anymore, Allison explained without elaboration. (I later found out that several of that generation left the church because of a scandal with the former pastor.) Allison said that at first her grandson didn't like it either. "He wanted to know nothing about nothing that was going on with the church, because they had nothing to do with him." But over time that changed. "He's an usher, he sings in the choir. He loves the church, he loves the youth group, he loves going on mission trips."

Allison now travels frequently for her job, so she can't always get Jordan, fourteen, to church. But, as she explained, Jordan now pushes his father to get him there. "'Dad, I've got to go to church. Dad, I've got to go to choir rehearsal.' So now it's not so much pushing church on him as bringing him to church and allowing the Holy Spirit to just work through him, and to see his church family, because this is a family. We're small, but we're a loving family and a serving family of the community as well as the Lord. He just loves it."

"It sounds like it took," I commented.

"Yes, it did. It did. I'll fight the streets over him, but I think that once we get our kids grounded in the church and under the faith with Jesus Christ, it's not that they're sheltered from the streets, but they know their right and wrong. They know which side of the fence they're supposed to be on. They know that temptation and that sin. Whether you do it or not, you know that it's wrong. You know how you were raised and how you were brought up here. Our children and youth here I consider brothers and sisters."

Allison went on to explain how important the church has been to the surrounding community. "We have a lot of children from the community. A lot of the parents don't come, but that's okay. We have the children. We'll get the parents later. Let's just go ahead and get these kids in."

"I've seen that happen," I commented. "The kids end up being the ones bringing the parents back." Allison nodded. Here the congregation was serving as a community of alloparents.

To wrap up the interview I asked what else Allison thought would be helpful to know about her or the church. "This has been really helpful,"

I said, "because I turn around and teach people who are going to be pastors. So, with that in mind, are there things that you think could be helpful for pastors to be thinking about when they go to churches and they begin to think about Christian education with children, the importance of grandparents, parents in their lives? What kinds of things would you want me to share with future pastors?"

Allison responded: "One thing I want pastors to do is meet children and young adults right where they are. Meet them right where they are. Don't make them to be something that you would want them to be." She said that she's heard from young people not to just use them "as techies." That is, don't just ask kids to do the church Facebook page or run computers. "Use them for other things. They want to be a part. They want to be a voice." Allison told me how she and her friend Veronica, another grandmother of the church, were planning a brainstorming session with the kids and teens of the church. "That will be happening next month. We will ask them what they want. 'Write it down if you don't want to share, if you think somebody might laugh.' We want to see what they want out of the church."

As the conversation went on, it became clear that the idea was more than simply getting kids engaged in the life of the church, though that was certainly part of it. But meeting them where they are was more about understanding what they may be going through. "You don't know what they're dealing with right now. You have a lot of suicides, a lot with our young adults and a lot of our teens. You have a lot of this bullying going on." Allison summed up her advice: "just be a listening ear."

* * *

Veronica, the friend Allison referred to, the one helping to organize the listening session, has twelve grandchildren. Several of them are in the area, and most of them come to church with her, with the help of a church van that picks them up. She keeps several of the grandchildren every other weekend: "It's nothing for me to have eight or nine kids at once there, but it's fine. I love it." Like Allison, Veronica hopes church will provide a supportive and constructive foundation for the kids. "I want them to know about God, and that's the whole purpose," she said. "If you start them off young, maybe when they get to be teenagers, they might go away, but they'll come back. So, my mama raised me, when I was young, through the church. I raised my three boys through church and I'm trying to get my grandbabies." She mentioned how important it's been for them to be involved in multiple aspects of the church, from Sunday school and worship to community service, ushering, singing in choir, and hearing good preaching.

Of the dozen grandbabies, one of them is a teenager now, Melanie, who is fifteen. But more than raising her through the church, Veronica has been raising Melanie in her home since she was seven. Before that, Melanie was raised by her other grandmother—a Seventh-day Adventist—until that grandmother got sick and could no longer do so. Veronica said, "When I got her at seven, she was really going through a lot, but she really came around to be a young lady. She really has." However, Veronica explained, "She's stuck again right now because her father just got murdered in July." I let her know that the pastor had told me about this and how sorry I was. "So, she's mad at God right now." And, as if it weren't enough for her son to have been murdered, Veronica revealed that her own mother had just died, at eighty-six, of leukemia. "So, Melanie's mad because God took both of them. . . . She's trying to forgive him [God], but she's still mad about her daddy, which she doesn't understand."

In addition to getting some counseling for Melanie, Veronica tells her granddaughter to talk to God, to pray about her anger. "I told her, 'God will hear you. If you're mad at him, talk to him. He'll listen to you. . . . It's not always good things you talk to him about or thanking him for. You're mad, explain to him why you're mad. Maybe that will help.'"

Melanie's anger at God led her to want to stay away from church. But for Veronica, staying home from church was not an option. "I said, 'No, we're going to church and we're still going to go to Bible study.' I said, 'I still have to guide you.' Because she got baptized. When she was young, she got baptized." She turned her head as if talking to her granddaughter: "'I told the Lord that I was going to make sure I guide you, I promised to guide you through church.' I said, 'When you become eighteen, it's up to you. But I'm hoping that you would still keep church in your life.'" Turning back to me, she said, "But we come, we come to church, we come to Bible study. She's mad. She's still mad. But I've been trying to talk to her about it. I said, 'Melanie, I'm not trying to tell you, you shouldn't be mad.' I said, 'But we all are just going to be on this earth for a short time anyway.'" Veronica gave me a poignant look, admitting, "She already knows that," then concluded, "We're just here and it's a gift."

Realizing how much suffering Veronica herself has recently been through, I gently asked her whether she talks to God, whether that was her practice.

"Yes," she said. "I've been talking to him. Yes. Because I'm hurting. They took my son too, but he's in a better place." She began to cry.

We sat together quietly for a few moments. Veronica eventually continued. "I pray every night before I go to bed, and I still pray. I pray for everybody. I pray for people at work—when they're going through stuff. I pray for people here. I pray for my family and my grandbabies, my siblings. Then I ask God to touch me, help me. Whatever sins, forgive my sins for that day. I might've been mad, or I might have been hollering. Just help me. Make me more calm, make me understand more, and help guide me. Every night I do it. Sometimes I'll be praying and I fall asleep. I wake up in the night, I'm like, did I get everybody? Did I get everything? Then I might start again."

Veronica's tears as well as her prayers are a powerful reminder that grandparents who care for their grandchildren—when something has gone wrong—are suffering intensely even as they step up for the sake of loved ones. We can also glimpse in Veronica how thoroughly the love of God that she knows through prayer and her church sustains her. We can witness the wisdom at work in this grandmother to pass that love along to another generation that faces hard times.

* * *

Carol is a professor of nursing at a college serving rural Appalachia. She is also a nurse practitioner specializing in alternative, or integrative, medical practices. Her work focuses upon depression and digestive issues, which, she says, more often than not go hand in hand. She was raised Episcopalian but at thirteen converted to Roman Catholicism and is still deeply committed to the Roman Church and its spiritual practices. For example, she discussed with me how important Thomas Merton, the Trappist monk and theologian, had been to her over the years—having read all his books, including *Seven Story Mountain*, which she said she'd read at least twenty times.

Carol is also a grandmother of two. Her granddaughter, a two-year-old, lives hundreds of miles away but they FaceTime nearly every day. The other grandchild, seven, lives in the same town as Carol, and, as she told me, is on the autism spectrum. His name is Leo. "He is just the most joyful, magical child that you could ever meet. I mean, he is so full of life and joy." She took out her phone to show me pictures. "He's amazing." Tears came to her eyes talking about their relationship. "It's like he has trouble just staying tethered to this world. You know what I mean?"

"I think so," I said tentatively. I wasn't sure I did.

"It's like he's just—I can't really describe it. I mean, it wouldn't surprise me to see him just rise up. He's made from other stuff. I don't know." I was beginning to get the picture. Carol, deeply immersed in her Catholic spirituality as well as her medical knowledge, saw something more in her grandson than simply a label. It was as if "trouble staying tethered to this world" were both a medical and spiritual determination, a kind of spiritual realism. But, it became clear through our conversation, this insight had not come without some struggle along the way.

"I have to admit," she said, "in terms of him being on the spectrum, I used to be very contemptuous of parents and grandparents who refused to own what was going on with their children. 'That's not autism.' But I did the very same thing. I was the world's worst." Part of the trouble in accepting it was that "he had so many characteristics that were nothing like autism. He makes great eye contact. He's super affectionate, full of joy, and all these things. He expresses himself extremely well, but he also has classic autistic behaviors, and my daughter and son-in-law were the same way—they wouldn't call it autism either. We thought something else was going on with him, and of course when he was real little, it's hard to evaluate that anyway."

Carol explained that when Leo was four, they all realized that he was not developmentally where other four-year-olds typically are. "It was just a process of recognizing how far behind he was with certain things. He has tons of language. He can say whatever he wants to say. It's more in his processing what you say to him. That's where the breakdown occurs. Now, if you say something he's really interested in, I've noticed he's right there with you and he'll respond, but just normal everyday conversation, he just sits there and looks at you like you're nuts if you try to talk to him. And of course, someone like that, it's very hard for him to learn because that's the whole ball game. A child has to be able to listen and reproduce certain things. And we noticed that he couldn't—like two-step commands, two- or three-step commands. 'Leo, could you go in the kitchen and get a . . .' That wasn't computing. He couldn't do that or wouldn't do that." Leo also has sensitivity issues and gets overwhelmed by too much noise or loud talk. He wears headphones at school to mute out the other children in his special education class. After telling me more about the situation, Carol finally confessed that she was still somewhat baffled by trying to describe it all. "I'm not an autism expert."

I asked Carol how often she is able to spend time with Leo. She explained that her daughter, Lacy, Leo's mother, works part time for a law firm but can do that from home. "Basically, she's home all the time, but she needs a break from things because he's a challenge and so three days a week, I take care of him from about three until seven in the afternoon. That gives her and my son-in-law time to have a life of their own." Carol also spends Sunday afternoons with the family.

Carol and her daughter go to church together, but they don't take Leo. He stays home with his father, a nonpracticing Jew. Going to church without Leo has been hard for Carol, but Lacy believes Leo would be too disruptive either for a Sunday school class or for worship. Carol said, "Something that I looked so forward to is being part of that religious formation with my grandchildren just like I was with my children, and of course it's a challenge." She explained, "Those [religious ideas] are pretty complex concepts. He knows who Jesus is. I very intentionally wear my religious jewelry, and I buy him books that talk about Jesus, coloring books that have religious themes. When he sees Jesus, he knows that's Jesus, but to try to explain to him what that really means is impossible at this point. . . . Now, the thing with autism is you never know what's going to happen even next week. Children can suddenly—parts of their brains can start to wake up, parts that they haven't even been using. And I don't know five years from now, even a year from now, what kinds of strides Leo might make." Carol paused to think, then resumed. "I'm trying to be, I guess, a spiritual person around him to expose him to the kinds of things in the world that I feel are deeply spiritual that don't require words, different types of intelligence, natural intelligence, being outside, trying things that don't require an explanation. I try to do a lot of things like that with him." Nonetheless, Carol admitted, she wishes she could do more to help "to embrace things that he's just not able to right now."

Even so, Carol recognizes in Leo a deeply spiritual presence that has affected her deeply. "I still feel like he's an intensely spiritual person. I feel that from him all the time, and I feel like it's so easy for him to be that and to do that." Carol quoted from the wedding vows that her daughter and son-in-law took: "'You carry the light of God like it was nothing at all.' And that's how I feel about Leo. It's like it's so effortless for him to just be this shining being. He's not trying to be anything. He just is."

I wondered if Carol were describing another example of "lantern consciousness," and the glow of "just is," of "this shining being" reflecting the soft light of God's image.

"One of my questions," I said to Carol, "and you're in that territory already, is: How has being a parent, in this case a grandparent, affected your own spiritual life?"

Carol reflected a moment, then offered, "Being a grandparent in general has affected me deeply in a spiritual way. It's the cycle of life, the beauty of creation, how you can become part of creating human beings and then seeing them create human beings. I mean, it's mind-blowing really, to be perfectly honest with you, and I feel so lucky to have been able to give birth and then see my daughter give birth." She continued, "Those things have deepened my spirituality in ways I can't even describe, but having Leo has taken that to even another level in that I do feel like he has been entrusted to us in a really important way, and I don't think it's a way that any of us completely understand yet." She paused for a moment, then offered, "I just think he's been entrusted to us, but that he has a tremendous amount to teach us as well. And I think that's only just begun. I've learned so much from him already, but I think as time goes by, I really think it's going to be amazing what he has to teach us."

* * *

I don't know whether it is an empirical fact or simply folk wisdom, but the importance of grandparents in the religious imagination of children is often profound. I have frequently asked my students—most of whom become church leaders—about the role of grandparents in their spiritual lives. Overwhelmingly they name at least one grandparent who mattered deeply. Maybe they went to church with Grandma and can still hear her singing, slightly off-key, "How Great Thou Art." Perhaps they took turns reading the psalms together with Grandaddy as he healed from a heart attack. Maybe Pawpaw was the first family member to accept their sexual orientation. Or perhaps Mamaw was an avid defender of civil rights and took them to their first protest. From personal piety to social justice, the grandparents—relationships with grandparents—have been a spiritual treasure to these theological students, bearers of love.

And, as we've witnessed through the grandparents in this chapter, the grace flows in both directions.

Epilogue

EARLIER THIS YEAR, in the spring, my grandchildren—Jacob and Elly—and I went to the wide-open field behind their school to fly kites. At first there wasn't enough wind to sustain them, and I was disappointed. But not Elly and Jacob. They each created their own wind by running. And running and running and running. They were so excited to look behind them and see the kites in the air, maybe ten feet, as they ran. I was tickled that they so easily found a way to play.

Some twenty minutes later, a breeze blew in. I helped them get their kites up and showed them how to let the string out without getting too tangled. They each got their kites soaring. Jacob reached the end of his string, maybe 150 feet of line, and his kite was little more than a dot in the sky. Elly was nearing the end as well. They both had huge smiles on their faces, as did I. Jacob turned to me and said with the enthusiasm of an energetic six-year-old, "This is great!" He was enchanted.

"This *is* great!" I agreed.

* * *

Reflecting upon this afternoon with Jacob and Elly somehow captures the feeling I have for the project you've been reading about here.

Is the project great? I'm not saying that. I'm claiming that the time with children and their parents, the conversations and connections, the smiles and tears, the stories and surprises, the thoughtful reflections and sharing of time—overall, the opportunity to listen. All this was great.

The hunch driving the research was that children's religious imaginations are more complex than we typically realize. By "we" I mean those working with inherited theories that oversimplify childhood, with psychological assumptions that paint young minds as irrational, even with spiritual attitudes that, like those of the disciples, prevent children from approaching Jesus.

I leave it to you whether you believe the hunch was confirmed (but it was for me). Along the way my own spiritual life has been deepened by the experience, by the relationships—often lasting no more than the blinking by of an hour—that nonetheless helped me see the world in fresh ways.

I kept a notebook throughout, with ideas, quotes from interviews, themes, or ideas to follow up on for a book. I wrote lines like "greeted by child in robe with censor," "kids animated about *aluxes*," "God not he or she," "Freud's 'development' is dis-enchantment," "Elly and Curious George," "God in origins and endings." You get the idea. These are expanded upon in the book.

Other ideas were not. For example, at one point I wrote, "Play is the gravity," but now I'm not sure what I meant. I don't think it was a quote. I suspect it was an instruction to my future writing self. Perhaps it had to do with the discussion in chapter 4, about play and grace. Or maybe it was in reference to play and creativity—like Michael making up stories with his nephew in chapter 9.

I could have been thinking about the book of Zechariah, from which I had preached about the time I began the research. Zechariah returned from exile to a devastated Jerusalem, and though it seemed unimaginable at the time, he declares: "Thus says the LORD of hosts: Old men and old women shall again sit in the streets of Jerusalem, each with staff in hand because of their great age. And the streets of the city shall be full of boys and girls playing in its streets" (8:4–5). The word for streets is sometimes translated parks, or fields, or broad places. Children are playing in open spaces. Old folks will be there too. Grandmas and Pawpaws delighting in the joy of the next generation. The peaceable world depicted by Zechariah is a place where God is at home, where the Holy One dwells and delights and—who knows?—plays a game with kids.

In all, the reference to play in the note to myself is not baffling. But gravity? Gravity is sometimes a metaphor for sin—those temptations and ways of being always pulling on us and dragging us down. But there is no way I meant that. If anything, play is the opposite. Play suggests a freedom from such burdens. Because it's impossible to play when you are weighed down, overwhelmed, or afraid. Play is flying kites despite gravity. So, what was I thinking?

Maybe I saw a connection between gravity—which holds you to the ground—and children, who live and play near the ground, if not in the dirt and sand and mud puddles. More than once the Gospels tell us that Jesus invites us to lower our sights from mountaintops and power, to children and the least among us.

Then again, gravity is a fundamental force of the universe—attracting and holding together anything with mass—whether our bodies to the ground or planets orbiting the sun. What would it mean to think of play as a fundamental force of reality? Play as the force attracting us together, around which life orbits. More than a few theologians have described the life of the Trinity—the inner relations of the persons—as a playful dance of delight, and creation as God's desire for the cosmos to join the dance.

* * *

If this divine dance is the deep nature of play, then it is tightly associated with love. The love of God for the world, the love of parents for children, the love of children for others. If there is a deep theme to the conversations in this book, it is love. Parents want their children to know that they are loved not only by them but by the one who created life. God's love, a kite string connecting the heavens to the earth, to the body of a child. Children not only get it, but they help their parents—if not researchers—understand this love in ever deeper ways.

I am enchanted.

Acknowledgments

THANK YOU TO all the children, parents, grandparents who were willing to talk with us and share their understandings of faith and love. If I could name you without betraying confidentiality, I would. Likewise, thank you to the many unnamed church leaders and friends who helped arrange these interviews across the country and the Yucatan. I'm deeply grateful for the researchers who helped conduct these conversations: Jane Larsen-Wigger, Joanna Hipp, Megan McCarty, Daniela Bartlett-Asenjo, and Annie Williams as well as translator Cathy Harrison (in Mexico).

This project would not have been possible without support from several institutions. Initial funding came through the Henry Luce III Fellows in Theology program, followed by support from the Lilly Endowment (funding the Mapping Children's Faith Formation Project at Union Theological Presbyterian Seminary as well as the Christian Parenting & Caregiving Program of Louisville Presbyterian Theological Seminary). I am grateful to the board of the seminary as well as to my colleagues for providing the time and support to carry out the research and writing.

This book is derived in part from the article (2019) "The Religious

Imagination of Children Project: An Initial Research Report," *International Journal of Children's Spirituality* 24, no. 3: 228–42, copyright Taylor and Francis, available online: http://www.tandfonline.com. https://doi.org/10.1080/1364436X.2019.1652572. Versions of two stories in this book (David's dream and Cora's birth) are drawn from my book *The Power of God at Home: Nurturing Our Children in Love and Grace* (San Francisco: Jossey-Bass, 2003). All rights have since reverted to the author. All biblical quotes are from the New Revised Standard Version Bible unless otherwise noted.

I am grateful to the terrific team at Eerdmans for shepherding this work to publication: Kimberly Benedict, Tom Raabe, Laurel Draper, Jeff Dundas, Amy Kent, and James Ernest. Thank you for giving the book and all its voices a home.

Notes

Introduction

1. I first told this story in J. Bradley Wigger, *The Power of God at Home: Nurturing Our Children in Love and Grace* (San Francisco: Jossey-Bass, 2003), 23–24.

2. On the banking method, see Paolo Freire, *Pedagogy of the Oppressed* (New York: Seabury, 1970).

3. Funding for this research over the years has come from the University of Oxford Cognition, Religion, and Theology Project; the John Templeton Foundation; the Luce Foundation; and the Lilly Endowment.

4. Janis Clark Johnston, *It Takes a Child to Raise a Parent: Stories of Evolving Child and Parent Development* (Lanham, MD: Rowman & Littlefield, 2013), 16.

5. In addition to the 151 children for the Religious Imagination of Children Project, I interviewed over 500 children for the earlier Invisible Friend Project (which is described more fully in chapter 1).

Chapter 1. Imagination

1. A version of the story of Elly and Curious George was published in J. Bradley Wigger, "The Religious Imagination of Children Project: An Initial Research Report," *International Journal of Children's Spirituality* 24, no. 3 (2019): 228–42, https://doi.org/10.1080/1364436X.2019.1652572. In the article, identities in this story were disguised for anonymity, but here, permission was granted to use real names.

2. Over the past hundred years the imagination has been berated, celebrated, ignored, or explored, depending upon the mood of the times or the mind-set of the psychological circle. Behaviorists like James Watson or B. F. Skinner more or less denied any inner life, while Sigmund Freud thought early psychic life was all fantasy. Others with more Romantic bents, such as Carl Jung or his mentor, Eugen Bleuler, understood the imagination as an important contributor not only to individual well-being but to cultural and religious vitality as well.

3. See Sigmund Freud, *An Outline of Psychoanalysis* (New York: Norton, 1949).

4. For more on God as a Freudian fantasy, see Sigmund Freud, *Totem and Taboo: Resemblances Between the Psychic Lives of Savages and Neurotics* (London: Routledge & Kegan Paul, 1950). Freud traces the "development" of humanity as a whole from the infancy of a magical animism through the moralistic codes of formal religions to the emergence of the clear-eyed rationality of scientific thought that sloughs off the fantasy figure of God.

5. "The child's mind," Piaget writes, "is full of these ludistic tendencies up to the age of 7 or 8, which means that before this age it is extremely difficult for [the child] to distinguish between fabulation and truth." Jean Piaget, *Judgement and Reasoning in the Child*, trans. Margorie Warden (New York: Harcourt, Brace, 1928), 202.

6. Both observations regarding Jacqueline are in Jean Piaget, *Play, Dreams, and Imitation in Childhood*, trans. C. Gattegno and F. M. Hodgson (New York: Norton, 1962), 131–32. Jacqueline also had a shape-shifting imaginary creature, Aseau (similar to the French *oiseau*, for bird), when she was four. Aseau could be a bird or a dog, and after

about two months became a girl who continued to take on new forms and names over time. Aseau was created, according to Piaget, in order to have a "sympathetic audience" whenever she wanted one and served as "a mirror for the ego" (129–30). At a more technical level, Piaget says what is typically called imagination or an imaginative symbol in young children is a misnomer. "In reality the child has no imagination, and what we ascribe to him is no more than lack of coherence, and still more, subjective assimilation" (131).

7. Examples of this newer generation of research include the following figures and works. Howard Gardner, *Frames of Mind: The Theory of Multiple Intelligences* (New York: Basic Books, 1983), makes a strong case that intelligence itself is multiple rather than the singular phenomenon measured by an IQ test. Marjorie Taylor, *Imaginary Companions and the Children Who Create Them* (Oxford: Oxford University Press, 1999), and Marjorie Taylor and Stephanie M. Carlson, "The Relation Between Individual Differences in Fantasy and Theory of Mind," *Child Development* 68 (1997): 436–55, doi:10.2307/1131670, show the constructive role of pretend play in childhood and contribute deeply to my own work on the subject: J. Bradley Wigger, *Invisible Companions: Encounters with Imaginary Friends, Gods, Ancestors, and Angels* (Stanford, CA: Stanford University Press, 2019). Justin Barrett, *Why Would Anyone Believe in God?* (Walnut Creek, CA: AltaMira, 2004), and *Born Believers: The Science of Children's Religious Belief* (New York: Free Press, 2012), shows how complex children's understanding of God is. Paul Harris, *The Work of the Imagination* (Oxford: Blackwell, 2000), and Maria Dias and Paul Harris, "The Effect of Make-Believe Play on Deductive Reasoning," *British Journal of Developmental Psychology* 6 (1988): 207–21, doi:10.1111/j.2044-835X.1988.tb01095.x, demonstrate how fundamentally social and logical young children are. All these have deeply shaped the picture of childhood described here as well as my own research.

8. For more about the prevalence of IFs, see J. Bradley Wigger, "Invisible Friends Across Four Countries: Kenya, Malawi, Nepal and the Dominican Republic," *International Journal of Psychology* 53 (2018): 46–52, doi.org/10.1002/ijop.12423j.

9. On children imagining invisibles, see Paul Harris, *Trusting What*

You're Told: How Children Learn from Others (Cambridge, MA: Belknap Press of Harvard University Press, 2012).

10. In the case of Hindu and Buddhist children in Nepal, we asked what "a god" would think, then followed with "what god were you thinking of?" Out of eighty-nine interviews, thirteen different deities were named.

11. For more, see Wigger, *Invisible Companions*; J. Bradley Wigger, Katrina Paxson, and Lacey Ryan, "What Do Invisible Friends Know? Imaginary Companions, God, and Theory of Mind," *International Journal for the Psychology of Religion* 23 (2013): 2–14, doi.org/10.1080/10508619.2013.739059; as well as Emily Burdett, J. Bradley Wigger, and Justin Barrett, "The Minds of God, Mortals, and In-Betweens: Children's Developing Understanding of Extraordinary and Ordinary Minds Across Four Countries," *Psychology of Religion and Spirituality* 13 (2021): 212–21, doi.org/10.1037/rel0000285.

12. On understanding God based on humans, see Jean Piaget, *The Child's Conception of the World*, trans. Joan Tomlinson and Andrew Tomlinson (London: Kegan Paul, 1929). Unlike Freud, Piaget did not go so far as to describe God or religion as a ludistic compensation or product of wish fulfillment. But drawing on Piaget's theory that children base their understanding of God upon their understanding of humans, the influential religious educator Ronald Goldman believed that children generally move from "gross materialistic and crude anthropomorphic thinking to the view that God is unseeable because of his spiritual nature." Drawing on examples from children six to eleven years old, Goldman summarizes, "God is seen in purely physical and human terms." In other words, children are "concrete thinkers" about God until adolescence. Ronald Goldman, *Religious Thinking from Childhood to Adolescence* (New York: Seabury, 1968), 88–90. The work was originally published in 1965 by Humanities Press.

13. The most plausible explanation I find for why young children did not differentiate types of minds in the surprising-contents task has to do with the development of executive function in young children, the part of the mind that learns to inhibit behavior. In this case, knowledge of the surprise tends to override their reflective ability.

14. For a fuller description of perception theory in a historical perspective, see J. Bradley Wigger, *The Texture of Mystery: An Interdisciplinary Inquiry into Perception and Learning* (Lewisburg, PA: Bucknell University Press, 1998).

15. For a summary of the core kinds of knowledge and expectations of babies, see Elizabeth S. Spelke and Katherine D. Kinzler, "Core Knowledge," *Developmental Science* 10, no. 1 (2007): 89–96, and Annette Karmiloff-Smith, *Beyond Modularity: A Developmental Perspective on Cognitive Science* (Cambridge, MA: MIT Press, 1992), chapter 5.

16. For more on pretend play in the second year of life, see Harris, *The Work of the Imagination.*

17. Alison Gopnik, *The Philosophical Baby: What Children's Minds Tell Us About Truth, Love, and the Meaning of Life* (New York: Farrar, Straus & Giroux, 2009), 110.

18. Gopnik's question (the title of chapter 4) is a clever play on a famous philosophical question posed by Thomas Nagel, "What Is It Like to Be a Bat?," *Philosophical Review* 83 (1974): 435–50, doi.org/10.2307/2183914. As Nagel points out, we can describe all kinds of aspects of a bat's life, from its ability to fly to feeding habits to its primary reliance upon echolocation to navigate the world, but we cannot know or describe what being a bat feels like to a bat. There is an irreducible, subjective, first-person (or first-bat) experience that those of us who walk along the ground on two legs without sonar and avoiding mosquitoes cannot access.

19. Quotes come from Gopnik, *Philosophical Baby*, 114, 125, 129, and 130. For more on the "I don't know" state, see Wigger, *Texture of Mystery*, 98.

20. "Transcript: Ezra Klein Interviews Alison Gopnik," *New York Times*, The Ezra Klein Show, April 16, 2021, https://tinyurl.com/dza5j5cv. In addition, the science writer Annie Murphy Paul finds that adults can experience this lantern form of attention through time in nature, when "we're not focusing very intently on anything but we're just kind of allowing the gentle movements and the sort of soft contours of the things that we see outside just entertain our attention but in this very diffuse way." In contrast to a "hard-edged concentration,"

she refers to "a kind of soft fascination that you might experience when you're looking at leaves rustling in the wind or watching waves on the ocean." "This Conversation Will Change How You Think About Thinking," interview with Annie Murphy Paul, *New York Times*, The Ezra Klein Show, July 20, 2021, https://tinyurl.com/mtar555t.

21. I first told of this experience of Cora's birth in Wigger, *The Power of God at Home*, 72.

22. Charles Taylor, *A Secular Age* (Cambridge, MA: Belknap Press of Harvard University Press, 2007). Taylor discusses the "porous self" beginning on p. 35.

23. Abraham Joshua Heschel, *Man Is Not Alone: A Philosophy of Religion* (New York: Farrar, Straus & Giroux, 1951), 13.

Chapter 2. Origins

1. For more on the logic experiments, see Dias and Harris, "Effect of Make-Believe Play," 207–21. See also Maria da Graça B. B. Dias et al., "Logical Reasoning and Fantasy Contexts: Eliminating Differences Between Children with and Without Experience in School," *Revista Interamericana de Psicologia/Interamerican Journal of Psychology* 39, no. 1 (2005): 13–22. The 2005 study was conducted cross-culturally and found that the effects were no different whether the children had been in school or not. Piaget (*Judgement and Reasoning in the Child*) thought children had to be much older, on the cusp of formal operations, to be able to correctly solve syllogisms with premises incongruent with experience (that is, that cats bark).

2. For the record, the Presbyterian Church (USA) denomination, to which Hannah's church belongs, affirms "that there is no contradiction between an evolutionary theory of human origins and the doctrine of God as Creator" (*Minutes of the 214th General Assembly, 2002*, resolution item 09-08, 2, p. 495).

3. *The Doctrine and Covenants of the Church of Jesus Christ of Latter-day Saints: Containing Revelations Given to Joseph Smith, the Prophet with Some*

Additions by His Successors in the Presidency of the Church (Salt Lake City: Church of Jesus Christ of Latter-day Saints, 2013).

4. *The Book of Moses* is part of *The Pearl of Great Price: A Selection from the Revelations, Translations, and Narrations of Joseph Smith, First Prophet, Seer, and Revelator to the Church of Jesus Christ of Latter-day Saints* (Salt Lake City: Church of Jesus Christ of Latter-day Saints, 2013).

5. For the story of Er, see Plato, *The Republic*, trans. Benjamin Jowett (New York: Modern Library, 1982), 10.617.

6. Harris, *Trusting What You're Told*, 2.

7. For the testimony experiments, see Harris, *Trusting What You're Told*, chap. 1.

8. Harris, *Trusting What You're Told*, chap. 5.

9. Harris, *Trusting What You're Told*, 87.

10. Harris, *Trusting What You're Told*, 210.

Chapter 3. Faith Communities

1. For more on social support measures, see Robert G. Crosby III, Erin I. Smith, and Thomas V. Frederick, "The Kid-Friendly Church: What Makes Children Feel Loved, Valued, and Part of a Supportive Church Community," *Journal of Family and Community Ministries* 28, no. 1 (2015): 87–109.

2. Crosby, Smith, and Frederick, "The Kid-Friendly Church." Quotes from children regarding the ways they feel support are from pp. 91–97.

3. For their study, see Erin Smith and Robert Crosby III, "Unpacking Religious Affiliation: Exploring Associations Between Christian Children's Religious Cultural Context, God Image, and Self-Esteem Across Development," *British Journal of Developmental Psychology: Special Issue Paper* (2016): 1–15, doi:10.1111/bjdp.12156.

4. Christian Smith, Bridget Ritz, and Michael Rotolo, *Religious Parenting: Transmitting Faith and Values in Contemporary America*

(Princeton: Princeton University Press, 2020), quotes from p. 267 and appendix.

Chapter 4. We Need a Place

1. Alison Gopnik, *The Gardener and the Carpenter: What the New Science of Child Development Tells Us About the Relationship Between Parents and Children* (New York: Picador, 2016), 108.

2. Albert J. Raboteau, *A Sorrowful Joy: A Spiritual Journey of an African-American Man in Late Twentieth-Century America* (Eugene, OR: Wipf & Stock, 2012), 41–42, 50.

3. Frank Marangos, "Storytelling and Children," in Zoe Kanavas, *The Bible for Young People*, trans. Spencer T. Kezios, illustrated by Christos Gousides (Northridge, CA: Narthex, 2005), 9.

4. Katherine Paterson, *Bridge to Terabithia* (New York: HarperCollins, 1977), 38–40.

5. Pannenberg points out that playing and games can be used simply to entertain and distract people from the abuse of power by leaders and unjust systems. In this case, "games become a compensation for the meaninglessness of life in the modern world of labor and professional work. The separation of work and play makes it especially clear that life in the modern industrial societies is alienating." Wolfhart Pannenberg, *Anthropology in Theological Perspective*, trans. Matthew J. O'Connell (Philadelphia: Westminster, 1985), 334. In other words, the very act of separating play out from other aspects of life allows it to be twisted into an escapist opiate.

6. Courtney J. Goto, *The Grace of Playing: Pedagogies for Leaning into God's New Creation* (Eugene, OR: Pickwick, 2016), 49. Goto's thought here is playing off the theology of J. Moltmann, but her linking of play to love is her own contribution, consistent with Moltmann's theology of play and creation.

7. Goto, *The Grace of Playing*, 128.

8. Raboteau, *A Sorrowful Joy*, 48.

9. The quotes are from an interview for National Public Radio by Merrit Kennedy, "44,000-Year-Old Indonesian Cave Painting Is Rewriting the

History of Art," NPR, All Things Considered, December 11, 2019, https://tinyurl.com/4v6w9eh9. For the original publication of the discovery, see Maxime Aubert, Rustan Lebe, et al., "Earliest Hunting Scene in Prehistoric Art," *Nature* 576 (2019): 442–45, doi.org/10.1038/s41586-019-1806-y.

10. On Ninkasi, see J. A. Black et al., "A Hymn to Ninkasi," in *The Electronic Text Corpus of Sumerian Literature*, t.r.23.1, 2nd ed. (Oxford: Faculty of Oriental Studies, University of Oxford, 2006), https://etcsl.orinst.ox.ac.uk/.

11. Abraham Joshua Heschel, *Israel: An Echo of Eternity* (New York: Farrar, Straus & Giroux, 1967), 11.

Chapter 5. Capillaries of Presence

1. To be precise, the children interviewed in Mexico were Yucatec Mayan, as there are many ethno-linguistic groups within the Mayan world. But in the Yucatan, there is only one indigenous ethnic group, so they refer to themselves as simply "Mayan." The one child not Catholic was from a Pentecostal tradition.

2. For the Mayan deity Itzamna, see Karl Taube, *The Major Gods of Ancient Yucatan* (Washington, DC: Dumbarton Oaks Research Library and Collection, 1992), 31ff.

3. For more on the history of Mayan temples and their construction, see Takeshi Inomata et al., "Monumental Architecture at Aguada Fénix and the Rise of Maya Civilization," *Nature* 582 (2020): 530–33, https://doi.org/10.1038/s41586-020-2343-4.

4. On the roots of the Black Christ in Guatemala, see Douglass Sullivan-González, *The Black Christ of Esquipulas: Religion and Identity in Guatemala* (Lincoln: University of Nebraska Press, 2016).

5. Robert A. Orsi, *History and Presence* (Cambridge, MA: Belknap Press of Harvard University Press, 2016), 61–62, 68.

6. Franz Rosenzweig, *Der Stern der Erlosung*, 3rd ed., vol. 3 (Heidelberg, 1954), 192ff., quoted in Jürgen Moltmann, *Trinity and the Kingdom* (San Francisco: Harper & Row, 1981), 29.

7. On the pathos of God, see Abraham Joshua Heschel, *The Prophets*, vol. 2 (New York: Harper & Row, 1962), 39.

8. Moltmann, *Trinity and the Kingdom*, 30.

9. For more on the Day of the Dead, see *Hanal Pixán Yesterday and Today: The Mayan Ritual of the Dead* (Merida, Mexico: Editorial Dante, 2004).

10. For more on the role of ancestors, see Wigger, *Invisible Companions*, chapter 7, "Ancestors and Angels."

11. T. M. Luhrmann, *When God Talks Back: Understanding the American Evangelical Relationship with God* (New York: Knopf, 2012), preface, quote from ix.

12. Luhrmann, *When God Talks Back*, chapter 3, quotes from 73–74.

13. Here Luhrmann (*When God Talks Back*, 100) is quoting Johan Huizinga, *Homo Ludens* (London: Routledge & Kegan Paul, 1949), 25.

14. Quotes are from Luhrmann, *When God Talks Back*, 100.

15. On widespread belief in guardian angels, see Susan R. Garrett, *No Ordinary Angel: Celestial Spirits and Christian Claims About Jesus* (New Haven: Yale University Press, 2008), 143.

16. While Sally was happy to call Deen and Elisabeth imaginary, neither she nor her parents called Pawpaw John "imaginary." This is another example of why I tend to use the term "invisible friends" rather than "imaginary friends."

17. Will Rodriguez, *The Great Book of Mayan Legends*, trans. David Phillips (Merida, Mexico: Dante, 2015), 24.

18. See Wigger, *Invisible Companions*, 42. The comedian Jay Ellis speaks to this anxiety in his entertaining *Did Everyone Have an Imaginary Friend (or Just Me)? Adventures in Boyhood* (New York: One World, 2024), especially chapters 1 and 2.

19. For a description of the *alux*, see Rodriguez, *Great Book of Mayan Legends*, chapter 1.

20. The shelter or small temple is under the Nizuc-Cancun bridge near the international airport and connects the city to the beachfront hotel zone.

21. On shamanism, see Bruce Love, *Maya Shamanism Today: Connecting with the Cosmos in Rural Yucatan* (San Francisco: Precolumbia Mesoweb Press, 2012). The quote is from the Kindle edition, location 111. It is not unusual for devout Catholics to also visit a shaman for

help. For example, Natalia's grandmother told of taking Natalia to a shaman because she'd had a several-day bout of diarrhea. The shaman traced the problem to a turkey Natalia had encountered, and he had the family bathe the turkey, then use the same bathwater to wash Natalia. According to the grandmother, the illness was gone within two days.

Chapter 6. The Way of Parenthood

1. Glenys Nellist, *I Wonder: Exploring God's Grand Story*, illustrated by Alessandra Fusi (Grand Rapids: Zonderkidz, 2021). Quotes are from 178–80.

2. Heschel, *Man Is Not Alone*, 12.

3. Nancy Fuchs, *Our Share of Night, Our Share of Morning: Parenting as a Spiritual Journey* (San Francisco: HarperSanFrancisco, 1996), 3.

4. Martin Buber, *I and Thou* (New York: Scribner, 1958), 18.

5. Smith, Ritz, and Rotolo, *Religious Parenting*, 129ff.

6. Gopnik, *The Gardener and the Carpenter*, quotes from 18–19, 23–24.

7. See Michael Tomasello et al., "Understanding and Sharing Intentions: The Origins of Cultural Cognition," *Behavioral and Brain Sciences* 28 (2005): 675–735, esp. 679, doi.10.1017/S0140525X05000129. See also J. Bradley Wigger, *Original Knowing: How Religion, Science, and the Human Mind Point to the Irreducible Depth of Life* (Eugene, OR: Cascade, 2012), chapter 13.

8. Gabriel Marcel, *The Mystery of Being*, vol. 1 (Lanham, MD: University Press of America, 1950), 216–17.

9. Craig Dykstra, *Vision and Character: A Christian Educator's Alternative to Kohlberg* (New York: Paulist, 1981), 36–37.

10. Craig Dykstra, "A Way of Seeing," *Christian Century*, April 8, 2008, 26–31, quotes from 28–29.

Chapter 7. Dreams

1. On dreams and counterfactual thinking, see Patrick McNamara, *An Evolutionary Psychology of Sleep and Dreams* (Westport, CT: Praeger, 2004), 106–8.

2. Taylor and Carlson, "Relation Between Individual Differences."

3. Taylor, *Imaginary Companions*, 47.

4. Wendell Berry, "Manifesto: The Mad Farmer Liberation Front," in *The Country of Marriage* (New York: Harcourt Brace Jovanovich, 1973).

Chapter 8. Stretching Religious Imaginations

1. David Shelf, *All We Are Saying: The Last Major Interview with John Lennon and Yoko Ono* (New York: St. Martin's, 2000), 212. Thank you to my pastor, Christine Coy-Fohr, for putting me on to this story.

2. Like all the churches discussed in this book, Garden Church is not the real name of the congregation. To protect anonymity in such a small, unique situation, I have not identified the denomination of which it is a part either.

3. See the Farminary website, Princeton Theological Seminary, accessed May 30, 2025, https://ptsem.edu/academics/departments/farminary/. The quote is from the Farminary Vision page.

4. Wild Church Network, accessed May 30, 2025, www.wildchurchnetwork.com; quotes from the "About Us" page.

Chapter 9. Countercultural Rhythms

1. Quotations come from Smith, *Religious Parenting*, 42–43.

2. For Fromm on love, see Erich Fromm, *The Art of Loving* (New York: Harper & Row, 1956), esp. chapter 2.

3. See Robert Coles, *Their Eyes Meeting the World: The Drawings and Paintings of Children* (Boston: Houghton Mifflin, 1992), quotes from 1, 3, 7–8.

Chapter 10. Endings

1. David Bentley Hart, *That All Shall Be Saved* (New Haven: Yale University Press, 2019), quote from 204–5. Hart asks if we can imagine

"that someone still in torment after a trillion ages, or then a trillion trillion, or then a trillion vigintillion, is in any meaningful sense the same agent who contracted some measurable quantity of personal guilt in that tiny, ever more vanishingly insubstantial gleam of an instant that constituted his or her terrestrial life" (203).

2. Erich Fromm quotes are from *The Art of Loving*, 8–9.

Chapter 11. Grandparents

1. For alloparenting, see E. O. Wilson, *Sociobiology: The New Synthesis*, 25th anniversary ed. (Cambridge, MA: Belknap Press of Harvard University Press, 1975/2000), 349–52. Specific examples of alloparenting behavior vary widely from species to species. Mother langurs (a type of old-world monkey of India) allow other females to handle a newborn almost immediately—allowing as many as eight individuals to pass the infant back and forth on the first day. Baboon mothers, on the other hand, resist such access, even when others try to harass them into compliance. Among other primates, such as chimps, mothers show preference for older siblings of the infant to help with care.

Bibliography

Aubert, Maxime, Rustan Lebe, et al. "Earliest Hunting Scene in Prehistoric Art." *Nature* 576 (2019): 442–45. doi.org/10.1038/s41586-019-1806-y.

Barrett, Justin. *Born Believers: The Science of Children's Religious Belief*. New York: Free Press, 2012.

———. *Why Would Anyone Believe in God?* Walnut Creek, CA: AltaMira, 2004.

Berry, Wendell. *The Country of Marriage*. New York: Harcourt Brace Jovanovich, 1973.

Black, J. A., G. Cunningham, J. Ebeling, E. Flückiger-Hawker, E. Robson, J. Taylor, and G. Zólyomi. *The Electronic Text Corpus of Sumerian Literature*. Oxford, 1998–2006. http://etcsl.orinst.ox.ac.uk/.

Buber, Martin. *I and Thou*. New York: Scribner, 1958.

Burdett, Emily, J. Bradley Wigger, and Justin Barrett. "The Minds of God, Mortals, and In-Betweens: Children's Developing Understanding of Extraordinary and Ordinary Minds Across Four Countries." *Psychology of Religion and Spirituality* 13 (2021): 212–21. doi.org/10.1037/rel0000285.

Coles, Robert. *Their Eyes Meeting the World: The Drawings and Paintings of Children*. Boston: Houghton Mifflin, 1992.

Crosby, Robert G., III, Erin I. Smith, and Thomas V. Frederick. "The Kid-Friendly Church: What Makes Children Feel Loved, Valued, and Part of a Supportive Church Community." *Journal of Family and Community Ministries* 28, no. 1 (2015): 87–109.

Dias, Maria, and Paul Harris. "The Effect of Make-Believe Play on Deductive Reasoning." *British Journal of Developmental Psychology* 6 (1988): 207–21. doi:10.1111/j.2044-835X.1988.tb01095.x.

Dias, Maria da Graça B. B., Antonio Roazzi, David P. O'Brien, and Paul L. Harris. "Logical Reasoning and Fantasy Contexts: Eliminating Differences Between Children with and Without Experience in School." *Revista Interamericana de Psicologia/Interamerican Journal of Psychology* 39, no. 1 (2005): 13–22.

The Doctrine and Covenants of the Church of Jesus Christ of Latter-day Saints: Containing Revelations Given to Joseph Smith, the Prophet with Some Additions by His Successors in the Presidency of the Church. Salt Lake City: Church of Jesus Christ of Latter-day Saints, 2013.

Dykstra, Craig. *Vision and Character: A Christian Educator's Alternative to Kohlberg*. New York: Paulist, 1981.

———. "A Way of Seeing." *Christian Century*, April 8, 2008, 26–31.

Ellis, Jay. *Did Everyone Have an Imaginary Friend (or Just Me)? Adventures in Boyhood*. New York: One World, 2024.

The Farminary. Princeton Theological Seminary. 2025. https://ptsem.edu/academics/departments/farminary/.

Freire, Paolo. *Pedagogy of the Oppressed*. New York: Seabury, 1970.

Freud, Sigmund. *An Outline of Psychoanalysis*. New York: Norton, 1949.

———. *Totem and Taboo: Resemblances Between the Psychic Lives of Savages and Neurotics*. London: Routledge & Kegan Paul, 1950.

Fromm, Erich. *The Art of Loving*. New York: Harper & Row, 1956.

Fuchs, Nancy. *Our Share of Night, Our Share of Morning: Parenting as a Spiritual Journey*. San Francisco: HarperSanFrancisco, 1996.

Gardner, Howard. *Frames of Mind: The Theory of Multiple Intelligences*. New York: Basic Books, 1983.

Garrett, Susan R. *No Ordinary Angel: Celestial Spirits and Christian Claims About Jesus*. New Haven: Yale University Press, 2008.

Goldman, Ronald. *Religious Thinking from Childhood to Adolescence*. New York: Seabury, 1968.

Gopnik, Alison. *The Gardener and the Carpenter: What the New Science of Child Development Tells Us About the Relationship Between Parents and Children*. New York: Picador, 2016.

———. *The Philosophical Baby: What Children's Minds Tell Us About Truth, Love, and the Meaning of Life*. New York: Farrar, Straus & Giroux, 2009.

———. "Transcript: Ezra Klein Interviews Alison Gopnik." *New York Times*, The Ezra Klein Show, April 16, 2021. https://tinyurl.com/dza5j5cv.

Goto, Courtney J. *The Grace of Playing: Pedagogies for Leaning into God's New Creation*. Eugene, OR: Pickwick, 2016.

Hanal Pixán Yesterday and Today: The Mayan Ritual of the Dead. Merida, Mexico: Editorial Dante, 2004.

Harris, Paul. *Trusting What You're Told: How Children Learn from Others*. Cambridge, MA: Belknap Press of Harvard University Press, 2012.

———. *The Work of the Imagination*. Oxford: Blackwell, 2000.

Hart, David Bentley. *That All Shall Be Saved*. New Haven: Yale University Press, 2019.

Heschel, Abraham Joshua. *Israel: An Echo of Eternity*. New York: Farrar, Straus & Giroux, 1967.

———. *Man Is Not Alone: A Philosophy of Religion*. New York: Farrar, Straus & Giroux, 1951.

———. *The Prophets*. Vol. 2. New York: Harper & Row, 1962.

Huizinga, Johan. *Homo Ludens*. London: Routledge & Kegan Paul, 1949.

Inomata, Takeshi, Daniela Triadan, Veronica A. Vázquez, et al. "Monumental Architecture at Aguada Fénix and the Rise of Maya Civilization." *Nature* 582 (2020): 530–33. https://doi.org/10.1038/s41586-020-2343-4.

Johnston, Janis Clark. *It Takes a Child to Raise a Parent: Stories of*

Evolving Child and Parent Development. Lanham, MD: Rowman & Littlefield, 2013.

Karmiloff-Smith, Annette. *Beyond Modularity: A Developmental Perspective on Cognitive Science*. Cambridge, MA: MIT Press, 1992.

Kennedy, Merrit. "44,000-Year-Old Indonesian Cave Painting Is Rewriting the History of Art." NPR, All Things Considered, December 11, 2019. https://tinyurl.com/4v6w9eh9.

Love, Bruce. *Maya Shamanism Today: Connecting with the Cosmos in Rural Yucatan*. San Francisco: Precolumbia Mesoweb Press, 2012. Kindle edition.

Luhrmann, T. M. *When God Talks Back: Understanding the American Evangelical Relationship with God*. New York: Knopf, 2012.

Marangos, Frank. "Storytelling and Children." In Zoe Kanavas, *The Bible for Young People*, translated by Spencer T. Kezios, illustrated by Christos Gousides. Northridge, CA: Narthex, 2005.

Marcel, Gabriel. *The Mystery of Being*. Vol. 1. Lanham, MD: University Press of America, 1950.

McNamara, Patrick. *An Evolutionary Psychology of Sleep and Dreams*. Westport, CT: Praeger, 2004.

Minutes of the 214th General Assembly, 2002. Presbyterian Church (USA). Resolution Item 09-08, 2.

Moltmann, Jürgen. *Trinity and the Kingdom*. San Francisco: Harper & Row, 1981.

Nagel, Thomas. "What Is It Like to Be a Bat?" *Philosophical Review* 83 (1974): 435–50. doi.org/10.2307/2183914.

Nellist, Glenys. *I Wonder: Exploring God's Grand Story*. Illustrated by Alessandra Fusi. Grand Rapids: Zonderkidz, 2021.

Orsi, Robert A. *History and Presence*. Cambridge, MA: Belknap Press of Harvard University Press, 2016.

Pannenberg, Wolfhart. *Anthropology in Theological Perspective*. Translated by Matthew J. O'Connell. Philadelphia: Westminster, 1985.

Paterson, Katherine. *Bridge to Terabithia*. New York: HarperCollins, 1977.

Paul, Annie Murphy. "This Conversation Will Change How You Think About Thinking." Interview. *New York Times*, The Ezra Klein Show, July 20, 2021. https://tinyurl.com/mtar555t.

The Pearl of Great Price: A Selection from the Revelations, Translations, and Narrations of Joseph Smith, First Prophet, Seer, and Revelator to the Church of Jesus Christ of Latter-day Saints. Salt Lake City: Church of Jesus Christ of Latter-day Saints, 2013.

Piaget, Jean. *The Child's Conception of the World.* Translated by Joan Tomlinson and Andrew Tomlinson. London: Kegan Paul, 1929.

——. *Judgement and Reasoning in the Child.* Translated by Margorie Warden. New York: Harcourt, Brace, 1928.

——. *Play, Dreams, and Imitation in Childhood.* Translated by C. Gattegno and F. M. Hodgson. New York: Norton, 1962.

Plato. *The Republic.* Translated by Benjamin Jowett. New York: Modern Library, 1982.

Raboteau, Albert J. *A Sorrowful Joy: A Spiritual Journey of an African-American Man in Late Twentieth-Century America.* Eugene, OR: Wipf & Stock, 2012.

Rodriguez, Will. *The Great Book of Mayan Legends.* Translated by David Phillips. Merida, Mexico: Dante, 2015.

Shelf, David. *All We Are Saying: The Last Major Interview with John Lennon and Yoko Ono.* New York: St. Martin's, 2000.

Smith, Christian, Bridget Ritz, and Michael Rotolo. *Religious Parenting: Transmitting Faith and Values in Contemporary America.* Princeton: Princeton University Press, 2020.

Smith, Erin, and Robert Crosby III. "Unpacking Religious Affiliation: Exploring Associations Between Christian Children's Religious Cultural Context, God Image, and Self-Esteem Across Development." *British Journal of Developmental Psychology: Special Issue Paper*, 2016, 1–15. doi:10.1111/bjdp.12156.

Spelke, Elizabeth S., and Katherine D. Kinzler. "Core Knowledge." *Developmental Science* 10, no. 1 (2007): 89–96. doi:10.1111/j.1467-7687.2007.00569.x.

Sullivan-González, Douglass. *The Black Christ of Esquipulas: Religion and Identity in Guatemala.* Lincoln: University of Nebraska Press, 2016.

Taube, Karl. *The Major Gods of Ancient Yucatan.* Washington, DC: Dumbarton Oaks Research Library and Collection, 1992.

Taylor, Charles. *A Secular Age*. Cambridge, MA: Belknap Press of Harvard University Press, 2007.

Taylor, Marjorie. *Imaginary Companions and the Children Who Create Them*. Oxford: Oxford University Press, 1999.

Taylor, Marjorie, and Stephanie M. Carlson. "The Relation Between Individual Differences in Fantasy and Theory of Mind." *Child Development* 68 (1997): 436–55. doi:10.2307/1131670.

Tomasello, Michael, Malinda Carpenter, Josef Call, Tanya Behne, and Henrike Moll. "Understanding and Sharing Intentions: The Origins of Cultural Cognition." *Behavioral and Brain Sciences* 28 (2005): 675–735. doi.10.1017/S0140525X05000129.

Wigger, J. Bradley. *Invisible Companions: Encounters with Imaginary Friends, Gods, Ancestors, and Angels*. Stanford, CA: Stanford University Press, 2019.

——. "Invisible Friends Across Four Countries: Kenya, Malawi, Nepal and the Dominican Republic." *International Journal of Psychology* 53 (2018): 46–52. doi.org/10.1002/ijop.12423j.

——. *Original Knowing: How Religion, Science, and the Human Mind Point to the Irreducible Depth of Life*. Eugene, OR: Cascade, 2012.

——. *The Power of God at Home: Nurturing Our Children in Love and Grace*. San Francisco: Jossey-Bass, 2003.

——. "The Religious Imagination of Children Project: An Initial Research Report." *International Journal of Children's Spirituality* 24, no. 3 (2019): 228–42. doi.org/10.1080/1364436X.2019.1652572.

——. *The Texture of Mystery: An Interdisciplinary Inquiry into Perception and Learning*. Lewisburg, PA: Bucknell University Press, 1998.

Wigger, J. Bradley, Katrina Paxson, and Lacey Ryan. "What Do Invisible Friends Know? Imaginary Companions, God, and Theory of Mind." *International Journal for the Psychology of Religion* 23 (2013): 2–14. doi.org/10.1080/10508619.2013.739059.

Wild Church Network. www.wildchurchnetwork.com (2016).

Wilson, E. O. *Sociobiology: The New Synthesis*. 25th anniversary ed. Cambridge, MA: Belknap Press of Harvard University Press, 1975/2000.